DATATHEFT

Hugo Cornwall is the pseu[...] Sommer who combines th[...] [...] computer security consultant with that of writer. He read law at Oxford and spent thirteen years in mass market book publishing before entering the computer industry in 1978 via electronic publishing where he acquired wide experience of financial services and commercial computing environments. Since the publication of his best-selling *Hacker's Handbook* (now in its fourth edition) he has worked for many leading corporate security companies. He also runs the consultancy Virtual City Associates which principally provides services for lawyers, and the insurance and private security industries.

Hugo Cornwall's journalism appears in a wide range of national and specialist newspapers and magazines; he is a frequent conference and seminar speaker and often appears on television and radio.

HUGO CORNWALL

DataTheft

Computer fraud, industrial espionage
and information crime

Mandarin

A Mandarin Paperback

DATATHEFT

First published in Great Britain 1987
by Heinemann Professional Publishing Ltd
This edition published 1990
by Mandarin Paperbacks
Michelin House, 81 Fulham Road, London SW3 6RB

Mandarin is an imprint of the Octopus Publishing Group

Copyright © 1987, 1989 by Hugo Cornwall

A CIP catalogue record for this book
is available from the British Library
ISBN 0 7493 0217 8

Phototypeset by Input Typesetting Ltd, London

Printed in Great Britain
by Cox & Wyman Ltd, Reading

Contents

We are shortly moving into the phase where computers will become one of the cheapest pieces of technology on earth – cheaper than tv sets (they already are), cheaper than portable typewriters, cheaper even than transistor radios. They will also, for exactly the same reasons, become the most common pieces of technology in the world, and the most useful.

Dr Christopher Evans,
The Mighty Micro, 1979

The medium, or process, of our time – electric technology – is reshaping and restructuring patterns of social interdependence and every aspect of our personal life. It is forcing us to reconsider and re-evaluate practically every thought, every action and every institution formerly taken for granted.

Marshall McLuhan,
The Medium is the Message, 1967

Information is the manager's main tool, indeed it is the manager's 'capital', and it is he who must decide what information he needs and how to use it. Managers will also have to come to grips with some critical questions about the role of information in their organisations. Who shall have access to what information? How can information be protected against fraud, industrial espionage, or prying and gossip-mongering? How can personal privacy be guarded? How can confidential information be confined to those who are legitimately entitled to it, without a secretiveness which encourages scuttlebutt and demoralises?

Peter Drucker,
The Changing World of the Executive, 1982

What was called computer security in the 1960s and data security in the 1970s is today more accurately called information security. Information security underscores the value of information in today's society – the recognition that information is a valuable resource, that is more than discrete data elements.

President's Council on Integrity
and Efficiency Prevention Committee, 1986

Computer-related crime is not just one type of crime; it is a ubiquitous variant of all crime. Ultimately the variant will become the dominant form, and most non-violent and even some violent types of crime will involve computers.

Donn B Parker,
Fighting Computer Crime, 1983

In a nutshell, there are several good reasons why you might consider a career in computer crime. First of all, no one will ever know if you commit one. Second, no one will ever tell if you do. Third, no one will ever punish you. Fourth, you don't really have to know an awful lot about computers to commit this crime. Fifth, the opportunities for advancement are phenomenal. And, finally, there's no time like the present.

Jay BloomBecker, US National Center
for Computer Crime Data, 1985

Preface

It is two and a half years since the hardback edition of *DataTheft* first appeared and I have taken the opportunity of the book's appearance in paperback to carry out a number of revisions. As you might expect, I have added a number of relevant new cases and updated the sections on law and insurance where there have been a number of significant developments.

But, re-reading the text, I decided that public perceptions about certain aspects of computer security – notably hackers and viruses – had undergone enough change for it to be necessary for me to address them specifically. Accordingly, I decided to carry out a few new interviews or re-interviews with my sources and to rewrite whole sections of chapters, including the introduction and conclusion. It also seemed to me that some of the tables inserted in the body of the hardback edition could be revised and placed, more usefully, in appendices at the back of the book.

This edition has been updated to late Summer 1989, with some further alterations made during proof reading in October, 1989.

Although the subject-matter of *DataTheft* is about things that go wrong with computers, there's no doubt that a great deal goes right with them. Revising books between new editions is vastly easier if you use a good word-processor, you can organise your ideas and lists of items to research with 'outliners', and it is possible to maintain a huge archive of source material on computer 'incidents' – the lifeblood of this book as well as my consultancy – on a large, fast PC hidden under my desk.

Hugo Cornwall

Introduction

Over the last few years a rather odd competition has been playing out across the pages and screens of the popular media to find the most definitively frightening computer scare. If you believe what these stories have claimed, the contenders are:

- **Hackers** – a group of maverick explorer/programmers, to whom every computer must eventually yield admission, whereupon its innermost secrets and wealth are lost. Hackers, originally student pranksters, may now, it is alleged, have links to organised crime and even to national espionage agencies.
- **Viruses** – rogue programs of considerable destructive power which have the capacity to replicate themselves through computer systems and networks. The virus has near-relatives called logic bombs, worms and trojans which, while lacking the virus's self-reproductive qualities, share its ability to hide until called upon to destroy.
- **Computer fraud** – Computers can hide the process of deception that is at the heart of fraud so effectively, and so speed it up, that, according to one calculation, the entire reserves of a middle-sized first world country could be siphoned off in fifteen minutes or less.
- **VDU radiation** – it's no longer necessary to break into a computer in the traditional sense in order to gain access to its secrets: stray radiation from the screens of visual display units can be readily captured and re-assembled on a modified television screen; alternatively, radiation can be detected from cables and networks, the signals cleaned up and analysed, and then converted into characters which can be fed into a hostile computer.
- **Computer-aided industrial espionage** – even without elaborate technical tricks, the enormous amount of data held on computers, and the very compact storage methods used

mean that huge quantities of valuable information can be siphoned off at great speed with little or no risk of detection.

- **Techno-terrorism** – the very dependence of companies – and indeed sovereign states – on their computer systems makes them particularly vulnerable to threats from techno-logically qualified terrorists, who can either aim to destroy a system or extort by threatening to do so.
- **Organised crime** – why go for the mess and danger of the traditional bank heist when much larger sums of money can be extracted, with no fuss, little chance of being caught, and from the comfort of one's own home?

While these are the favoured runners in the track athletics, there are field events also: are the bulletin boards favoured by computer hobbyists being used for the dissemination of pornography, or unpleasant political ideas, or as a contact point for paedophiles? Could disaffected trade unions with members in key computer operations roles hold companies and countries to ransom?

This approach to 'computer security' has not been of much help to those whose organisations are dependent on computers. For there turns out to be another contender in the 'computer scare' competition – moral panic. Moral panic is what happens when reaction to an event is out of all proportion to the immediate threat actually faced, to the point where the most imminent danger is from the consequences of the panic itself. A typical non-computer example of moral panic is the individual who breaks a leg in their hurry to get away from a mouse. Later in this book, we'll see what the computer equivalents are.

Within each of the popular computer scare stories is an element of fact: there *are* viruses; there may be dangerous conse-quences to unauthorised computer explorations by students; computer fraud can be uniquely easy to execute; it is possible, though not easy, remotely to read the contents of vdu screens; computer-aided espionage of both the industrial and inter-government varieties is a reality; there are verified cases of techno-terrorism; there are a handful of instances where traditional organised crime has become involved with computers.

But all of these stories, by concentrating on the unusual, are guilty of considerable distortion:

- Computer owners are persuaded to protect against risks they are relatively unlikely to face
- Computer owners don't protect against commonplace, but relatively unnewsworthy threats
- Some computer owners disregard or dismiss the issue altogether
- Managers of companies dependent on computers end up not in control of their businesses
- Politicians, police, and so on have a distorted view of priorities

This book seeks to redefine the subject of 'computer security'; it argues that the focus on exotic manifestations of 'computer crime' – whatever that phrase actually means – has dangerously distracted attention from the rather broader risks faced by all of us from information crimes of every kind, of which computer crime in general forms merely the most important and fastest growing sub-set. The simple equation – 'more computers means more computer crime' – appears to summarise all that can usefully be offered to explain the modern phenomenon of datacrime: information crimes of all types and in particular: datafraud – computer assisted fraud; dataspying – theft of computer-based information; datatheft – theft of the computer's corporeal and calculating resources; and physical attack on computer facilities. I propose to demonstrate that datacrime is now an all prevalent hazard for every organisation that makes use of computers. I will be showing how nearly all present accounts of 'computer crime' are guilty of considerable understatement in terms of the risk that commercial undertakings, public authorities and private individuals face. These crimes are now as commonplace and banal as house-breaking is in the suburbs, pilfering is in retail outlets, warehouses and workshops, and petty embezzlement is in offices.

I aim to show that computer risks, those that are publicity worthy as well as those that are not, can be managed in the same way as any other aspect of business. That is to say, you can learn to make rational assessments of the risks which a particular computer system could face; you can make a judgement of how likely a given risk is to occur, and how much it could impact the business the computer is serving if it does. Based on this, you can decide what sort of preventative and other measures are appropriate – and have a cost-justification for them.

Computer disasters, accidental or intended, are not freakish random events; they can be predicted. They have a context within the history of management as well as within the history of computers. Without an awareness of that context, there will never be any adequate understanding of what could threaten a computer-dependent organisation.

The uncomfortable fact is that nearly all organisations and individuals that use computers – and that tends to include nearly all organisations and enormous numbers of individuals – underestimate the extent to which they have become dependent on them. The commodity of information is itself an essential asset of all organisations – accurate information about markets, raw materials, production processes, the position of inventories, the management of accounts – all contribute to making an organisation efficient in the utilisation of its tangible, physical assets. 'Information' in this sense is produced and held within an organisation's computers; if they fail, are abused, are suborned to assist fraud, or if they leak, the organisation itself can collapse. In many senses, money too has become 'information'; often it is the representation of money on a computer, together with the authority to move it, that has become critical to the way in which business is conducted. That is why fear of vulnerability to datatheft should be in the forefront of the minds of every executive, manager, director and individual whose organisation uses computers.

But datacrime is an issue which affects more than just the manager of an organisation. For the manager, the prime concern must be that loss by datacrime can hit profits directly, not just turnover. If a manager is not in proper control of his data resources, then he is not in control of the organisation. If, as a result of a spectacular fraud or manifest leakage of information, this becomes apparent to others, then customer and client confidence will be sorely tried. If, in addition, the organisation is commercial and has shareholders, then their lack of confidence can lead to a fall in share price. Even if the existence of the fraud or leakage remains a secret, the resulting loss has the same effect as a large drop in productivity. It can easily lead to loss of market share. In any event, the manager's job will be on the line.

The manager must also guard his data not only against misuse by his employees and rivals, but must also protect those on whom data is maintained. Computers have unique abilities in acquiring, sorting and regurgitating information about individuals. Many legislations now require collectors of such data to list their activities in a publicly available register and, upon suitable demand from the individual affected, to make available the records maintained. If such records are incorrect, the individual can use threat of legal sanction to get the record corrected. One of the cardinal features of these same data protection laws requires the database managers to take steps to maintain the security of their data.

However the consequences of datacrime extend far beyond this. Companies have gone out of business or undergone severe reduction in size. The veteran analyst Dr Ken Wong tells of a Hong Kong-based bank that had to close down following a fraud that swallowed up too much of its reserves; no one knows how many companies have quietly folded because one day the computer failed beyond recovery or how many enterprises have become bankrupt or asset-stripped because vital internal data was allowed to leak. There is a view among insurers that the first serious computer disaster a company suffers is also their last. Market research analysts Dataquest say that 80 per cent of disaster victim companies who experience extensive computer down-time are bankrupt within eighteen months. Employees, blameless and unaware of the insecurity of the computers that help run their organisations, can lose their jobs. And for individuals with skills in declining industries and living in geographic areas already suffering from high unemployment, datacrime can lead to long-term joblessness. Datacrime deserves to be as much a social issue as more traditional areas of 'law and order' such as crimes against the person, crimes against property and the maintenance of public peace.

Those who earn their living from advising on computer security are aware of a paradox: popular perceptions of computer crime suggest that it is only a real hazard for very large computer systems and/or those handling financial transactions. However, in contrast to the sensational claims that were paraded at the beginning of this introduction, every single serious survey of computer crime shows that the criminal is usually employed by the victim, that the crimes are not particularly sophisticated in pure computer terms and that the typical crime would previously have been described as an 'average' embezzlement or betrayal of confidence. Further, small computers are much more vulnerable than large ones and are far less likely to be adequately secured. The existence of these computer crime surveys is not secret; it is almost as though there has been a wilful disregard of their conclusions. Datacrimes are important not because they are new and strange, but precisely because they have now become so banal.

This book, therefore, is not going to be a mere collection of 'Dreadful Tales of Computer Crime'. I want, among other things, to place datacrime in the unambiguous historical and social context of change within corporations and businesses because it is only in this way that the subject can be rescued from the Scylla of sensationalism and the Charybdis of management ignorance. In fact, we will be concerned with one of the least anticipated by-products of the on-going information revolution.

The first seven chapters, therefore, deal with these issues and, among other things, show how the 'computer' has emerged from its shrine in the ascetic Computer Room to permeate, as PCs, intelligent machinery, cash-tills, automatic teller machines and networks, throughout the organisation that owns it, and how the organisation has changed out of all recognition in consequence. We will examine the main sources of case material of computer crime. We will look at the published surveys and statistics, assess their reliability, and wonder why media accounts, typified by those scare stories diverge so strongly from what the academic research actually says. We will also examine the phenomenon of the white collar criminal; I believe it is this archetype, rather than that of the 'hacker' which should guide perceptions of what computer crime is about.

The following three chapters are the only 'computer-technical' ones; they describe how to analyse a business and a computer system from a security perspective. The next sequence of chapters is concerned with the principles of risk management – how to identify risks, put a value on them, and hence how to match preventative measures. Much of the money that is spent on computer security products is entirely wasted because no one has decided what they really want to protect against. When a computer disaster occurs, victims often compound the damage by lack of adequate previous planning or by allowing themselves to be consumed by – that phrase again – moral panic.

From there we move to issues of public policy: many countries have persuaded themselves that the way to 'deal' with computer crime is by passing new, computer-specific laws. Is this the right way? How effective are policing methods? Where are the weak points in the current system of justice? Indeed, how far is it worth the while of victims to report to the authorities?

The book concludes with a series of check-list type appendices.

DataTheft the book, is intended for all those that rely on computers to manage organisations, or a part thereof. In this introduction I have used the word 'organisation' rather than 'company' or 'corporation' because datacrime is a problem in the non-profit-seeking world as well as in the overtly commercial one. In fact the absence of profit-orientation can make an organisation even more vulnerable to internal corruption. Most of the material I have, however, comes from the commercial world, but the words 'company', 'corporation' and their synonyms can nearly always be interpreted to include the non-profit organisations, utilities and services in public ownership and indeed many government and federal departments. Whilst we are on the subject of synonyms: I recognise that women as well as men run, and have responsibility for, organisations and computers; I have tried to use language that makes no assumptions about the gender of the reader. I haven't always been successful so, where appropriate, 'he' can also mean 'she'.

You do not need to know much about computers in order to benefit from this book. There are, alas, still too many people who have decided that they will never 'understand' computers and eagerly delegate responsibility for them to others. The idea of 'understanding' computers is a chimera, no one any longer 'understands' all about computers in the way that a dedicated scholar can become an authority on, say, Mozart concerti. Coping with computers consists in knowing enough for your own immediate purposes and having sufficient self-confidence to believe that you can, from time to time, extend your knowledge as needs arise.

Most of *DataTheft* is concerned with managements and administration in their very widest meanings; the computer's involvement is almost incidental. There are certain arguments which must be made, certain hazards which must be described, which require a level of technical explanation if they are to be useful. But even here, no person of reasonable managerial competence need fear being left adrift.

The assumption I have made about you as a reader is that you have some responsibility or concern for an operation – company, public authority, educational establishment, voluntary organisation, supplier of professional services – that makes use of computers; you may be a chief executive officer, a manager, or self-employed professional; that every now and then you are prepared to think conceptually about your job and environment as well as getting on with day-to-day tasks; and that you suspect that the prevention of datacrime is something for which you should take precautions.

Much of my raw material has come from the casebooks and observations of others. The diligent researcher can soon track down published collections of computer crimes though, as will become apparent later, many reports need to be examined with scepticism.* Further reports, available from the handful of specialists in computer crime investigation and from insurance underwriters, have never been published and probably never will because the victims fear that the one way in which to compound their existing loss is to promote alarm among their customers. I keep a full text database of as many computer crime and disaster reports as I can lay my hands on. Also useful have been a series of risk assessment surveys prepared by consultants so that organisations have been able to obtain insurance cover. These are interesting because they show an organisation's attitudes towards computers away from the trauma of having just been ripped off.

I have been fortunate to be able to prepare most of this book in London where, for a variety of reasons, a great deal of the world's expertise in computer security is concentrated. British pioneering work in computing, decryption and coding is well known through publications about the wartime eavesdropping and decoding activities at Bletchley Park, the parent of both the NSA and GCHQ. Britain had, in LEO – Lyons' Electronic Office, one of the first purely commercial computers. Far less well-known, though, has been the work of the British 'clearing' or retail banks which, because of their large individual size, small number and the way they bestride the British national economy, were very early users of computers. Banks have always had to take special care both to avoid fraud and to preserve client confidentiality. Many of the commonplace disciplines of computer security in the commercial environment – technical and administrative – were first developed by UK banks. Finally, Lloyds of London has always been the place

*A number of frequently reported cases almost certainly fall into the category of modern urban myth – stories and themes which re-appear repeatedly in different locations and for which precise evidence of their occurrence never seems to be forthcoming. Jan Harold Brunvard quotes the vanishing hitch-hiker, the cement-filled Cadillac and Kentucky-fried rat as examples. It seems likely that, among stories from the world of computer fraud, the Zwana/Sal-ami case and the 'Pay me half of what I stole and I'll show you how I did it' programmer are candidates. For a case to be treated non-sceptically here I have hoped to find at least one fairly detailed contemporaneous report written by someone who appeared to understand a reasonable amount about computers. In some instances, of course, I have been able to rely on personal knowledge or have interviewed participants.

where new forms of insurance policy have been developed. Part of my own professional practice serves the Lloyds community of underwriters, brokers and loss adjusters.

Some information has been available to me only after signing non-disclosure agreements such that I must disguise the identity of the victim or simply use the information as general background. Computer crime investigators from both the private and public sectors have, to varying degrees, been willing to discuss their work informally but often on a non-attributable basis. There are a number of statistical surveys but all of them much more defective in formal methodology than most crime statistics. How on earth do you gauge what is often not reported – or deliberately concealed?

All this leaves me as an author in the position of making a series of claims and assertions for which I cannot publish all the evidence and where I have to rely intuitively on my own experience in deciding which evidence to accept, which to reject. Of course I am uncomfortable in this stance but it is not unusual for certain types of writer. Those newspaper correspondents who specialise in politics or defence know that often the only way in which they can write a story is by agreeing to terms set by their source – a source whom they ought, in other circumstances, to be exposing. Their justification is the same as I will make: it is better to offer the best partial truth you can than to publish nothing at all. There are two tests the reader can, in these circumstances, apply: first, do the assertions make sense in terms of what is already known? Second, do later events show that the stories and perceptions must have been true?

Readers of my earlier effort, *The Hacker's Handbook*, may be curious to know how it fits in with this present work. *The Hacker's Handbook* was written – very quickly – for an audience of computer hobbyists at a time when many of them were in the process of making their first purchase of modems to enable their home machines to talk to the outside world. They needed books to fill the gaps of explanation in the documentation provided with the equipment they had bought. The hacking theme was chosen because, in the form in which I described it in the book – the word's usage has changed somewhat since, it is a fascinating and more-or-less harmless pastime for a certain sort of fanatic. Those who condemn hacking usually operate on a different definition of the activity from mine.

The book's publication coincided with one of a series of peaks of public fascination with hackers who, by and large, were believed to possess a level of skill and achievement far in excess of anything that I actually ever came across. The psychological reasons for the attractiveness of hackers as public heroes is almost worth a book in itself. Not the least disconcerting aspect of the book's success – it was in the *Sunday Times* Bestseller List for seven weeks – was how I found myself being described. 'Hugo Cornwall', as he appeared in the press and in computer magazines, was much more a product of what people wanted him to be like than anything else.

One more pleasant consequence, however, was a series of invitations from top-line computer security consultants to carry out freelance assignments for them. The first such was to assist in a fraud where over £900,000 had disappeared. It was a combination of my annoyance at misconceptions about the importance of hackers as security threats and the lack of overall public understanding of the problems of information security that first lead me to want to write this book.

The following people and organisations provided material, gave me interviews, read parts of the manuscript, or otherwise helped in the preparation of this book. Other people and organisations helped but asked specifically not to be identified. The errors and omissions of fact, as well as the opinions, are my sole responsibility.

4–What It's Worth; Frank Austin; BIS Applied Systems; Jay BloomBecker; Richard Brickwood/C T Bowring; Paul Burden; Duncan Campbell; Control Risks Group; Sir James Crane; Data Integrity plc; DataLink; Peter Emms; Doug Fox; Steve Gold; Peter Hamilton; Patricia Hughes; Alan D Jones; Alistair Kelman; Janet Kollek; Jules Kroll; Dr Michael Levi; Simon Mann; Sir Robert Mark; Roy Mills; Gary Murray; National Center for Computer Crime Data; Network Security Management Ltd; David Newman; Professor Joseph O'Donoghue; Donn Parker/SRI; Martin Samocuik; Robert

Schifreen; Martin Short; Jim Smith; Mark Tantam/Serious
Fraud Office; Glenn Tenney; Peter Warren; Ted Wassell; Dr
Ken Wong; WBK International Ltd; Rupert Villers and
Lorraine Adlam/Spreckly Villers Hunt & Co Ltd.

These are the main sources used for case material and articles;
books appear in the bibliography.

Attitudes of Companies in Britain to Fraud: Ernst & Whinney
Computer Fraud Surveys: Audit Commission
BIS Computer Crime Casebooks
BIS Computer Disaster Casebooks
BIS Computer Related Fraud Casebooks
Banking Technology
British Library: Science Reference Division
Computer Insecurity: Adrian D Norman
Computers & Security
Computer Security Digest
Computer Fraud & Security Bulletin
Computing
Computer Law & Security Report
Computer Talk
Computer Weekly
Datalink
Dialog: Inspec. Microcomputer Index, The Computer
    Database, The Magazine Index, Newsearch, National
    Newspaper Index, Sociological Abstracts, Harvard Business
    Review
Home Office, Police Foundation & Arthur Young: *Incidence,
    Reporting and Prevention of Commercial Fraud*
Donn Parker
Economist
Financial Times
Guardian
Home Office Research Bulletin No 21
Information Security Monitor
Mercy College Report on Computer Crime
NCCCD
New York Public Library

Observer
PC Week
Profile
Sunday Telegraph
Sunday Times
Telelink
The Times

CHAPTER ONE

Setting the Scene

Entering a large supermarket or department store in the 1990s is an experience superficially hardly different from visiting the same establishment ten or more years earlier. The particular pattern of selling – attractively presented and well-lit shelves from which you load a trolley or wire basket, a wide range of carefully selected goods, the general absence of staff compared with the traditional retail outlet and the check-out where your money is taken – had been well established in most Western countries several years before the mid 1970s. Indeed, there was nothing unusual or abnormal about self-service fifteen years before that at the beginning of the 1960s.

For the observer, asked to compare the late 1980s appearance of the store with how it had been in the 1970s, the most obvious feature upon which to light would be the change in prices. All would of course have gone up in the absolute units of currency – inflation will have seen to that – though using the more accurate measure of determining how many hours a customer must work in order to earn enough to purchase a given item, many goods will actually prove to be cheaper. Product lines will have changed slightly in line with fashion and innovation. In a food store, it will probably be possible to detect changes of emphasis rather than essentials – more fresh, additive-free goods, for example, a tribute to greater concern about health. Again, the range of products will have increased but the number of competitive brands in each category may have diminished. Overall, some smaller and medium-sized supermarkets and department stores near traditional town- and city-centre shopping areas will have been closed down, although their parent companies are still highly profitable. Large, out-of-town mega-warehouses or hypermarkets have become more important. But such alterations seem natural and evolutionary; some stores are managed well and prosper, others fail to detect changing consumer interests and go into decline.

The check-out system superficially appears more-or-less unchanged over the ten-year period. The queues are the same, the level of attention from the clerk or assistant – usually very low – is the same. Many products now carry printed bar-codes containing product identification and price information, but only a very few stores are beginning to use them. Some stores do operate semi-automated price entry into the tills – often using wands to read magnetic strips on the price label or lasers to read product bar codes and here and there are (at the time of writing) sporadic experiments in full-scale EFT/POS: electronic funds transfer at point-of-sale, where a bank or credit card is wiped into a machine and your credit status is checked; after your bill has been calculated, an automatic and immediate deduction is made from your bank current account or credit card account. But these are mainly experiments and although they will be with us properly in the next few years, nationally recognised and widely adopted systems for EFT/POS have yet to come into being.

This observer, unless primed beforehand, would have missed the most important transformation. For the changes that have taken place behind the scenes have been profound. Competition between all such stores for access to the consumer's household purse has been intense; the principal form of that competition has been an extended and continuing price war – with comparatively minor battles being fought in terms of product quality and store 'image'. The only substantive strategies in the war have been to become ever more efficient in the use of shelf-space, in the management of stock turnover, in the accuracy and sharpness of identifying customer requirements, in the assessment of areas of marginal profit and in the squeezing of suppliers for keener and keener pricing. The weapons in the war have been computers.

In the efficient supermarket or retail store, computers watch everything – not only reporting on every item that is sold so that it may be re-ordered in exactly the right quantity and at exactly the right time, but also assessing product lines against each other: how much turnover and profit is a given length of shelving providing, is one brand being preferred against another, and if so, is this due to a special promotion or an advertising campaign? Would a given range of products do better at another site within the store – and if this is the case, what are the implications for all the other in-store 'sites' that must now be reallocated? What longer term trends can be detected? How well is the test marketing of the new product launch progressing? How is one branch of a supermarket chain doing against another? What regional or cultural differences can be found between stores in different neighbourhoods or geographical locations – and what can be learnt from that? Finally, the computers will be managing the cash-flow with particular care. Bills will be paid at the last possible moment, the existence of any spare pool of cash at the end of the trading day being placed in the hands of the company's treasurer, who, if the Group is large enough, may seek to earn a little overnight interest from a bank.

Not only do the computers produce endless reports, they even make some of the actual decisions about when to re-order. Why leave such matters to a human who may not notice that demand is up and the shelves are emptying? Or that capital is being tied up and shop-space wasted by slow-moving lines? When introducing a new product-line, an external data-feed can provide demographics – information about the social profile of given catchment areas – the proportions of young families to childless couples to single people, of high wage-earners to unemployed, of old to young, and so on. By taking a data-feed from an agency supplying long-term weather forecasting, a store can ensure that its stocks react to changing purchasing patterns when the climate becomes suddenly hot, or cold, or wet or drought-ridden. Using 'expert systems' software (sometimes misleadingly called artificial intelligence), computers can detect patterns of stock turnover that might be missed by mere mortals – and can act on them. In fact, why not get the computer in the supermarket warehouse to talk direct to the computer in the warehouse of the supplier? Such a linkage avoids double-keying of orders made and fulfilled, and also enables the supplier to have the information with which to anticipate his customer's needs, plan production accordingly and hence offer a keener price. In the case of food, the traditional supply chain of the farmer, the wholesale market and the retail outlet is being by-passed. Farmers, now themselves very industrial creatures in their methods, supply direct, saving the supermarket the margins of any intermediaries and getting fresher produce to the shopper.

Though it's a subject for another book, the retail trade has seen a profound shift of power: ten or fifteen years ago, power lay with suppliers and manufacturers; today, it is those organis-ations that control the distribution networks and the places-of-sale that can dictate terms to the manufacturers. It couldn't be done without computers. The supermarket has been providing 'superhuman' services for some time while still preserving an unchanged outward appearance. The growth of the use of computers in supermarkets in fact started properly in the early 1960s but has come a very long way since then. Sainsbury's, one of the largest UK operators, serves six million customers a week and has an annual turnover of £3.5 bn. It has 260 outlets and 60 warehouses. In addition to all the check-out tills, over 1000 screens and printers are necessary for managerial, supervisory and programming requirements. 180 of its stores have their own minicomputers and there are two computer centres with large mainframes. An ICL report in the UK in 1987 stated that 20 per cent of British points-of-sale were backed by electronic systems, but, by the following year, the figure would be 36 per cent. By 1993, 40 per cent would have laser-readers. These statistics include small single-unit retail outlets as well as the large multiples. A simple set of statistics from the UK High Street grocery giant Sainsbury shows the benefits they have reaped – between 1977 and 1987, their stock ratio, the number of times it turns over its stock in a year – has doubled. At the same time, stock availability, the proportion of products actu-ally on the shelf at any one time has risen from the mid 70s to the mid 90s.[1]

Supermarkets and department stores are not usually thought repositories of 'high tech'. You can visit one and never see anything that looks obviously like a computer terminal. The branch managers and staff of supermarkets don't often think of themselves as being involved in computers or information technology. Whereas the first generations of computers were often undoubtedly acquired by commercial companies of all kinds with little clear view as to how they were to be used – the 'reason' often was that a computer salesman had told them that they were 'on the point of' selling a machine to their most obvious rival – computers are now bought as a matter of essential survival. Competitive companies have to become ever more efficient and the computer is what provides that efficiency.

What has happened in retail distribution has been replicated in many other industries and professions. Superficially the essential business activity appears unaltered, but the computer has long been providing a huge range of services in support of efficient management. The Information Revolution, fifteen years ago a phrase used by academics and parroted by office equipment salesmen, is now well advanced. It would be an unwise social critic who, at this point, tried to calculate all its effects up to date and an even less wise one who attempted much detailed prediction.

In this book we have more narrow concerns: nearly every organisation is changing important aspects of its information and decision-making systems every three years or so, some even more frequently. Traditional controls over the organisation's affairs and assets are having to be scrapped as competition forces the introduction of newer and newer systems. The Information Revolution has brought many benefits; it has also made every participant, conscious or otherwise, unbelievably vulnerable. For the priority of the new systems has been efficiency in the management of resources; security is hardly ever properly considered.

Understanding the information revolution

A book with the title *DataTheft* ought, at first sight, to be limited to descriptions of appalling computer crimes and prescriptions of methods for their prevention. It wouldn't do the job. Profound changes are under way in all businesses and organisations as a result of the mass availability of computing power. Because so much has been written in anticipation about this emerging revolution there is a considerable danger that people believe they understand what is happening; what needs to be said now is that the changes already identifiable are importantly different and other from those predicted, even a very few years ago. It is almost impossible to live in the middle of an extensive social and cultural revolution and keep alert to all the consequences; indeed, our instincts for survival, as Alvin Toffler identified in his 1970 book, *Future Shock*, make us want to hope that change – the process by which the future invades our lives – is much less profound than is actually the case. Many of the present problems of datacrime result from a failure of system owners to understand how the computer has changed for ever the range of criminal opportunities and motives.

So, some form of instant historic recapitulation and reinterpretation of the Information Revolution, still only in its very early stages, is unavoidable. Every so often, particular technical inventions have triggered a series of events with such an enormous impact on society that the only appropriate adjective is the overworked word 'revolutionary'. In the countries of the northern hemisphere these transforming breakthroughs of the last two-and-a-half centuries have included the discovery of crop rotation, the process of learning how to manufacture machinery, the powered rotary printing press (which made mass-market newspapers, magazines and books possible), the coming of the railways, electric power, the techniques of the mass-assembly line and the telephone. For the countries of the Third World you would single out the arrival of large ships able to carry cargo – thus enabling the advanced world to commence its (initially) one-sided trade of exploitation – and the coming of the mass media which taught the Third World what advanced countries were like and that they could, if they wished, try to become like them.

Such revolutions as these technologies cause are different from their political counterparts: there is no direct equivalent of: 'One month you are being ruled by a Czar, then there's fighting in the streets; after a short while, things settle down, the President of a Committee of People's Representatives says he is in charge, and everyone addresses each other as "Comrade".' By contrast, changes in technological revolutions are non-linear and highly unpredictable, each small change causing many others.

The direct consequence of Trevithick's road locomotive of 1801 was not simply Stephenson's success with The Rocket on the Stockton & Darlington railway in 1825 nor even the world's first passenger railway between Liverpool and Manchester in 1830. It was that, for the first time, it was no longer necessary for manufactured goods to be produced from raw materials all found in one location, assembled at that location and sold and consumed at that location. Materials could come from anywhere, be assembled at the most convenient point and sold everywhere. Certain industries received special stimulus: the output of pig-iron in Britain was 678,000 tons in 1830 and 2,701,000 by 1852; coal output was 10m tons in 1800 and 100m in 1865. Exports rose from £69m in 1830 to £197m in 1850, the emphasis shifting from textiles towards coal and iron fabrications. Vast quantities of population movement took place, nearly 200,000 being directly employed constructing railways by 1848, but at least ten times as many taking advantage of easy communications to migrate to where the new industrial work was. In this sense, Trevithick's steam-driven road vehicle stands in direct line as the begetter of both the modern industrial city and the British Empire. It also introduced, for the first time on a nationwide basis, a synchronised clock time. Before the regular running of railways, what use was 'the exact time'?

These revolutions are also different in the time-scale of their effects. Although they do touch all parts of society eventually, they act on different sections at different speeds, whereas a political revolution tends to hit all areas of a nation almost simultaneously, or none. This is why living through a technological revolution seems at times deceptively placid and gives sceptics the chance to argue that the enthusiasts have got it wrong: whilst change can be perceived all around, the lives of many individuals and groups will for extended periods appear relatively unaltered. One reason for this is that technical change has its impact initially at a commercial level on an industry by industry basis, with demographic effects following afterwards. If the industry in which you earn your living is sufficiently remote from the new technology, your life-pattern could remain the same for some considerable time. A second reason is that these revolutions are more exponential in their growth than linear. A simple illustration of exponentialism is the old one of the lily in the pond which doubles in area coverage every day. Five days before the day the pond is completely covered, under exponential growth, only one-thirty-second of the surface has any lilies on it at all and on the day before the pond is engulfed, only half its area is covered.*

The Information Revolution is not directly about computers and data communications: it is about their effects. The collection of information of all kinds and its subsequent intelligent processing is the equivalent (though don't make the mistake of pushing the analogy too far) of the Victorian railway line. The people directly employed in the obvious computer industries are not those upon whom the eye ought to be fixed; it is what they are making possible for everyone else.

Even if the computer industry provides not a jot more innovation over the next twenty years but merely carries on the production lines of the existing models (an event unlikely in the extreme), the changes already triggered – and their chains of consequences – the specific revolution which I identify as having really started in the late 1970s – are going to be astonishing.

The integrated computer resource

As we saw in the opening section of this chapter, the changes in the supermarket industry are not visibly being driven by computer-derived or any other technological innovation. The impetus comes from competition between the industry leaders as they struggle to identify ever more accurately what their customers want and how to deliver it. In industry after industry, office after office, the pattern is repeated. It is the computer's ability to collect and manipulate data in useful ways – and the effective utilisation of that power by managers – that has made the strides of the last decade possible.

Most organisations believe that they have installed computers

*This is not a description of how lilies actually behave in ponds – their development rate is slower and a pond's natural ecosystem tends to hold growth in check as the lilies expand – nor is it an assertion that all revolutionary technological change takes place at pure exponential rates; it is however, a vived image of what exponentialism means.

to carry out particular tasks; on the contrary, their computers now perform such a range of functions to optimise the benefits of the resources employed and to provide assistance to management decisions – in some cases effectively making those decisions – that the proper phrase for what has happened is *computer integration*.

Originally, computers were *installed* to carry out particular, well-defined functions: inventory, order processing, payroll, accounts. Once all the data required to carry out these functions are fed into computers, many more facets of the company's activities can be examined. Questions can be asked that would not have been worth formulating before computerisation because deriving the answers would have been impossibly tedious and expensive. Marry together the data from a warehouse inventory/stock control system with information from salesmen's orders and you can determine, among other things: what is selling where, what seasonal and regional sales patterns exist, how far the inventory needs to anticipate consumer demand, how late the purchase of raw materials and the commitment to manufacture can be timed and still please the customer, how to manage the organisation's working capital more effectively, and so on. The marginal cost of most of these extra items of information, once the basic systems have been installed, is often remarkably low. And once a company has come to rely for its decision-making on the availability of these answers, the word 'installation' is no longer adequate: the computers have become *integrated* into the very fabric of the organisation's existence.

The change and significance from having computers *installed* in order to service specific functions for organisations to regarding them as fully *integrated* within them has been largely unperceived and unrecognised. There has, of course, been no clearly identifiable event in the life of most organisations that definitively marks the passage from installation to integration.

A computer which is merely installed can genuinely be regarded as just another item of machinery, and its operators can be seen as particularly skilled and inventive specialist machineminders. Once a Chief Executive Officer recognises that the organisation's computer resources and data networks are integrated with and indivisible from the organisation itself, then managing those resources and the assets they contain takes on a substantially different cast. And the risks associated with computer malfunction or abuse – however caused – become vastly more critical.

Information in many different forms is therefore as much an asset of a company as its buildings, stock, proprietaries, goodwill, staff and cash. If the information flow stops, the company stops. If the information is corrupted, the management lose their ability to make proper decisions. If information representing sales figures and market projections ends up in the hands of a rival, the company can lose competitive edge. If the information is misleading in its totalling up of the company's physical assets – or can be made to mislead – the company can be defrauded. If the information is money itself – the automated drawing of cheques, authorisations for payment, the validation of credit lines, or (just seriously beginning) EFT/POS, fraud can happen again. If the company's facilities for collecting and processing information are abused because someone is using the computers and data network for personal enterprise, the company loses yet again.

There is a further change that takes place in organisations that are computer-integrated, one that will be examined in the next chapter: decision-making becomes quite different and new centres of power and authority arise, threatening traditional managers. Some of the displaced managers will turn to datacrime as a form of covert or overt revenge for disappointed careers.

Computer-supported manufacture/computer-aided manufacture

There are degrees to which the integration of computers has taken place within organisations: ask most people about computers in manufacturing and they will initially think of robot-dominated assembly lines and the development of new products using vdus that present the designer's ideas every which way in a cascade of brilliant visuals. The general name for this is CAD/CAM – Computer-Aided Design/Computer-Aided Manufacture.

But this is simply to look at the glossy, glamorous end of

current possibilities. What is now commonplace for many manufacturing concerns is computer-*supported* manufacture – to determine critical resource flows, to quantify materials requirements, to optimise the use of machinery (even if the machines themselves are run by humans and not robots), to control the movement of materials, to advise management and sales when products will be ready for dispatch. Such computer facilities, even for quite large manufacturing concerns, can be run on relatively insignificant-looking desk-top micros supported by semi-specialised software packages.

Just as in the supermarket where computer resources originally introduced to smarten up warehousing, re-ordering and accounts procedures grew into a powerful management instrument which transformed the whole business, so in manufacturing 'Job Progress Reporting', 'Materials Requirement Planning,' and 'Sales Order Handling' facilities are beginning to enable managers in manufacturing to change the whole emphasis and thrust of their businesses. In many traditional mechanical and electrical engineering concerns of all kinds, it is usually considered necessary to maintain stocks against demand not only of finished goods, but also of components and raw materials. Only in this way is there a guarantee that customers' demands can be quickly met. However these inventories can represent considerable sums of tied-up working capital. Further, the company's sales staff may find what they have in the warehouse is not precisely what the customers are asking for. It may even be that the company doesn't have in stock all the components to assemble the required product. What computer-based information systems in manufacturing offer is the opportunity to Make to Order, rather than Make to Sell.

There have always been industries, of course, where customers have been prepared for long waiting periods to get delivery of what they want. As the new information systems become ever cheaper, more and more factories have been able to tailor manufacture more precisely to demand. Consumer goods – kitchen, home appliance, DIY, home entertainment – are all affected by fashion to a remarkable degree. Competitive manufacturers need to be able to offer the precise range of finishes and features that customers want. Should the maker of microwave ovens concentrate on basic switch on/switch off models at the lowest possible selling price, or offer knobs and lights, delayed action timers, temperature probes and combinations with other forms of cooking? Do the paying public want their home stereos in discreet matt black with slider controls, in shiny chrome with rotary knobs and multi-coloured displays, or concealed in fake Chippendale? The later the manufacturer can postpone commitments about his final production line, the more up-to-date can be the sales market research data upon which the decisions are made.

In a more extreme form, the information process can be developed into what is called Just In Time (JIT) methods. Here, the manufacturer, often in association with his key suppliers, maintains no stock of anything. All he provides is the production environment and skills. When the order arrives, the computer system works out a set of carefully timed materials requirements and associated work-flows. Every item is delivered and handled Just In Time and the manufacturer can offer his customer very quick supply of exactly what was asked for – and retain the savings of not having to maintain speculative stocks of materials. These techniques are now in use within some of the world's leading vehicle manufacturers as well as in a number of well-known heavy engineering companies. Just In Time, in its purest form, can only work for certain sorts of manufactured goods serving particular areas of demand, and obviously there are many situations in which the costings simply don't make sense – too much machinery, skilled labour and other fixed costs may be left idle so that what is gained from minimal stockholding is lost in expensive under used overhead. But elements of the JIT approach can be seen in very many companies. As with the supermarket, the final appearance of the products of the manufacturing concern may be little altered by the new management technique; in fact, decision making and the utilisation of human and machine resources will have been drastically mutated.

Process control, where a machine tool is run by a computer, is also much more unexceptional than is often imagined. Numerically controlled machine tools date back to the early 1950s and computer-controlled machine tools started being installed in the early 1960s. Many of today's machine tools don't look very different from their purely mechanical predecessors. They certainly don't have the appearance of the traditional humanoid robot of decades of science fictionalising. Computer-driven machine tools are often simply machines which use computers for repetitious and detailed accuracy; they are much more reliable than purely mechanical control mechanisms and much easier to reprogram for other purposes.

Slightly more advanced, but also increasingly commonplace are machine tools with sensing capabilities, able to modify their actions in the light of what is perceived to be happening in the outside world and so make their own decisions about adjustments. The future of this technology depends on the developing of a whole range of sensory probes, including reliable pseudo-visual devices, and the software to interpret what is happening. Once this has been done, the software to link together a large number of manufacturing modules and meld them into a harmonious whole already exists.

Not very far down the line is Computer-*Integrated* Manufacture, or CIM. Here the ambition is to tie together CAD/CAM design and manufacture techniques with Materials Requirement Planning and Sales Office facilities. Some of the leading computer manufacturers are already using such processes to assemble their own products. In some cases, this is linked in to automated (robotic) delivery of materials within factories and, ultimately, to 'pick and pack' warehouse technologies, where robots locate the required elements of a finished order, pack, and deliver to a dispatch bay. GM's Detroit production facilities contain some 40,000 intelligent devices. They are not yet (1989) all linked together as they come from a variety of suppliers each of which implement their own command language. However, agreement of a universally accepted protocol for all such machines and controllers is not far off. Computer manufacturers already have in place the beginnings of an agreed industry-wide standard to enable equipment from different suppliers to be easily connected. It is called MAP – Manufacturing Automated Protocol.

But what has already happened, even without this extent of sophistication, is that there are large number of apparently everyday objects on sale that could not have been designed or manufactured (or at least at an affordable price) other than by computer aid.[2]

Computer Integration
One History of Computing is about the movement from installation to integration

Standard applications

Order processing
Warehousing/inventory/stock control
Payroll
Corporate finance plans

Early forms of management information – in the form of standardised computer print-outs

Sales analysis
  by product
  by territory
  by salesman
  by time period

Cost analysis
Target/actual comparisons
  sales
  production
  corporate finance

Later forms of management information – the manager can design his own requirements – formulate his own questions and the way in which the answers are presented

Sales analysis – as before, but in much more detail
  by product
  by territory
  by salesman
  by time period

Cost analysis
  raw materials

      production process
      warehousing
      distribution
      cost of sales
      retail discounts

Market research findings
Marketing analyses
    cost of research
    product development
    production costs
    sales costs
    distribution costs
    retail discounts costs

Input from suppliers and customers
    suppliers production lines/warehouse inventory
    customers actual requirements

Projections of possible future activity – using computer modelling packages
Target/actual comparisons
    sales
    production
    corporate finance
    sensitivity analyses

Management data that is allowed to 'feedback' decisions without human intervention

re-ordering of standard stock lines
ordering up of contingency stock lines
generating mail-out lists
initiating sales pushes based on past performance
delivering stock to customers based on past performances

Computer-Controlled production lines – extended mass production lines under computer administration

labour supervision
supplies supervision
individual machine supervision

break-down reporting
timings supervision
reports to top management
reports to warehousing
reports to sales
reports to corporate finance
reports to suppliers
reports to customers

Automated production lines – extended mass production lines substantially under computer control – and using robots as well as computer-aided administration

labour and robot supervision
supplies supervision
individual machine supervision
break-down reporting
timings supervision
reports to top management
reports to warehousing
reports to sales
reports to corporate finance
reports to suppliers
reports to customers

Computer-aided manufacture > computer-aided design

products that can only be made by computer-driven machines (or can only be made at acceptable costs using computer aids)
products which require computer-aided design, either to permit conception in the first place, or to give variety and detail to a basis idea, or to deliver at an acceptable cost

Services that could not exist but for computer aid

market research analysis
customised and individualised services
high-speed response services
specialised publishing

What is being developed, at great expense, for the world's largest manufacturing companies, is likely to appear in much cheaper form a few years' hence. In even small specialist factories, general purpose programmable sensing machine tools will receive their instructions from programs developed on cheap CAD work-stations on which the software 'fills in' the rough ideas of the designer – and then, from a few basic concepts, produces designs for a whole range of notional alternative versions. The process whereby these facilities move down-market will be little different from the way in which word-processors have, within ten years, dropped to 3 per cent (in money units, more allowing for inflation) of the cost of the original offerings.

What will also have happened will be a vast increase in dependence on the computer information systems. As we will see later on, a small act of sabotage at a critical point could bring the entire company to an unseemly and permanent halt. These new schemes tend to need fewer human operators and though in the longer term some redeployment may take place, in the immediate future, resentment – and worse – could be common. Adding productivity measurement routines to these sophisticated programs is a trivial matter in terms of pure technical achievement; they could be a source of even more resentment.

Only very few manufacturers will be able to withstand the blandishments of the new combinations of technology; competition from their rivals will see to that. But, without a very carefully thought-out security policy, they will become fearfully exposed. Their survival will depend on the continuous reliability of the flow of data through the factory floor and beyond. And increasingly, it will be the designs of the products rather than the existence of a large pool of skilled workers that become the key asset for the long term. Those designs will exist as software and data – complete instructions to be fed into off-the-shelf general purpose computer-driven machine tools – and a malign individual could walk out with them all on a few square centimetres of magnetic or laser disk storage.

DataTheft and the information revolution

The other great area apart from the retail and manufacturing industries where the information revolution has had uncalculated effects has been the office and the ways in which organisations make decisions. In particular we must look, in the next chapter, at the profound and on-going reverberations from the arrival of the desk-top work-station and those who use it.

It takes time to test out thoroughly the byways of computer systems; modules which individually work in a perfectly satisfactory fashion by themselves turn out, when linked together, to exhibit all sorts of peculiar behaviour. The rate at which new systems are being introduced is increasing all the time. The drive behind the Information Revolution is competition, not pure technology. Almost the last consideration to be introduced into all these new systems has been security; almost no thought has been given to the extraordinary exposure of risk that the hapless acquirers of these new systems now face. It is with this omission that the remainder of this book is concerned.

CHAPTER TWO

The Desk-top Revolution and End-User Computing

The arrival of the computer on the corporate desk-top has not only democratised computing and destroyed for ever its quality as an esoteric skill, it has spread the extent and availability of the vital data upon which key corporate decisions can be made. And this in turn has had profound effects on how organisations are run – and how corporate information is controlled.

There are already many ways of writing computer history. The favourite seems to be by reference to successive generations of hardware: the move from thermionic valve (tube) technology to transistor, from transistor to integrated circuit, from IC to large-scale integrated microprocessor; the sequences by which central processors became more sophisticated, how the price of random-access memory plummeted, how mass production made the costs of essential peripherals like vdus and disk-drives ever lower, and so on. Hardware has got steadily smaller and smaller, another theme goes: in his 1979 book *The Mighty Micro*, Dr Christopher Evans calculated the decreasing physical size of electronic circuitry with ten thousand million switches, the same number as the human brain has neurones. In 1950 under thermionic valve technology, this unit would have covered Greater London; ten years afterwards, bipolar transistors would have brought the size down to that of the Albert Hall; ten years thereafter you would be contemplating a double-decker bus; in the mid 1970s it would be the size of a domestic television. In the mid-to-late 1980s, you can cram all that circuitry onto one printed circuit board. If the circuitry is simply used for memory storage, the size comes down to that of the compact disc.

A similar theme is that of declining costs, all the way down to the Sinclair (Timex) ZX-81, a complete computer for a few days' work at average earnings levels and requiring the addition merely of a home tv and low-cost cassette player. The

ZX-81 was really too stripped down to be particularly useful and subsequent machines had much more extensive facilities – like keyboards that could be used without personal injury to the fingertips. The table shows falling costs simply over the last ten years in terms of micros; in fact, the fall has been even steeper in real terms, as the figures take no account of inflation.

Another strain of history examines the development of software – operating systems and applications programs – and their various functions.

The historic process which is most relevant to this book, however, is the story of how control of corporate computing became removed from the Electronic Data Processing Department and became, up to a point, potentially the property of everyone within the organisation. How, in consequence, the ways in which decisions are arrived at within the organisation have become drastically altered, with new centres of corporate power emerging while certain traditional middle management skills have become displaced. And how, by corollary, the opportunities for datacrime have ceased to be the sole perk of computer operators and programmers.

The personal corporate computer

The first of the threads to this story is the arrival of 'end-user' or 'desk-top' computing. In other words, the stages by which it became possible for relatively ordinary, untrained individuals to tell computers what they wanted them to do and, with very little external help, get the results they required. 'End-user' computing can happen on any sort of computer; it is most obvious on the hobbyist micro, but, with the right sort of system 'front-end', the business executive user of a mainframe or large minicomputer can also specify his own applications without having to go back to the DP department every time. One of the less well-publicised consequences of the arrival of the micro, as we will shortly see, has been the demand that mainframe software should look a lot more attractive.

There's nothing new, of course, in the notion of non-specialists using computers – airline staff have been taking bookings for more than twenty years, nearly every big computer ever built has had its support army of 'key punch operators' to transfer written documents into computer-readable format; we are all used to interrogating banks via ATMs to get cash withdrawals or be told our 'balance'. What separates 'end-user' computing from these operations is the power, within limits, to be in charge of what the computer (or part of it, anyway) does.

In the mid 1970s, some of the best research and marketing brains in what was to become British Telecom were deciding to develop a mass market public access database service. It was to be available down ordinary telephone lines and the display would appear, screenful by screenful, on a modified domestic television receiver. The service was eventually launched in 1979 as Prestel. The design criteria then selected now make extraordinary reading. It must be remembered that the designers were not stupid men; they solved a number of quite tricky computing problems – the most obvious of which was how to run a reliable service with a very large number of people simultaneously making an enormous number of requests for different types of information and while several hundred suppliers of information were updating their material in real time. And all of this was to operate on unmodified public telephone lines. Prestel was designed around assumptions about public knowledge of computing that were fully accepted in the mid 1970s.

'People' it was decided, would not be able to cope with anything more complicated than a numbers-only keypad. It was rash to conceive of the untrained typing in whole words or simple commands. The on-line retrieval databases that existed in the 1970s were strictly for professional computing users: to obtain information from them you had to type in a precise series of grunts, usually abbreviations of English words. Get the spelling, punctuation or even the word-spacing wrong, and the computer would throw back a **?** or **syntax error** message at you. Not having anything else to compare with, Prestel's designers decided that everything its customers would want must be available simply by keying in the numbers on a series of 'choices' menus. It might take a little longer to find the desired item of information, but it would be safer. The second design decision was to make all information appear as a series of electronic file cards or pages. Traditional on-line retrieval services used a 'scrolling' method of display. This means that the information, however long or short, starts to appear at the top of the screen (or printer) and carries on till it has finished. 'Scrolling' seems very sensible compared with an electronic file card which may be too long or too short for the information, in which case more file cards have to be located and displayed. But scrolling services imply the ownership of a printer and in 1976, computer printers were extremely large, noisy and expensive. Prestel's method of display was to be the slightly modified domestic television set.

But by the time of Prestel's public launch in 1979, these assumptions were beginning to look drastically wrong. The hobbyist micro revolution had started in 1975. It had already passed the point where you had to build your own machine from a kit in order to participate. Ready-made computers, with displays and (initially) cassette drives, complete with BASIC programming capability, could be bought easily. Various forms of software, including primitive business applications, were available. The Great Untrained, those who had never had any proper computer education, it turned out, were not only coping with the keyboards of micros, they were managing to teach themselves programming.

In fact, at almost the same time as Prestel was being launched, the first item of serious business software for a personal computer was being released. Moreover, it did not merely mimic something that had previously been available on mainframes or minis. It was for the Apple II and was called VisiCalc.

The VisiCalc effect

The program presented a grid of cells on the screen into which the user could load letters, figures and calculation formulae. Its value was that it made it incredibly easy for the user to set out a simple model of a business plan, sales forecast or whatever and then try out variants in terms of operating costs, sales expenditure, commissions and so on. Adjust one figure in a single cell, and all the other cells were automatically amended. In other words, its forte was the 'What if . . . ? calculation all managers must play with if they are to get a grip on the dynamics of running their business or department.

It is almost impossible to overestimate the significance of VisiCalc. Not only had nothing quite like it existed before on mainframes or minis, it was almost the first PC program not intended either for the pure computer hobbyist or the games player. The documentation, certainly by the standards of the day, was outstanding . . . it did not assume that the user knew much about computer programming – or indeed was ever likely to become interested. For at least two years afterwards an overwhelming majority of business people selected the Apple II as the definitive personal computer because it was the machine upon which VisiCalc ran – and for no other reason. And for many of those who learnt VisiCalc, the investment paid for itself very quickly. It genuinely gave, for the first time, individual computing power to the corporate executive, independently from the efforts of the EDP Manager. It created a new sort of computer buff, one who had no formal computer training, who had little interest in games or programming languages but was attracted to the latest applications programs that boosted productivity. Finally, it caused irretrievable cultural changes in the business use of all computers, a notion we will examine further.

VisiCalc spawned imitations and improvements. Soon it was joined by high-quality database packages to replace file cards of information – dBase II was an early and prolonged success.

Word processors, specialised machines that combined keyboard, display unit and printer and provided an infinitely correctable typewriter and the ability to generate thousands of almost identical documents, but uniquely customised, appeared in the early 1970s. By the end of the decade, software products that had all the features any professional might wish were available on the personal computers originally designed for the hobbyist market. Another element in the desk-top revolution was in place.

And at about the same time, the first affordable modems – devices for connecting a desk-top machine to the telephone line and thence to other computers in the outside world – and the associated communications software – surfaced as well. Database services for the new generation of communicating personal micros were started up shortly afterwards. In the first years of the 1980s, in the US there was CompuServe for the hobbyist and domestic user and for business customers, Dow Jones provided almost instant share prices and company news. In the UK, Prestel had its first proper commercial success after failing in the TV set-based domestic market by opening a specialist service for personal computer buffs called Micronet; soon it was joined by specialist services for the financial service sector, for travel agents, and for agriculture. For executives in companies with their own mainframes, the ambition became to get corporate data from there on to their own desk-top machines where it could be analysed and re-presented – a task which in many cases has turned out to be easier to describe than achieve.

These four elements, spreadsheet, database, word-processing and external communications, have been the essential ingredients of the desk-top revolution. They all appeared in fairly mature versions in 1979 or 1980. Further new forms of personal software followed within the next few years – schedulers that assisted in the planning of projects, 'thought processors' or 'outliners' which produced nested lists of ideas that could be assembled into coherent plans (some of the material in this book was generated with the help of one), presentation graphics that let the user paint a series of displays onto a PC screen and then run them as a slide show to illustrate a set of ideas, desk-top publishing – wordprocessing that ends up looking as though it has been professionally designed and printed in an expensive magazine, and so on. Almost no one had predicted it, not even the hacker pioneers who had conceived the possibility of assembling personal computers from the microprocessor devices that had been originally developed for industrial process control and 'advanced' calculators. Right into the early years of the 1980s decade, management consultants' predictions about 'the electronic office' – they still don't exist by the way – were based on master mainframe installations graciously feeding data out to a series of satellite workstations at which the office worker of the future would sit. The workstation exists, and it is autonomous, with the individual user determining its use and applications.

When the IBM PC was launched in 1981, despite the fact that

it had a rather less impressive technical specification than many other personal micros of that year, on the strength of its provenance it rapidly became the favourite of the corporate PC user, displacing the Apple II within about a year. Soon, new software packages, capable of exploiting the IBM PC's facilities, appeared; Lotus 1–2–3 became the best-seller.

IBM PC users represent a key new influence in the development of computing within corporations. At the beginning of 1986 there were 5.4m PCs installed in US business alone, of which 1.9m had been purchased in the previous year; a further 2.3m were expected to be sold in the following twelve months. The survey that provided these figures – by Romtec – showed that 24% of US businesses had at least one PC and that among companies with more than 500 employees, penetration was 90%. As a computing subculture PC users are quite different and distinct from both the mainframe-trained systems or programming specialist and from the traditional micro-computer enthusiast. In fact, many of them cannot program in the usual sense of writing code in languages like BASIC, Fortran, Pascal or C. However, they are a whiz at stringing together ready-made programs and utilities so that they can develop their own unique applications. They have built up a considerable skill in the byways of the one machine that every corporation owns. They have their own clubs – User Groups – through which gossip and special public domain software are distributed. These people can contribute much to the corporations in which they are employed but also present a considerable challenge both to the EDP manager, whom they criticise because he is slow to respond to the desk-top revolution, and to senior management.

The corporate computing environment

The second strand takes us away from the personal micro back to the corporate mainframe, the changes that are being demanded of it and the way in which it is managed and controlled.

For fifteen or twenty years until IBM PCs started to appear in quantity on corporate desk-tops, the role of the DP or EDP department in a large organisation was clear: it operated apart

– geographically and culturally – from the mainstream activities that provided the justification for the organisation's existence. Its temple – still to be seen widely in organisations across the world – consisted of three large rooms: one was double-sealed and air-conditioned, full of clean grey boxes upon which lights winked or within which tapes whirred; one was a library and consisted of row upon row of tapes; the third was open-space but divided into many cubicular work areas at each of which a programmer sat in front of a vdu. The man who ran it provided the sole link between his machinery and his staff and the rest of the organisation. He did not expect – and mostly did not get – much questioning of his decisions. The organisation's top management's role was simply to wince and pay up when he quoted prices and lead times for the introduction of new facilities – or stated that the announcement of new hardware from the manufacturers compelled the organisation to go in for a complete upgrade if they wished to keep pace with technology.

These upgrades would have taken the company through a series of computer architectures and methodologies, from batch to realtime, from single user to time-sharing, from multi-user/ multi-tasking to virtual machines, from flat databases to relational databases, from punched cards to paper tape to magnetic tape to disc and Winchester drives, from magnetic core memory to silicon memory, from line printers to laser printers, from vdus that were glass teletypes to graphics workstations.

In some circles it is now fashionable to mock this DP priesthood and its acolyte programmers, who were reckoned often to be too in thrall to the succession of technological novelties produced by computer hardware salesmen. It was not only the arrival of the desk-top micro that demystified and dethroned the priesthood: simultaneously other events were beginning to change the political status quo within organisations using computers.

One of them has been referred to in Chapter 1, information processing was becoming simply too important to the future of ambitious and competitive companies for line management to feel that they could merely await suggestions from DP managers as to the 'next move'. Managers had become used to receiving print-outs of sales activity, budgets and profit margins; they realised that with more detail and greater speed and accuracy they could improve the organisation's industry position. The performance of mainframe computers was looking increasingly sick compared with the apparent ease and savviness of the PC. PCs have created expectations in terms of speed of response, flexibility and alterability of result, and slickness of presentation. Couldn't the newly acquired desk-top machine – which its owner now knew how to handle – be linked direct to the mainframe so that central data could be input direct into the experimental spreadsheet? The new end-users might not realise the work involved in producing the new facilities, but they knew how they could transform the information thereby derived into profits. It was in the seeds of this managerial discovery that DP departments began to come under the same pressures to perform as all other section of the organisation.

Increasingly, the most aggressive and competitive of line managers would not accept 'impossible' as an answer; they wanted results in their time-scale and not that of the DP department. As the price of hardware and software fell – the minicomputer revolution of the 1970s saw to that – so it became more feasible for the individual department to say that they weren't interested in getting their information from the central mainframe, they would buy their own minicomputer complete with ready-to-run packaged software instead – out of existing departmental budgets. The departmental secretary typed in the raw data. By the early 1980s, it wasn't even necessary to buy a mini, a desk-top PC with a hard-disc would do the job – and that could be purchased out of petty cash.

Within a few years the inherent security of a centralised data processing facility disappeared in most companies, as DP departments could no longer keep all an organisation's activities on one large mainframe. The mainframe became relegated to big 'number crunching' activities and the maintenance of huge databases; all the sensitive innovative work – the key research data – migrated to the micro. And with it, the task of securing the company's secrets became considerably greater.

But, as organisations expected their computing power to become accessible over an ever wider geographic scale, DP managers had to become alive to two other threats.

The telecommunications manager

During the early 1980s large companies began to realise that their bills for telephone and telex, if left to themselves, were becoming unacceptably large. In the United States, the Federal authorities embarked on a series of judicial decisions which had, by 1984, resulted in the ending of the traditional quasi-monopolies of AT&T – Ma Bell; first competition was permitted on long-distance connections, then Ma Bell was forced into dismembering itself into a series of regional utilities. In the United Kingdom, the government used different legal devices to break up the British Telecom monopoly, but the effect was to allow competition among suppliers of equipment and to license one alternative, Mercury, to compete in the main types of service area. These new commercial opportunities within telecommunications, the chance for a skilled manager to make careful assessments of his company's actual requirements and to play the field in terms of suppliers, came at the same time as the technology itself was changing. The telephone conversation between human beings has, until recently, relied on analogue techniques. Increasingly even on public networks, the conversations are digitised because it is then possible to utilise more reliable and flexible switching and communications methods. An adept telecommunications specialist can take advantage of this and cram several conversations – human and machine – along the one physical path, thus lowering the bill payable to the telecommunications authorities. Analogue telecommunications technology requires ultimately that there be one physical path per conversation. Similarly, telex traffic can be converted into electronic mail and perhaps handled by a message switch for optimum advantage of the tariffs. Satellite links and cable tv technology also can offer competition to more traditional forms of communications link.

In short, the 'man who orders the phones' has been replaced by a new sort of technological expert. And his territory keeps encroaching on that of the DP manager. The demand for having computer power delivered to every last corner of an organisation's geographic locations – the 'end-user' revolution – has meant the use of telephone and other communications lines.

Human telephone conversations are being digitised both for convenience and economy and thus resemble computer conversations.

The security consultant isn't concerned with the bigger political battle here, the questions he will want to ask are: Where does the demarcation line between the two jobs – DP manager and telecommunications manager – fall? Who is responsible for what? And if you see the organisation's system security as depending on the resilience of both computers and telecommunications – who carries out the supervisory security function? But this is not the end of the story.

Management information services/information resource management

By the late 1970s, it was also becoming evident that the largest corporations were beginning to suffer from information overload. The computers were producing so much data that managers were in danger of being overwhelmed with print-out, most of it not particularly useful.

So it was, in a movement parallel to the arrival of the first personal computers with usable business facilities, but actually independent from it, these corporations started to set up what were called Management Information Services (MIS) Departments or to speak of IRM – Information Resource Management. The purpose of the department was to mediate between the EDP department and line and top management. Part of the job was to prevent the rise of the independent departmental mini (see p40 above), but more creatively, to use management skills to handle information overload. John Diebold, one of the more reliable of computer gurus, set the scene in 1979:

Information, which in essence is the analysis and synthesis of data, will unquestionably be one of the most vital of corporate resources in the 1980s. It will be structured in models for planning and decision making. It will be incorporated into measurements of performance and profitability. In other words, information will be recognised and treated as an asset.

MIS/IRM departments, in other words, were a recognition that the EDP staff weren't particularly good as systems analysts and traditional line managers not sufficiently trained to articulate their requirements clearly to computer staff.

When the personal computer arrived, many MIS departments made a successful bid to seize control of corporate policy over their implementation. EDP managers lost out in this battle, by and large, because of their contempt for what they regarded as the low-specification PC. Yet some form of management control was needed – the PCs and their associated software had to be set up correctly for their end-users: an in-house PC-help facility was obviously required: managers didn't have time to learn how to connect up the various boxes and peripherals involved and in many cases didn't want to have to learn how to program in dBase II – they simply wanted the results. Where in-housing training was required, for example in the use of spreadsheets like Lotus and Symphony, the MIS department stepped in. MIS staff were also able to make sure that there was some coherence in the purchase of hardware and software – so that information and analyses once generated could be shared.

By 1986 it was being suggested by the Systems Security Technology Manager of Xerox Corp, James Schweitzer, that MIS/IRM should expand to include information security; however there is very little sign that this has actually happened. In the short term, security responsibility ends up being divided between resentful EDP manager, ambitious telecommunications and MIS/IRM managers and the traditional 'physical' security chief who guards the buildings. In a few short years, the inherent security derived from the fact that sensitive knowledge belongs only to a clearly identifiable elite has been replaced by a free-for-all.

The battle for control of corporate information

There is a third major theme to this story about the desk-top computer revolution: it has also brought into reality a prediction of the 1960s about the way in which business organisation and management would develop. The forecast, most vigorously promulgated by Peter Drucker in a whole series of articles and books, concerned the coming primacy of what he called the 'knowledge worker': in *Technology, Management and Society* in 1969, he said:

> A primary task of management in the developed countries in the decades ahead will increasingly be to make knowledge productive . . . The basic capital resource, the fundamental investment, but also the cost centre of a developed economy, is the knowledge worker . . . To make knowledge productive will bring about changes in job structure, careers, and organisations as drastic as those which resulted in the factory from the application of [Frederick Winslow Taylor's] Scientific Management to manual work.

In the same book of essays, he explained the historic process at work as an extension of the automation argued for in Taylor's classic tract:

> Between 1910 and 1940 the machine operators became the largest single occupational group in every industrial country, pushing both farmers and labourers out of first place. The consequences for mass consumption, labour relations and politics were profound and are still with us. [Taylor's] work resulted in a tremendous expansion of the number of educated people needed in the work force and, ultimately, in a complete shift in the focus of work from labour to knowledge.
>
> What is today called automation is conceptually a logical extension of Taylor's Scientific Management. Once operations have been analysed as if they were machine operations and organised as such (and Scientific Management did this successfully), they should be capable of being performed by machines rather than by hand.

It is, however, his prediction of the effects of this on organisation structure that are of most immediate interest:

> There is sufficient reason to wonder whether the traditional organisation structure, with which we are all familiar, is going to work tomorrow the way it has worked for the past forty

years. Everybody is familiar with the pyramid. We took our organisation structure from the military, and so it is a rank-focused structure. When you look at the high-technology and high-knowledge businesses, this structure does not work. You do need the authority of the decisions. There has to be somebody who finally can say 'yes' or 'no' after which debate ceases. You do need an orderly process for on-going work. But ideas do not observe these channels, or they die.

What we see emerging are, essentially, very complex structures, the analogy to which is not mechanical, as has been the traditional organisation, but biological . . . The high-technology companies are simply showing the way. Their problem is very acute. You may have a physicist next to a cell biologist, next to a communications engineer, and you cannot say that one is more important than the others . . . So you need to be able to have spontaneous teams, with a high degree of purpose and order and self-discipline, within a framework of orderly decision making and procedure . . . As we move from an organisation where there were a few people at the top who had all the decision-making power and all the knowledge, while the rest were at their machines, to an organisation where the bulk of people are paid for knowledge input and, above all, for innovative input, we are going to see more of this development.

By 1982, Drucker was beginning to see the implications for information security. In *The Changing World of the Executive* he says:

Information is the manager's main tool, indeed it is the manager's 'capital', and it is he who must decide what information he needs and how to use it. Managers will also have to come to grips with some critical questions about the role of information in their organisations. Who shall have access to what information? How can information be protected against fraud, industrial espionage, or prying and gossip-mongering? How can personal privacy be guarded? How can confidential information be confined to those who are legitimately entitled to it, without a secretiveness which encourages scuttlebutt and demoralises?

Top management

The final element in this examination of the desk-top revolution is to scrutinise the impact of all of this on Chief Executive Officers and other members of top management.

The people who make the key decisions within most organisations are in their fifties and sixties. Theoretically, any information which the organisation possesses or produce is theirs for the asking – always supposing they know what to ask for and how to make useful interpretations. Their formative experiences took place either in a totally computer-free environment or within a company in which the computer was a simple processing machine. Most of them have not adapted; anything that smacks too much of using a computer is thought demeaning; either it is too much like secretarial work or it fills the mind with useless clutter. These are common findings in surveys carried out by consultants. In a study at the end of 1985, management consultants Kepner Regoe, Inc asked the chief executive officers of the Fortune 500 companies about their attitudes towards computers. 52% said they never used computers; only 18.5% said that they personally used computers 'often'; 27% said that they studied computer print-outs 'often' and 13% said they never looked at print-outs. Only 27% of chief executives had a computer terminal in their offices.

The situation is neatly illustrated by a double-edged story about the European head of Wang, the mini-computer manufacturer, Arend Vleggeert, which he seemed astonishingly happy to spread. 'I refused to use my own equipment for 16 years in a row. It was too complicated,' he told the *Financial Times*, 'I asked them how long it would take to teach me to use it and they replied: one week. I said I was too busy and they should come back when they could teach me in a day.' By 1985, Vleggeert was told it was now possible to teach him how to use Wang machines in a day. 'I told them my time had become more valuable and I wanted to be taught in two hours.' And so matters continued, until 1986, when his colleagues were able to teach him the mysteries of the machines in an hour.

A 1986 report by Eosys backed by the UK Department of Trade and Industry confirmed the other side of this equation: although many of the respondents to its questionnaire claimed that progress in information technology was being driven by top management, many managements were less in the driving seat than they felt they ought to be.

The story of the consequences of the desk-top revolution – so far – is now almost complete. In organisation after organisation, the benefits of democratic information availability have been accompanied by corporate warfare for control over computer and systems resources as departments both old and new have fought to show that they alone have proved their right to be in command. Standing above them, but not really in control, are top management who, through a combination of fundamental computer illiteracy and a lack of awareness of the profound changes that the last ten years have brought about, seem unprepared for the vulnerabilities that their businesses face. In too many cases they do not appreciate that the changes they have overseen have resulted in an extensive abandonment of traditional hierarchical methods of responsibility and reporting, that information processing and management has become such a crucial element in their future viability, that much incipient discontent exists in lower managerial ranks as individuals come to realise their loss of importance and status, and that their security policies are wholly inadequate to cope with the new circumstances.

In the next chapter we must look at the ways in which people have attempted to quantify the range of risks that exist.

CHAPTER THREE

The Extent of the Problem

The earliest reports of computer crime can be traced back to the end of the 1950s. The veteran computer security expert Dr Ken Wong describes a 1959 case involving a large catering chain. Although the crime took place on a computer that must today be regarded as antique, there's nothing obsolete about the details and methods. In many ways it's as typical a computer-aided embezzlement as you will find. The company had a series of standing orders, maintained on computer, with a large number of suppliers. From time to time some suppliers would lose their contracts. An applications programmer employed by the company replaced these suppliers' names with fictitious ones. He amended the program so that only the invoicing file with the fictitious suppliers was updated, without any corresponding check on the inventory file. The 'new' suppliers' revenue ended up in his pocket, via a series of specially set-up bank accounts. The crime was uncovered when management became suspicious of the programmer's extravagant life-style.[1]

By the first half of the 1960s, a small but significant casebook of incidents was being built up. One of the most reported of these early cases, and one which is still frequently cited, involved the use of bank deposit slips. Customers usually deposited money with slips from a ready-made book which contained details of the customer's name and account number printed in a machine-readable code called MICR. However, for the convenience of those who wished to deposit money when they didn't have the right documentation with them, the bank provided blanks which were left out on desks in the public area. The fraudster replaced the blank forms with deposit slips bearing his own account MICR code. Subsequent customers used these forms as though they were regular blanks. In reconciling the day's transactions, the bank's computer checked the MICR code and sent the funds into the fraudster's account. Donn Parker of SRI, who is generally regarded as having the world's most

48

extensive collection of computer crime cases, dates this event to Boston in 1964 but similar accounts appear from other cities.[2]

Initially, these and other cases throughout the 1960s merely formed anecdotal evidence of the inherent unreliability of computers as clerical aids and sat easily with 'computer horror' stories of small households receiving demands for payment of electricity bills sufficient to light and heat a medium-sized town or individuals being relentlessly pursued by word-processed threats over non-payment of infinitesimally small sums. It was not until 1973 and the Equity Funding case that the public imagination was properly caught.

The case has been written up many times and was indeed made into the TV drama documentary – a model of its kind – called *The Billion Dollar Bubble*.[3] It often forms a 'set piece' in books on computer security and so won't be repeated in detail here; the reader is referred to *The Impossible Dream* by Robert Soble and Robert Dallas, the official bankruptcy report by Robert M Loeffler and Chapter 13 of Donn Parker's *Crime by Computer*. In brief, the Equity Funding Corporation of America (EFCA) was an American attempt at using a device originated in the United Kingdom, linking the sale of mutual funds (unit trusts) and life insurance. The client bought mutual fund shares and then used them as collateral to borrow money with which to purchase life assurance. The idea required the belief that the projected growth in the value of the mutual funds would be more than sufficient to pay the entire costs of the life assurance policy, including the fees and interest payments of the borrowing with which it was financed. There was nothing particularly wrong with the underlying concept, provided you believed both in the relentless growth of the equity market and in the capabilities of the fund's managers. As in the other great mutual funds scandal of the period, Bernie Cornfeld's Investors Overseas Services, problems started when the underlying shares comprising the assets of the mutual fund failed to perform to the expected – and very exaggerated – levels. EFCA had to pay out dividends and life insurance claims to early purchasers without having the real income with which to do so. The fund's managers had to resort to a whole range of operations in order to maintain the facade of success.

A number of these moves had nothing to do with computers; in the early stages of its decline, inter-company deals were used to provide 'evidence' of the value of the fund and thus create bogus earnings. This helped maintain the share price of EFCA itself. As real cash became short, EFCA made its life assurance subsidiary sell some of the future income due on the life policies to reinsurance companies who supplied cash immediately against income in the future. After a while, EFCA's life assurance subsidiary no longer had any more real 'lives' to sell and so started to invent them. It was at this point that the computer – an IBM 360 series mainframe – came in. EFCA used the computer in two main ways. First, the computer was made to create data, usually by taking a file of the details of real people and then massaging them so that it created a new illegitimate file of non-existent policy holders whose lives could be sold to the reinsurers. In the final count, 64,000 fake lives were created by these means: at the height of the fraud, more than 65 per cent of all EFCA's policies were on 'invented souls'. Secondly, the computer was used to create misleading output; almost the entire records of EFCA were available solely from the computer and there was precious little in the way of audit trailing that an investigator could examine. The computer was able to provide the appearance of a healthy company.

At the time, Equity Funding was the biggest known corporate fraud at $1,000,000,000 but there had been a number of significant computer-related crimes well before that. $1,000,000 had been lifted in 1972 by Jerry Neil Schneider, a 19–year-old Los Angeles businessman who had acquired knowledge of Pacific Telephone and Telegraph's on-line ordering system – using two classic methods out of the industrial spy's technique manual – scavenging around in garbage cans for discarded internal manuals and instruction sheets and posing as a journalist. He would place orders for supplies and equipment to be delivered early in the morning at various PT&T depots. Schneider would then show up to sign for delivery of the goods which he then proceeded to load into his own vehicle, which conveniently bore the PT&T insignia, having previously belonged to them and subsequently been acquired at auction.[4] The year before that $6,000,000 had been at risk in a US domestic bank fraud and

$100,000,000 in a computer-aided theft of goods and supplies from the US Army in Korea.[5] In 1970 four student activists at the University of Wisconsin bombed a computer centre. A researcher was killed, physical damage of $2.4m was caused and data representing over 1.3m hours of staff effort destroyed.[6] Another datacrime in the same year involved tapes containing 2 million names and addresses owned by Encyclopaedia Brittanica.[7] As far back as 1964, a man called Robert F Hancock offered what was described as $5m worth of software to the oil company Texaco[8] and in 1968, analysts working for BOAC, the airline that later became the overseas part of British Airways, offered for sale details of IBM's PARS and the Boadicea seat reservation software package upon which they were working; contemporary valuations of the package were in the £2,250,000 range.[9]

In fact, already by the very early 1970s, many of the classic computer crime types – we will be examining them in more detail in subsequent chapters – had already been invented. The first salami (or 'round down') cases date from the late 1960s,[10] a French incident from 1970 centred around a logic bomb and in the same year is a case in Cincinnati involving theft of computer time and resources from a time-share bureau. The perpetrator had impersonated legitimate customers by using their passwords and, when caught, was apparently in the process of writing a security by-pass program.[11]

However, Equity Funding was the turning point: it was the combination of the enormity of that particular fraud and the accumulated previous cases of computer-aided crime that persuaded journalists and researchers that here was a new important subject all of its own. First off the mark appears to have been a British security consultant called Peter Hamilton in 1972; Hamilton isn't a computer specialist but his *Computer Security* holds up surprisingly well. The first popular accounts came from another Briton, the crime journalist Gerald McKnight in 1973 with *Computer Crime*. In the same year came an important high-price academic work by the computer-guru James Martin, *Security, Accuracy, and Privacy in Computer Systems*. Another book for a popular readership was Robert Farr's 1973 *The Electronic Criminals*. In 1976, Donn Parker, who had provided case material for some of the earlier journalistic efforts from his archive built up at the Stanford Research Institute, published the book which for a long time was regarded as the 'standard work' – *Crime by Computer*.

Definitions of computer crime

The trouble was, the more books and articles that were written, the less precise the subject–area became. Soon, on the basis of various surveys, statistics purporting to show the extent of computer crimes began to appear. One of the most frequently quoted figures of the early 1980s is attributed to the FBI: that only one in 22,000 computer criminals goes to prison. In a March 1986 official guide produced for use within US Federal Agencies, *Computers: Crimes, Clues and Controls*, the authors were happy to include the following: 'Computer crime is a growth industry . . . Some estimates peg the increase of computer crime at 35 per cent annually and the cost at $3.5 billion . . . The computer criminal is less likely to get caught than the bank robber – and less likely to get convicted, if caught. Estimates of detected computer crimes are as low as 1 per cent. And the likelihood of a criminal conviction for computer fraud is less than 1 in 10.' Outside the area of official statistics, there has been, and still is, a rather unhealthy competition involving organisations and consultants of various kinds to provide the most headline-grabbing estimates. An American Bar Association survey in 1984 reported that 25 per cent of its respondents had suffered 'known and verifiable losses due to computer crime during the last twelve months'. However, in the same year, the American Institute of Certified Public Accountants conducted a survey of banks and insurance companies and reported that only 2 per cent of the banks and 3 per cent of the insurance companies had found instances of computer fraud. Computer security consultant Robert Courtney Jnr told the US Congress Office of Technology Assessment in 1985 that, based on 1,406 cases known to him, the average loss was $500,000; that 89 per cent of cases are never taken to judicial process; that of the remainder that are, convictions are obtained in only 18 per cent. Other people have suggested that the whole matter has been ridiculously overblown.

An examination both of the well-known archives of case material and of surveys published over the last few years shows how little one can rely on any of the figures. Since there appears to be an enormous thirst for statistics it is worth spending time on showing their comparative worthlessness and to ask: how do you propose to use the statistics once you have them?

The first problem is to define what you mean by computer crime. Depending on whom you speak to, the definition can encompass anything from those activities which would require a system programmer's skills to perpetrate right through to any activity in which a computer is somehow involved. The narrow definition includes logic bombs, trapdoors, salamis, trojans, network viruses, compromised access methods and the use of zap utilities, but very little more. Bob Courtney, the IBM security specialist mentioned earlier, uses this sort of definition to say that the Equity Funding case, where the computer was used to generate fake data and misleading output, was not 'really' a computer crime at all. The widest definition could include having one's pocket picked while outside a store selling computers. Almost every variant between these two extremes has featured at one time or another in a book, article or survey. Some analysts have tried to draw distinctions between computer crime and computer-related crime, but here again each writer seems to operate their own definitions.

Computer Crime Definitions

Crimes which include specific references to computers

There are remarkably few of these, though there may be incidental references, eg in the Police and Criminal Evidence Act, 1984 and the Forgery and Counterfeiting Act, 1981

Crimes not possible outside computer context

computer manipulation
  datafiles
  applications programs

    systems programs
attack on hardware
theft of software
theft of hardware & peripherals
theft of computer resources
hacking

Crimes which computers make easier

fraud
    false inputting
    'dead souls'
    fake inventorising
forgery
impersonation
theft of information
eavesdropping

Crimes in which a computer is a bystander

fraud
consequential damage
    to a business
    personal damage to individuals

Crimes committed by computer-using criminals

using a computer to keep track of criminal business
using a computer to create a fake front

Which definition you accept tends to depend on who you are and your reason for collecting data. The police and courts have a not unreasonable bias towards activities for which there are penalties in the criminal law. Where, for example, the crime is computer-aided embezzlement, there may be no reason to record the conviction specifically as a 'computer crime' but as a form of theft – even 'fraud' is not a precise crime. Some, but not all, collectors of data include theft of computer hardware and software piracy, although most people would agree that misuse of a computer's resources for private purposes is properly a 'computer crime.' Again, the insurance industry is concerned with claims on policies. As we will see much later on, most computer insurance is simply an extension of existing forms of cover – protection of hardware against fire, flood and theft, and employee fidelity, for example. Computer consultants, not unnaturally, tend to prefer wider definitions, but then they have less hard-and-fast raw material upon which to rely.

There are also biases imposed by the nature of the agency collecting the data and the methods they use for accepting material. In the United Kingdom, the surveys currently regarded as the most 'official' are compiled by the Audit Commission and were published by Her Majesty's Stationery Office in 1981, 1984 and 1987. In the most recent, invitations were sent out to 1,000 public sector and 3,000 private sector organisations. There were 1,214 responses, 60 per cent from the public sector, 20 per cent from the private. A total of 118 incidents were reported. But the full name of the body is The Audit Commission for Local Authorities in England and Wales and one of its main functions is to oversee the way in which local authorities handle expenditure on education, housing, welfare and other services. There was a very heavy bias in reporting from central and local government organisations. Of the 1,214 who sent in replies, only 154 came from the finance sector and 193 from manufacturing. Although the survey is the best the UK has, no one can really accept that these responses accurately reflect Britain's range of commercial activity or locations of computers.

A form of survey often produced comes from management consultants and security specialists. Here, you will usually find that the respondents are drawn either from the consultant's existing clientele – or from those whom he would like to attract as clients. Not all such surveys are blatant forms of self-publicity, but at the very least the sample has another sort of bias built in: usually only the larger companies can afford to contemplate the services of such people. The surveys will nearly always exclude the small business.

Even where compilers of reports have stated explicitly the range of activities they propose to include, an examination of the *actual* cases described shows that they do not always stick to their announced charter; some of the incidents covered in the

UK Audit Commission reports in 1984 and 1987 are so scant in detail it is impossible to judge what role, if any, a computer played.

It's also possible to build up statistics utilising published accounts of cases. This is the approach used by Donn Parker's well established computer crime project at the Stanford Research Institute. Parker himself has grown increasingly sceptical about the value of statistical conclusions based on his raw material. In the UK, Dr Ken Wong's casebooks published by BIS Applied Systems and based partly on work commenced by him at the National Computing Centre in Manchester, have similarly been used as the basis of statistical work, sometimes by Wong himself. The twin problems: to be satisfied that the researcher's scouring of newspapers, magazines and journals is truly comprehensive and exhaustive; and which press accounts to accept and which to reject. The computer press in both the USA and UK no longer routinely cover all 'computer crimes', but concentrate on those with some news value – which results in a not unnatural leaning in favour of the exotic. Relying on national and local newspapers has particular hazards: the general news reporter and the local sub-editors' desks are simply not equipped to report accurately what has happened, even if they have been sitting in court.★ Between 1985 and 1989, many articles on computer security published in the UK reported that 'one of the big four clearing banks' had suffered an enormous loss – estimates varied between £1m and £9m – and that it had been stopped and covered up by the expedient of getting the perpetrator, a systems programmer, to close up the loophole he

---

★There are other reasons for being cautious about press reports: journalism thrives on the unusual, not the mundane. Anecdotes, often inaccurate to start off with having been gleaned from clippings libraries, are repeated and so acheive spurious authority from sheer repetition. At its worst, journalists look for stories which validate their preconceptions, so that a pundit like me has frequently received media requests for 'hackers – the younger the better'. tv coverage is biased towards the visual; but most computer crime methods lack visual qualities – what is interesting about them is their very invisibility. Few computer criminals, apart from the ubiquitous hacker, have particular television appeal. Items that are difficult to show on screen are usually not reported.

had discovered in return for a promise of non-prosecution and a fee of one-half of the money he had extracted. There are good grounds for believing that this incident may never have occurred and that the whole idea started out theoretical suggestion.[12] In the course of writing this book I had cause to talk to nearly all of the well-known London-based computer fraud investigators, the principal broker in the relevant insurance area (bankers' blanket bond) and to the leading Lloyds underwriters. No one has been able to confirm to me, on the record or off, that such an incident ever took place: the most these insiders will say is: 'It might have.' However, UK banks are required to carry certain types of insurance cover – and when they apply, or renew their existing policies, the underwriters ask them for a declaration of any relevant loss, whether or not that loss was the subject of a claim. Making a false declaration can lead to a voiding of the insurance cover. If such a crime was ever covered up, the bank involved faces all manner of penalties if it is ever found out. All this tends me to suppose that this story may have to join those other modern myths which never have direct witnesses but always turn out to have happened to a friend.*

In another famous instance, in mid 1985 newspapers and tv stations around the world reported that hackers in New Jersey had caused satellites to be moved in their orbits around the globe.[13] Nothing of the sort had gone on. An eager policeman had misunderstood something he had read on a hobbyist's bulletin board (electronic message centre), had passed on his conclusions to a local prosecutor, whose opening remarks in a trial were amplified and distorted as they were transmitted and interpreted through various news agencies. Eventually the 'hackers' agreed to plead guilty to minimal technical offences and the substantive charges were thrown out; only the very local press reported the fact.[14] Even the very reliable Donn Parker's material occasionally gives rise to anxiety: in his 1983 book, *Fighting Computer Crime*, he provides a graphic description of the climax of one London-based case as taking place 'on the curb of busy Oxford Street on Piccadilly Circus at rush hour', a circumstance as feasible 'as the sidewalk of Park Avenue

*See also p 10.

at Times Square'. The incident – which involved motor cycle riders in the attempted exchange of stolen computer tapes for cash – actually took place outside Selfridge's department store. If the researchers can't verify the geography why should one believe the technical account of computing processes?

Even with the best will in the world it is sometimes impossible to arrive at an account which one can consider truthful and complete: too many of the participants are misleading themselves – or pumping out disinformation. One of the more intriguing of the 1989 cases is the suggestion of a relationship between the KGB and the Hamburg Chaos Computer Club of 'master hackers'. I'll speculate about this in Chapter 7.

It is this mixture of authentic material, rumour and fable that too many statisticians rely on.

An alternative approach is to exclude all case material for which proper transcripts are not available for analysis. The US National Center for Computer Crime Data, based in Los Angeles, aspires to this aim. However, the ease with which such transcripts are obtainable, particularly for cases tried in lower courts, varies from jurisdiction to jurisdiction. As a result, the raw data tends to be both unrepresentative and thin.

There's another sort of statistical analysis: where companies are asked to report their experiences (eg 'Have you suffered a fraud in the recent past?') but without asking for specifics. Surveys of this kind concentrate on attitudes towards fraud, or whatever, and ask the respondents how widespread they think the 'problem' is in *other* companies, whether the authorities are doing sufficient, and so on. The raw data from such surveys – Ernst & Whinney produced one in 1985 in the UK and a US-based one in 1987 – is often useful in helping both individual companies and the authorities determine appropriate policies. It is interesting to know, for example, from the 1985 Ernst & Whinney UK study, that only 10 per cent of small firms (turnover under £5m) thought their computer systems lacked adequate safeguards – small computers are usually less easy to protect, in fact, and small companies find it more difficult to utilise the 'separation of duties' technique which is one of the most important defences against internal fraud. Another useful study was produced in 1988 by Coopers & Lybrand for the

European Commission and concentrated on data networks. The trouble is that these studies are too often used as the basis of unsubstantiated conclusions. Highly selective quotations are used to illustrate journalism – or to sell computer security products and services. By sheer weight of repetition these assertions acquire apparent authority.

Beyond the problem of definition there are others. First you must take into account the difficulties relating to crime statistics in general: different collectors of such data assemble material on different bases. Are you viewing actual convictions; offences 'taken into account'; cases brought before the courts; cases reported to the authorities; cases that are unreported but, for one reason or another thought to have occurred; or reports of behaviour which is anti-social but not necessarily against the law? The further the compiler moves from basing his conclusions purely from convictions, the more he is relying on subjective or conjectural judgements.

This is particularly true of extrapolations based on what is thought to be unreported. As far as street crime (offences against the person or property) is concerned, some estimates of the extent of unreported crime can be calculated from publications like the *British Crime Survey* which regularly interviews statistical samples based on British households and enquiries whether they have suffered from any crime which has not been reported. For example, according to the 1984 survey, only 8 per cent of thefts in a dwelling, 50 per cent of bicycle thefts, 8 per cent of thefts from the person (ie robbery and mugging) and 11 per cent of sexual offences. The best-reported crime was theft of a motor vehicle at 98 per cent. One of the prime reasons for reporting a crime to the police was that it was a condition of making an insurance claim. The most-given reason for non-reporting, at 55 per cent, was that the damage involved was either non-existent or trivial; 16 per cent said that the police would have been unable to do anything about the incident and 10 per cent said that the matter was not one for the police and would be dealt with privately. Intuitively one suspects that this last figure would be much greater if similar work had been carried out in the business world. However, no such comparable research has been done recently in the business community, either by Government bodies or academic researchers. One apparently must go back to a 1962 British study by J P Martin which found that in cases of employee theft, only 41 per cent were reported where the victim was a large firm, and a mere 24 per cent where the victim was a small company. A 1965 US study came to similar conclusions but also found considerable variations in employer policy: one company prosecuted only 2 per cent of apprehended employees whilst another prosecuted 34 per cent.

Other academic work has sought to identify how much employee crime is *undiscovered*, typically where retail outlets and warehouses have been unable to distinguish between wastage or spoilage of the product, employee pilfering and customer shop-lifting. The 1962 English study referred to above found that 82 per cent of large firms and 56 per cent of small firms admitted to thefts from employees, whilst the apprehension rate was 0.4 per cent of the workforce in large firms and 1.4 per cent in smaller firms. A 1971 study suggested that 75 per cent of retail employees stole and a 1979 investigation found that 91 per cent of the sample of industrial workers stole.

The amount of unreported information crime – let alone computer-related crime – is really quite unknown.

In cases of fraud and industrial espionage, attempts are frequently made to produce estimates of annual losses. In a straightforward theft of, say, jewellery, appraisals are relatively easy to make – you add up the items for which conviction has been secured, plus anything else that the convicts have admitted to. Your only technical problem is to decide whether to base your valuation on retail or resale prices. In fraud trials, where there is a requirement to avoid unnecessary complexity, 'specimen' charges are quite frequent, the official statistics, where they are properly collected, refer to 'sums at risk'. Unfortunately, there are grounds for supposing that different police forces have different ways of determining what 'at risk' means. At the end of 1988 the British Home Office published *The Costs of Crime*, an academically interesting but ultimately inconclusive attempt to review the various problems.

Outside the area of fraud, estimates are even more subjective – how far, for example, do you include *consequential* losses in your calculations? For the computer-dependent business, it is often the case that the greatest costs are in terms of interruption to the regular flow of business. Or, suppose someone destroys or corrupts some computer data representing an invoice for, say $1m. The false data is spotted before the invoice is paid, but some damage has occurred which has to be rectified at a cost of, say $2000 in consultants' fees and there has been some damage to the victim's reputation as a reliable business, but that is almost impossible to quantify. Which figures do the statisticians take in building up their picture of the totality of damage occasioned by computer crime? And how does the reader of those statistics know which judgements the statistician has made?

The largest estimates for computer crime include the consequences of industrial espionage. How on earth can anyone measure these losses? The main area of penalty for victims is in lost business opportunities – the new product that will now have an unsuccessful launch, the proprietary process that will now be cheaply copied, the exclusive mailing list now in the hands of a competitor – how do you put a realistic figure on any of these?

Computer Crime Statistics: The Problems

Crime statistics in general: problems

convictions
'taken into account'
reported
unreported, but likely to have occurred
behaviour that is anti-social but not against the criminal law

How are you going to use the statistics?

to determine public policy
effectiveness of laws, regulations etc
effectiveness of courts
comparisons with other sorts of crime
effectiveness of police
degree of personal risk exposure > decision to take precautionary measures or insurance

Fraud statistics in general: problems

definitions of fraud
   criminal liability
   civil liability
   regulatory offence amounting to neither of these
reported to police but not resulting in any legal action
reported by accountants, regulatory bodies etc
what is being measured?
   actual losses
   potential losses
   sums at risk

   consequential (and therefore indirect) losses

Statistics gathered by reference to crime

convictions
sums 'at risk'
reports to police, prosecuting authorities
extrapolated estimates

Statistics gathered by reference to insurable risks

physical loss of hardware & media
business interruption
fidelity insurance
bankers' blanket bond

Statistics gathered by survey

official bodies
   NB bias even here: eg Audit Commission and Local Authorities
management consultants/accountants
   bias towards big business
computer consultants
   bias towards users of large installations & networks
surveys by analysis of media reports
   which media – consumer or technical?
   bias towards the 'interesting'

Why do you want the statistics anyway?

The debate on definitions and statistics becomes significant if decisions involving public policy are to be made. There are in fact two things one can reasonably hope for from statistics: figures for the total numbers of incidents of a particular crime and proportions showing methods, perpetrators, and victims. If major political decisions are to be made, it is clearly important that like is compared with like and that problems can be properly sized so that a view can be formed of the resources required to tackle the problems identified. For politicians and public servants, the findings of statistics can be used for a variety of public issues: how far are the existing laws and regulations adequate? How effective are the police and other investigatory bodies? How well do prosecutors, judges, juries, cope with cases set before them? How does one sort of crime compare in this respect with the generality of criminal activity, or other specific related crimes? Should the government introduce new substantive legislation or more powers and resources for investigation?

For the individual businessman, however, the only real use of statistics must be in determining the extent of personal risk exposure and the degree to which precautionary measures – including insurance – should be adopted.* As we will see later, there are formal methodologies in risk assessment and risk management which depend on the existence of statistical data, but it is questionable whether any of them are needed in order to derive a proper security program. It should be enough that case material provides evidence of crimes or losses occurring in particular sets of circumstances which could easily be replicated within the manager's own organisation. If the primary threat in fraud is from employees inputting unchecked false data into a computer system and likewise if the main peril in industrial espionage is from employees supplying material to business rivals in return for offers of future work, then what the manager must be concerned with is the extent to which the organisation's computers lack adequate input verification and audit trailing and

*See Chapter 11.

the physical security of disc and print media. The non-availability of reliable statistics should not be an excuse for inaction.

What the surveys say

Although I am refusing to put any *total* figures on the extent of information crimes, I think it is worth reporting the extent to which the more reliable published surveys agree on the most frequent types of crime, and classes of perpetrator. Each of these surveys operates on its own set of definitions about 'computer fraud' in general as well as specific sub-sets which are often not explicitly stated; one survey's definition of 'clerk' may be different from another's; however some general trends can be seen:

First, as to **perpetrators:**

UK Audit Commission Survey of 1985 was based on 77 identified cases from 943 replies:

Clerk	29.4 per cent
Supervisor, Manager etc	37.7 per cent
Programmer	10.3 per cent
Customer	3.8 per cent
Other	3.8 per cent
Not known	9.1 per cent

The American Bar Association *Report on Computer Crime*, 1984, was based on 283 responses to a questionnaire sent out to 1000 private organisations and public agencies. 160 replies stated that they had suffered some form of computer crime:

Perpetrators not identified	39 per cent
Individuals within the organisation	
Executives not directly involved with computers	13 per cent
Computer ops, supervisors	14 per cent
Programmers, etc	41 per cent
Non-supervisory computer ops	26 per cent

| Non-supervisory staff, not directly involved with computers | 25 per cent |
| Others | 11 per cent |

Individuals outside the organisation

Competitors	10 per cent
Customers/clients	7 per cent
Outside consultants	14 per cent
Individuals with no prior relationship to organisation	23 per cent
Others	10 per cent

(NB in this survey, multiple responses were permitted, so the percentages are of those confirming that they had suffered one or more crimes).

A 1984 Australian report by *Chishom Institute of Technology-CARB* based on 123 cases:

EDP Employee	39.8 per cent
User Employee	29.2 per cent
Outsiders	14.6 per cent
Unidentified	16.2 per cent

A 1985 survey by the US *CPA's EDP Fraud Review Task Force* collected from 5,127 banks and 854 insurance companies:

Clerical	49.5 per cent
Managers, Supervisors	21.8 per cent
DP Staff	10.9 per cent
Tellers	7.6 per cent
Others	10.9 per cent

The 1986 Mercy College Report on *Computer Crime in the Forbes 500 Corporations*, collected from 184 US companies in the Forbes 500, 1–11–1984 to 1–11–1985:

| Non-supervisory staff, not directly involved with computers | 24.4 per cent |

Unknown individuals, believed to be non-employees	20.8 per cent
Computer programmer	12.7 per cent
Unknown individuals, believed to be employees	8.6 per cent
Former employees	8.1 per cent
Non-supervisory computer ops personnel	7.1 per cent
Managers, not directly involved with computers	6.6 per cent
Outside contractors	4.1 per cent
Customer or clients	3.6 per cent
Computer ops supervisors	3.0 per cent
Executives not directly involved with computers	0.5 per cent
Competitors	0.5 per cent

The *NCCCD Computer Crime Census* of occupations of computer crime defendants (1986):

Programmer	21 per cent
Student	14 per cent
Input Clerk	14 per cent
Bank Teller	10 per cent
Accomplice	10 per cent
Unskilled	7 per cent
Unemployed	7 per cent
Employee with Access	6 per cent
Computer Executive	5 per cent
Misc	9 per cent

(NB: these are individuals actually brought to trial in the USA, total number: 71)

Turning to fraud more generally, the 1986 Home Office report *The Incidence, Reporting and Prevention of Commercial Fraud* stated that in 73.8 per cent of the cases it surveyed, the offender was an employee. The breakdown was:

Manager	29.0 per cent
Accounts official	19.4 per cent
Salesperson/shopfloor operative	12.9 per cent
Director/partner	9.7 per cent
Distributor/driver	6.0 per cent
Computer operative	3.2 per cent

Next, as to **types and methods:**
UK Audit Commission Survey of 1985 based on 77 identified cases from 943 replies:

Input frauds	75 per cent
Output frauds	3 per cent
Resource misuse	22 per cent
Program compromise	-

A 1984 Australian report: by *CIT-CARB* based on 123 cases:

Computer-related fraud	52 per cent
Unauthorised use	24 per cent
Theft of output	9 per cent
Sabotage	6 per cent
Masterfile destroyed	2 per cent
Theft of equipment	7 per cent

A 1985 study by Dr Ken Wong of BIS Applied Systems based on the 95 cases in his *Casebooks*:

Theft of equipment	21 per cent
Covert sabotage	19 per cent
Arson, bombing	19 per cent
Theft of information & media	15 per cent
System penetration	10 per cent
Logic bombs	8 per cent
Overt damage	8 per cent

Wong further classified the crimes thus:

Manipulation of input/documents	63 per cent
Use of remote terminals	15 per cent
Abuse of input data	12 per cent
Exploitation of computer reports	7 per cent
Misappropriation of computer resources	7 per cent
Unauthorised program amendments	5 per cent

The 1986 Mercy College Report on *Computer Crime in the Forbes 500 Corporations*, collected from 184 US companies in the Forbes 500, 1–11–1984 to 1–11–1985:

Theft of computer hardware	23.8 per cent
Misuse of corporate computers for employee benefit	17.5 per cent
Theft of computer software	14.3 per cent
Destruction or alteration of corporate data	10.1 per cent
Embezzlement of corporate funds	7.9 per cent
Destruction of computer hardware	6.9 per cent
Destruction of corporate software	5.8 per cent
Fraud against the corporation	5.3 per cent
Theft of output data	5.3 per cent
Extortion or blackmail	1.6 per cent
Theft of input data	1.6 per cent

The *NCCCD Computer Crime Census* (1986):

Money theft	54 per cent
Theft of Data or Programs	16 per cent
Damage to Software	16 per cent
Alteration of Data	12 per cent
Theft of services	10 per cent
Trespass	2 per cent

If nothing else, the small sizes of the samples in each survey and the considerable variances show that all existing computer crime statistics should be treated with great diffidence.

Surveys by management consultants Ernst & Whinney in both the UK and USA carried out between 1985 and 1986 show the extent and distribution of fraud in general in larger corporations: in a 1985 UK survey of 401 companies, 56 per cent felt that they had either experienced fraud in the past or might be vulnerable to it in the future. Sixteen per cent suspected that they might be victims at the time they were being asked. In a follow-up study two years later, they were reporting 'around two in three companies in Britain' now considered themselves vulnerable to fraud and a fifth suspected they were current victims.

Looking at areas that companies believed were vulnerable to fraud:

Stock, stores	46 per cent
Bank account/petty cash	25 per cent
Expenses	19 per cent
Computer Fraud*	8 per cent
Contracts	6 per cent
International business	4 per cent
Purchasing	1 per cent
Accounts Dept	1 per cent
Other	7 per cent
None	16 per cent
Don't know	2 per cent

*No definition was provided as to what computer fraud encompassed; many of the other catagories might be managed *via* computer resources.

CHAPTER FOUR

DataFraud

Once an organisation has installed computers, it has almost no choice but to manage itself through its computer systems. 'Reality' for those making the critical decisions is determined, not by inspecting warehouses of raw materials and finished goods, or production lines, or offices, or retail areas, or the contents of cash boxes, but by reading a computer print-out or vdu display. If the computer has been persuaded not to tell the truth, by whatever means, fraud is almost certainly taking place.

Few new forms of fraud have been brought into existence by the computer; however, the computer's powerful abilities to simulate the appearance of normality have made it the best present a fraudster could imagine.

'If I take money from you without your consent – that's theft. If you give it to me willingly as a result of a deception – that's fraud,' says one senior City of London policeman at the lectures he gives to warn businessmen of their vulnerabilities. The essence of fraud is deception combined with the aim of gaining a dishonest advantage over another. Fraud, pure and simple, isn't a crime. Or rather, there are very few elements in the criminal law, either that part based on the common law or that found in statutes, which use the word 'fraud' directly. It's a whole collection of crimes, breaches of regulations and actions of ethical misconduct. The computer's role is to aid the deception.

If you can persuade a computer to accept a false input, if you can get it to generate false output or if you can creatively manipulate a program's inner workings – and if you have the means to turn that into money or assets which you can then walk off with, you have the essential ingredients of the basic computer fraud. There is almost no finer partner to the commercial deceiver than the computer. The computer separates the physical reality of an asset from the *representation* of that asset in an organisation's books and records. The computer print-out or vdu report are the means by which an organisation's management and staff knows what the organisation possesses and what it is doing. A deceiving print-out has the virtue of appearing totally normal; it looks its victim as squarely in the eye as a correct one. To perpetrate a successful computer-aided fraud, you have only to get away with a falsified input which is not subsequently identified by the system . . . and the computer will do the rest for you.

False inputting is the easiest and most common category of computer frauds, though definitely not the most spectacular or interesting in terms of technique. The computer can also be used to aid the confidence trickster by giving the impression of high-tech competence and wizardry; alternatively a computer breakdown can be blamed if it becomes necessary to avoid or delay payment. However, computer- or system-related fraud isn't primarily about technique, it's about opportunities to commit and avoid subsequent detection. As we will be observing throughout this book, the obsession of writers on computer fraud – and their readers – with ingenious methods of implementation does little service to those who want to prevent themselves being victims. The success of a fraud is not commensurate with the skill involved in its execution. Criminals, with the singular exception of hackers, tend to look for the path of least effort and risk in securing their loot. We begin, therefore, by developing an overview of the variety of fraud.

The variety of fraud

There are a number of ways of classifying fraud, by reference to legislation, by activity, by perpetrator, by victim, by method, but one of the more helpful is by reference to opportunity and situation, because this is how they usually arise in the perpetrator's mind. The following is an A-Z of some of the best-known types of fraud in which information systems can play an important role; any categorisation must to an extent be arbitrary; obviously a number of actual crimes could be fitted into more than one heading:

Accounts frauds. One of the reasons for the introduction of double-entry book-keeping was to make fraud easier to detect; the would-be fraudster has to make adjustments in at least two places – and balance them out – if detection is to be avoided. Modern book-keeping practice requires the maintenance of a series of journals and ledgers which should make fraud even more difficult to execute. A proper software package for accounts creates the journals and does the posting to appropriate ledgers automatically. However, such packages can be abused . . . This wide collection of frauds, which can appear in many guises, is available to anyone with access to an organisation's books – clerk, book-keeper, computer operator, finance director, chief executive. It consists of making a series of alterations in the ledgers to make them reflect what the fraudster would like others to see and is usually directed to concealing the disappearance of assets or cash. The simplest form of accounts fraud is to omit to place a transaction in the accounts at all; the most common is to make a series of erasures or alterations. In a typical case quoted by the UK Audit Commission[1] from the late 1970s, a clerk in a distribution depot of a manufacturing company took cash from customers over a six-month period in cash-on-delivery sales. He then destroyed the relevant computer-produced delivery notes and cancelled the orders on the computer. In another case from the same source, a rather different motive for accounts manipulation appears: a financial controller wanted to ensure that actual profits for the year approximated to the previous profit forecast. The computer was used to redo the accounts.

Advance fee frauds. This is one of the oldest known frauds; money is taken in payment or partial payment for goods or services to be delivered in the future, only they never are. One of the simplest forms uses mail-order: an advertisement is placed offering a bargain, the fraudster collects the cash and disappears. To be sure of success, the fraudster usually has to build up the confidence of the victim to persuade him or her to part with the advance payment. One method is to carry out a few legitimate transactions and then persuade the victim that some special bargain is in prospect – for which a large sum of money must be put up in advance. Other methods require the fraudster to build up a convincing 'front' – an impressive address, a yacht, an airplane, where appropriate, a model of the proposed 'development' or 'invention', references, bank accounts, and so on. In 1984, two Indian brothers set up a shipping business above a photocopying shop with a London, W1, address. They carried out two legitimate exports of tinned food for delivery to the United Arab Emirates for $200,000 and $500,000 respectively. The next shipment required an advance payment of $1.3m which was promptly sent to a Swiss bank account; the recipients received two container-loads of rubbish; the London 'office' was closed with a forwarding-address in Rio de Janeiro.[2]

Similar to advance fee frauds are 'seed money' frauds, where plausible entrepreneurs explain to gullible investors that they have identified a wonderful opportunity which, once an initial sum has been invested, will undoubtedly reward those sufficiently prescient to recognise the potential. In another case, a proposal to build a gambling complex complete with casinos, hotels and an airport in a small Southern African state netted fraudsters $5m from the government involved and from five large international companies. The scheme had included the founding of a new national airline – the existence of which is a matter of pride to many poor Third World countries. The trail to the fraudsters ended in a single grubby room rented above a take-away in Florida.[3] On a more modest scale, fraudulent overseas time-sharing schemes often are in essence advance fee frauds. Many of the fraudsters involved are never brought to book because of the international nature of the crime: the deception takes place in one country, the failure to deliver in another, and yet a third may act as host to the banking facilities whilst a fourth (perhaps to minimise tax) is formally nominated as the country, the legal system of which is regarded as the 'place of contract'. Computers can be used in such scams to increase the credibility of the fraudsters – elaborate cash-flows and pay-backs can be modelled on desk-top machines; CAD – computer-aided design – can be used quickly to prepare models and designs; use of cheque cross-firing (see below) can help produce phoney bank statements.

Banking frauds.

Cheque cross-firing is one of the most basic techniques for persuading banks and creditors that accounts have more substance to them than is actually the case. Predating the computer but mightily assisted by it, the fraud relies on the fact that it takes time for different banks – or different branches of the same bank – to clear cheques presented to them. What happens is that debits on one account are not posted until after the counterpart credits have been applied to the other. The fraudster has therefore at least a day, and usually three days, in which creatively to mislead creditors, would-be partners or bank staff. By using a large number of accounts and careful timing, substantial sums of money can be made to appear on bank statements. The fraud is completed either by withdrawing a large sum from one of the accounts and then letting the others collapse, or by using the bank statements as collateral for a loan or evidence of creditworthiness. In a 1971 case reported by Ken Wong, an Olivetti 101 desk-top computer and a stock control program were leased and used to run a company almost the entire purpose of which was to facilitate cross-firing. The fraudster didn't even pay the computer leasing charges.[3] There was an element of cross-firing, too, in a couple of frauds involving ATMs – automatic teller machines (see below p 80). Teaming and lading (see below p 96) is similar to cross-firing, but does not involve bank accounts directly.

False collateral. A financial institution is persuaded to advance a loan on the security of various assets. The assets may be those of the business – its buildings, machinery and stock – or shares in other businesses, or personal assets of the directors. Alternatively, the asset may be a house, as in mortgage fraud, where a bank or building society is persuaded to lend money on the strength of a false valuation by a corrupt surveyor and/or lend money on a property already mortgaged as a result of a false report produced by a corrupt lawyer. In the case of a business using its assets as collateral, the usual fraud is to fix the books either to ramp up the value, or to conceal the fact that some of the assets have been already pledged as security for previous loans. Here, the computer is used to generate a misleading, parallel set of accounts. In the case of shares, computers can be made to produce falsified statements as to their existence – though clearly this won't work if the bank insists on holding the physical certificates during the duration of the loan. If security is taken on the private wealth of the directors, again a computer can be used to create a spurious set of accounts.

EFT/money transmission. Traditionally, one of the weakest points in banking security has been the methods by which one bank transmits money to another or, rather, authorises another bank to make a payment which will later be covered. The systems for international money transmission have had to cater for the capabilities of the world's least sophisticated and poorest banks as well as those of the technology-rich US and UK. It is still the case that in many Third World banks, the only technology available to receive such instructions are battered telex machines. Instructions are sent between such banks in encoded form using a series of test keys and it is open to bank employees and ex-employees to abuse the system. Whether the old telex technology or its more sophisticated variants are used, the most vulnerable point is the stage at which instructions are input into the system.

The most spectacular known fraud of this type is the classic Rifkin case from 1978 which involved the Security Pacific Bank in Los Angeles and some diamonds. It features in many books and articles on computer and banking security – fairly full accounts appear in Adrian Norman's *Computer Insecurity* and Donn Parker's *Fighting Computer Crime* (where Rifkin is renamed Mike Hansen)) and so only a summary is given here. Rifkin, at the time 32 years old, was a systems analyst employed by a contractor to the bank to provide a backup system. He was able to go into the wire transfer room on at least four occasions and observe the procedures whereby authorised users of the EFT services were given identification codes. He impersonated an official and transferred $10.2m to his account at another bank in New York. From there he transferred most of the funds to a Swiss bank account owned by the official Soviet diamond broker, Russalmaz, and purchased $8m worth of cut diamonds, 9000 carats, which, according to some reports, he could have sold on the open retail market for $13m. Security Pacific didn't spot their loss for eight days. Rifkin was caught after he returned to the States and had tried to sell some of his diamonds. While out on bail, Rifkin, this time with an accomplice, tried to repeat the fraud and had hoped to turn the money into bearer bonds – securities which do not have the name of the owner on the certificate and which can be treated almost like cash. The Rifkin case ranks with the Equity Funding case (see p 49) in public notoriety, even though the involvement of computers was only incidental. One of the consequences of Rifkin was the creation of new forms of computer insurance at Lloyds of London.

The banks of the Western world no longer use telex between themselves but more sophisticated systems. Internally, the US has several electronic clearing house networks including CHIPS, FedWire (which was probably the service used by Rifkin), and Bankwire and the UK has one called CHAPS. Internationally, banks belong to SWIFT, the Society for World Interbank Financial Transactions which by-passes the telex system and uses its own communications network and a much more sophisticated encryption system. However, it is still vulnerable to tampering with by employees. In mid 1986, three fraudulent instructions totalling £440,000 were sent via SWIFT from the Whitehall branch of Barclays to European destinations. A fourth instruction worth £600,000 was awaiting transmission when the fraud was detected. The fraud had been perpetrated simply by forging signatures and both Barclays and SWIFT were at pains to stress that the computer and communications services were not at fault; the case illustrates that once a system has accepted fraudulent input, it will rush to complete the transaction.[4]

Internal frauds. Although all banks have extensive internal fraud prevention and detection procedures to limit the opportunities for criminal activity by their employees, there are still plenty of instances. One line of cases involves 'spoilt' cheques – cheques which are met by the bank but, because of some deficiency in making out, are rejected by the central computer and sent back to the local branch for action. In a typical case from 1977, a branch manager made out personal cheques to shops which he knew were likely to be queried by the central computer and returned to him at the branch for action. He then simply destroyed the cheques. In the same year a female bank clerk had also noticed the same administrative loophole in the system; she conspired with her husband and managed to collect enough cash to pay for a glamorous honeymoon, a house, three cars including a Daimler, and furniture.

Another line of bank internal frauds involves a form of 'teaming and lading' or 'cheque cross-firing': what is cross-fired are internal settlement notes so that cash that has been fraudulently paid out is concealed by a series of credit and debit documents that never catch up with each other. The most spectacular known example of this is the Wells Fargo case which went on between 1976 and 1981. The fraud involved a con-man and two bank employees who were seduced into collusion. The con-man was running a series of 'businesses' involved in promoting athletics and boxing. He claimed to be a close associate of Muhammad Ali and indeed the 'champ' received funds in return for permitting the use of his name; Ali, however, behaved entirely innocently. The two bank employees, respectively a banking and services officer and an operations manager, became extremely friendly with the con-man as they shared an interest in sport. The con-man arranged treats for the two men, including tickets to exclusive sporting events and a two-for-one holiday trip. The con-man's businesses had constant cash-flow problems and gradually the two employees allowed unacceptably large overdrafts to build up. Until quite close to the end, they persuaded themselves that their friend with the glamorous connections (and a life-style including an airplane, a yacht and an entourage of 40 which was being paid for by the bank) would sort himself out. In the meantime, they had realised that Wells Fargo was settling inter-branch reconciliations on a 10–day turn-around cycle. Provided they kept the flow of credit and debit documents so that no individual debit existed for more than 10 days, the computerised branch reconciliation system was happy. Eventually, some $21.3m on, the cross-firing broke down and the bank's auditing department began to unravel what had happened. The trials that followed were as spectacular as the frauds and the book co-written by the prosecutor, *Empire of Deceit*, shows just how many people were seduced into participating in propping up the con-man's life-style, and how they managed to justify their behaviour to themselves.

Laundering. Strictly speaking, this is not a fraud, but the process by which money earned from illegal activities – robberies, extortion, prostitution and drugs – can be made respectable or 'clean'. What usually happens is that the dirty money is passed through a series of transactions and bank accounts such that the eventual recipient can have the wealth and also a plausible explanation for possessing it. Import/export concerns, where the eventual recipient can be shown to have been successful in selling large quantities of goods he never in reality owned, or banks and investment companies, where successful financing deals can be invented, are favourite laundering mechanisms. The banking system of Switzerland, with its traditional secrecy, used to be the main intermediary for laundering operations, but more recently activity has switched to the Caribbean. In a single 14–month period, approximately $97m was laundered through just one bank account, according to the head of the Metropolitan and City Police Fraud Squad.[5] The British police, in particular, have said that they intend to increase pressure on UK banks to show more awareness of the occurrence of laundering.

Treasury systems. The world's largest companies can handle vast sums of money during the course of a working day; at any one time they will both be receiving large amounts of money and be called upon to pay out considerable amounts to meet their commitments. It is the function of their treasury departments to manage the availability of these large sums. Such funds as are not required immediately have to be put to use, usually overnight in the money markets to earn interest. The companies need to have reliable statements from their banks – amounts actually credited to each account, amounts expected within the next two or three days (cheques paid in but not yet passed through settlement) and amounts that will have to be paid out within the next few days (cheques the company has signed but which have not yet been presented via the settlement system or sums that are known will be payable) – and a computer program which tells them how much money they actually have 'spare' to invest at any one time. The company will usually have a number of dealers who play the money markets looking for the best deal in the various money market instruments to maximise the interest earned. The computer program will advise on the alternatives and show the earnings in each case. The treasury department thus becomes a profit centre for the company in its own right. Several sorts of fraud are possible: dealers, with confederates in the money market brokers, can use their employer's money to finance gambles of their own; increasingly, banks are introducing systems which allow their biggest customers direct access to their accounts, so that instructions to move sums between various accounts can be sent direct from desk-top computers, usually of the IBM PC family. The computer security specialists are awaiting the first instance of these new services being used for fraud.

Bankruptcy frauds. When a firm goes under, several sorts of fraud are possible. Sometimes a company is set up with the sole purpose that goods should be ordered, transferred to the direct control of the directors or their associates, and then the company closed down without paying any of its bills. In other cases, companies are started with good intentions but, when trading conditions become rough, the directors decide to sell off the assets for personal gain – either pocketing part of the cash or selling the assets below their real value to themselves or their associates. In yet other cases, directors of collapsing companies deliberately and recklessly fail to pay the Inland Revenue and Excise. Computers usually figure as a way of creating false books to disguise what really went on in the business or to falsify transactions.

Charity frauds. The fraud consists of diverting money donated to a charity – either a properly registered one or a completely bogus organisation – into the pocket of the fraudster. Large sums of money can be involved: a fairly typical example in 1986 involved an Indian entrepreneur who took advantage of the Hands Across America charity in favour of the American poor by selling T-shirts, the profits of which he had claimed would go to the charity. If computers are used, their purpose is to manipulate the books to disguise what is happening.

Charitable contributions are frequently tax-exempt and another area of fraud are schemes which exaggerate the size of contributions, or 'charities' which turn out to be for the benefit of the donors. In the UK, companies even set themselves up to advise private individuals how to reduce their burden of tax by setting up suitable (allegedly legal) charities. The best-known of these was Rossminster.

Cheque- credit-card and ATM frauds. Individually, these frauds are for very small sums of money but, because a great number of instances occur each year, large totals are involved.[6] Cheque-card fraud in the UK in 1985 was £26m, over £1 for each card issued. The typical crime is theft followed by impersonation and forgery: a bank customer loses a card (and sometimes also a cheque book) in a break-in or pick-pocketing exercise, the thief passes the card, cheque book and PIN (personal identity number) as available to a specialist who then uses the card as quickly and safely as possible until it is likely to appear on the 'hot sheets' or be stopped if anyone calls the card company for authority. One of the commonest credit-card frauds is to use someone else's card number to order goods over the telephone; employees in shops are well-placed to pick up valid numbers from transaction counterfoils. The credit-card issuers have sought to limit this particular fraud by requiring that mail order credit-card deals must always be delivered only to the registered address of the card-holder. A less well-publicised credit-card fraud is called 'merchant collusion', where a shop and a customer conspire to create a situation so that the customer gets the goods but the shop is able to persuade the credit-card company that the transaction should be voided, perhaps as a result of a deliberate 'mistake'. The credit-card companies attempt to maintain a database of their 'merchants' who seem to have a high number of voided transactions. Merchant collusion is likely to grow as debit cards, and their associated validation 'black boxes' become widely placed in retail outlets of all kinds.

The commonest form of ATM (automatic teller machine – hole-in-the-wall cash machine) fraud is also impersonation; a card and PIN is stolen and abused.

However, medium scale fraud on ATMs is possible by external criminals and is one of the relatively rare examples of successful computer crimes committed on banks by complete outsiders. I acted as advisor to a 1986 Channel 4 tv program showing one specific version.[7] The method took advantage of the fact that some of the big ATM networks operate, not in real-time instantly on the bank's central accounting facility, but via a disguised batch mode★. When a withdrawal is made via a real-time ATM, the customer's account is debited immediately, so that if the customer draws out more than the daily single-transaction or weekly limit, or pushes the account over its overdraft limit, it is the bank's central computer which stops the pay-out taking place. With a batch-mode ATM, the decision whether to allow a payment is made by the ATM, and not by any central computer. The ATM decides on the basis of information held on the magnetic stripe – which contains, among other things, the account number, the PIN (in an encrypted form), the weekly transaction limit, and the amount of that limit already used up that week. The magnetic stripe holds some data which is permanent and some which is changed each time the card is used. The ATM *is* able to contact a central computer facility, but cannot adjust the account itself – it can report the previous night's balance and also (sometimes) check if the card has been used at another ATM in the last 24 hours. It keeps a record of all transactions and sends these overnight, when called upon to do so, to the headquarters computer and it is only then that the data is incorporated into the customer's account. The reason for this convoluted process is to save computing power. ATMs face their greatest use during lunch-hours – around 1pm – and banks with very large numbers of customers find it difficult to maintain a mainframe able to adjust considerable numbers of accounts simultaneously; the batch-mode enables the updating process to be spread out – the mainframe calls each ATM at a time which suits the mainframe's processing activity. Since each ATM has quite a bit of intelligence (it is, in a sense, a computer in its own right), the customer gets almost the same service as would be the case if the mainframe were permanently updating the accounts. But the disparity, for several hours each day, between what has actually

★'Batch' and 'real-time' are explained in more detail on p 169.

happened at the ATM and what the main computer *thinks* has happened, gives the fraudster and forger an opportunity.

The fraud requires one genuine ATM card, preferably stolen at the beginning of the week so as to ensure it has a maximum withdrawal value still encoded on its stripe, the associated PIN (which so many people still keep on a piece of paper right next to the card), a personal computer, a mag-stripe writer/reader and a handful of blank mag-stripe cards. Total cost of this kit: around £1500, possibly less. The genuine card is fed into the writer/reader attached to the personal computer, where the contents of the mag-stripe are read – nearly all cards conform to a universal ISO-published standard. The writer/reader doesn't have to understand the contents of the card – although parts will be encrypted, the beauty of this method is that no decoding is required – it merely has to store them until a blank is put in and the data written onto the stripe. As many blanks can be written as necessary. The fraudster thus has a number of cards each of which can be used to withdraw a maximum amount – 100 cards each allowing £250 produces £25,000. You'll get the cards back again, of course, so if you can secure a further fresh genuine card a week later, you can do the same trick again, and again, and again. If you have a portable PC in the back of a car, you mightn't even need 100 blanks. The fraud might be a little more complicated than that . . . a single ATM might not let the same card (or what appears to be the same card) carry out more than three or four transactions at a time; it might even communicate to others on the same network. However, these networks are not 'up' all the time – for example, you can't always get a balance from the central computer although the ATM will allow you to withdraw – so you might need some careful observation and a bit of luck. Most of the large ATM networks currently operating in batch mode have plans to go over to real-time.

A small gang, based in Wolverhampton in the Midlands, but operating in London, used variants of this method in 1987 to carry out a potentially large-scale ATM fraud – up to £3m could have been involved had they succeeded. They opened up a large number of bank accounts with false references and teemed and laded money through them to build up for each one a record of reliability. In due course, each bogus account was rewarded with a cash card and associated ATM. All that was necessary to complete the fraud was to clone each card many times over. This was done with a NBS Magcoder 9401 reader/writer and a personal computer. The two couples involved were caught with 1,800 forged cash cards. Their activities had been spotted by a security supervisory program used by one of their targets, the National Westminster Bank. Three of the gang were jailed, with the fourth successfully claiming she had acted under duress.[8] The case is additionally interesting because none of the perpetrators had any particular computer expertise – the idea came from a magazine article.

A similar 'electronic dragnet' was also used in 1988 to capture Serge Jovignot, who had used what was called a 'credit window fraud', which involved drawing money from cash dispensers during periods following Christmas and Easter. He had approximately 60 building society accounts in false names and with addresses leading back to bedsitters. He would deposit stolen or unbacked cheques just before the holidays and take advantage of the fact that the computers would credit his account 3 days later, but before the moneys had actually been properly cleared. A trap was laid, arranged between a Scotland Yard officer and two building societies just before Easter 1988. The trap consisted of the ability to close down specific ATM terminals at will. Once Jovignot had used one, they tried to predict which ones he would try next and then sought to move him geographically into a place where he could be caught red-handed.[9]

ATMs have also been used in association with other frauds as a means of permitting the anonymous withdrawal of funds. In a 1986 case involving one of Britain's largest building societies (savings and loan institution) an employee transferred over £40,000 from customers' accounts into her own by using a standard employee terminal. One of the methods of withdrawing the money was to use the society's ATM network in the middle of the night. Another use of the ATM has been to pay out members of a gang after a robbery; each was given a card and a PIN and told that, at a certain time, they would be able to draw out, in cash (and presumably in clean money) the sums promised.

In all of these cases it is the bank or building society which loses; in the case of 'phantom withdrawals' – where a customer discovers from their bank statement debits of which they are unaware and from ATMs which they have never visited – it is the customer that loses. Banks and building societies have sometimes been extremely unhelpful to victims in these circumstances.[10]

Commission and discount frauds. These normally arise as a result of collusion between a clerk or salesperson who is in a position regularly to authorise a commission for a sale achieved or a discount on a sale made and a person who could be receiving such a benefit. The fraud usually requires some bogus documentation to be completed, and the proceeds are divided between the two colluders. The role of the computer is either to accept misleading input or generate misleading output. In one case, a fuel company used a computer to send invoices for supplies to garages. The program had a facility allowing the granting of discounts at the discretion of a regional manager. A data input clerk 'granted' the discounts to three garages from whom he received commission. It is possible for a systems programmer to modify a program so that unusually large commissions or discounts are granted only on certain very specific accounts.

Collusion with suppliers and customers. Commissions and discounts are only two areas where collusive action between a company's employees and its suppliers or customers can result in fraud. Another important form is the warehouse or inventory fraud, where suppliers under-deliver, or provide lower-quality goods, or where customers are given more than they have paid for. A 1979 case involved a pub licensee and an accounts supervisor at a brewery – the landlord received beer for which he was not invoiced, the supervisor modified input records and the landlord paid the supervisor in cash.[11] A variant is to arrange for goods to be 'delivered' twice, so that payment is made twice. The employee sees to it that the documentation camouflages what has actually happened and an inefficient computer-based warehouse system will aid the fraudster by concealing events in plausible computer print-outs. A good warehouse system should require frequent reconciliation between goods inward and goods outward so that, if discrepancies occur, a physical inspection can be carried out. The company's administrative procedures should not permit a single employee both to authorise the movement of goods and handle the payment procedures.

Discounting or factoring frauds. The victim here is usually a bank or finance house. The fraudster produces evidence of invoices sent against orders completed or in progress but not yet paid. The bank or specialist factoring house is asked to advance cash. The invoices are bogus; sometimes computer-generated output is used to demonstrate the 'cash-flow' the factoring is supposed to support. In a variant of this, the victim is a credit collection agency. The agency buys the promising bad debts of a company at a discount to their face value believing that, if pressure is applied to the debtors, most of them will actually pay up. The 'bad debts' may be non-existent, or may have been produced in collusion with the company that sold the debts to the collection agency: company A arranges to sell goods to company B on credit knowing that company B won't pay. Company A then factors the debt to a credit collection agency. Company B shortly afterwards goes into liquidation and the assets are acquired from the liquidator by the former directors at a fraction of their new cost. Company A has received the initial payments from company B plus the value of the debt, less the factoring discount.

Dummy account frauds. A sales manager, accounts manager, computer operator, or anyone with suitable authority creates an account – or several – in a fictitious name and arranges for money to be credited to it. In a typical case from 1974, a manager had created a number of 'bubble' companies which, so he instructed be entered into the computer terminal, had apparently supplied goods to his employers. He then authorised payments; cheques were automatically generated and then dispatched to a series of accommodation addresses. To balance the books up, the same manager arranged for bogus sales of the non-existent goods. The fraud was able to take place partly because too much authority was vested in the one individual and partly because there were insufficient physical checks on the inventory. According to the Data Systems report, the fraud provided £50,000, and was discovered by a chance query by an auditor. This appears to have been one of those cases where the culprit successfully blackmailed the victim into providing a letter of recommendation to enable him to get employment elsewhere.[12]

Embezzlement. Embezzlement is the felonious appropriation of property which is in the possession of the offender as trustee, agent, factor or other administrator. It covers both theft from an employer and, in the case of financial institutions and others who hold funds on behalf of clients, theft from customers as well. Embezzlement features in many forms of information theft.

Expenses frauds. Exaggerating personal expenses is one of the most widespread of all crimes by middle- and upper-range employees against their employers. It is compounded by the fact that no one really expects records of expenses to be kept accurately. Most employees find that a proportion of their legitimate expenses – public transport fares, drinks, tips are good examples – don't generate proper vouchers. Most employers allow for this either by allowing for an element of unvouchered claims or by turning a blind eye to receipts actually incurred during the non-business activities of the claimant but which 'balance up' the expenses that can't be claimed.

However, most of the larger-scale expenses frauds are committed by payroll clerks. It is only the clerks who regularly see the source receipts upon which the expenses claims are made and once they have told the computer that they exist, no further checking may take place. In a case involving the UK Health Service, a clerk took advantage of the fact that doctors' expenses could be repaid either as an addition to the monthly salary or as a separate cheque. The clerk in fact authorised some expenses twice, both as an addition to salary and as hand-written cheques – the latter she intercepted, altered the payee names and paid them into bank accounts she controlled. In another case, a clerk re-used genuine vouchers to support a set of claims, the cheque for which was sent to an accommodation address where it could be recovered.

Forgery/forged documentation/forged identity. Forgery is one of the basic weapons of the fraudster. In pre-computer days, the forgery was executed by altering an entry or name with pen and ink. To the skilled and not-so-skilled computer user, forgery is easy. A favourite document for forgery is a cheque or other authority to pay – a cheque made out in favour of 'I C L' can be altered to read 'I C Lambert' and an account opened in that name so that the cheque can be encashed. This technique was used by two people who attempted to steal at least $800,000 from the Hartford Insurance Group in the USA in 1988.[13] (A fraudster wishing to convert or launder a cheque will often open a receiving account not at a bank, where managers tend to want to know something about you and take up references, but at institutions like building societies in the UK and savings and loans banks in the USA; funds can then be withdrawn from such accounts by way of a cheque made out to the fraudster's own bank account).

Some so-called computer crimes have depended on manually altered input forms: the fraudster forges a favourable alteration which is then passed on to an innocent computer operator: the computer system then accepts the input as genuine. The £440,000 Barclays Bank fraud on p 76 is an example.

But a computer can also produce an entire forged document: a machine-generated cheque, for example. One particular trick is for a machine operator to purloin unused forms during working hours and then set up a small routine to print off some cheques made out to his account using the cheque printer out of hours. (To avoid this danger, all cheques and forms used ought to have serial numbers and a manual log should be kept to record 'spoilt' forms). A variant on this is to forge bearer bonds, which are exchangeable for cash (see p 76).

Computers can generate forged letters – genuine paragraphs in letters and memoranda can be adjusted and then printed out using the same printers that would have been used by the alleged author.

It's also possible to forge an identity: forged ATM and credit-cards have already been mentioned, but the courts in England have held that people who use passwords to which they are not entitled are guilty of forgery. In the celebrated 'Prince Phillip' Prestel hack of 1984, a couple of hackers who were trying out 'obvious' pass-numbers on British Telecom's Prestel service (a standard hacking technique, see p 157) and discovered they had acquired the identity of a BT employee and had access, not only to the part of Prestel available to ordinary subscribers but also to areas only accessible to BT's supervisory staff. Armed with the information they thus obtained, they were able to become the system manager of the entire system and so, among other things, read confidential mail and use the pass-numbers of any other Prestel subscriber. Among the identities they assumed was that of Prince Phillip. They were initially convicted under the Forgery and Counterfeiting Act, 1981 but successfully appealed.*

Franchise frauds. Investors are induced to buy a franchise of a chain of businesses; the promoters claim to offer expertise, specialist machinery, supplies of materials, business advice, perhaps a site from which to trade. There's nothing wrong with the concept of franchising – fast-food, printing, car hire are all well-established examples; however, when run by fraudsters, you have a variant on the advance fee fraud – see above p 72. Computers can be used to generate spurious business plans, fake references, and so on.

Government and other subsidy frauds. The fraud consists of making a false claim to a government or other department. Certain industries, like agriculture, defence and high technology, tend to operate with the aid of subsidies which they have persuaded governments or supra-national entities like the European Common Market, are essential if they are to flourish properly. Farmers can be subsidised to produce crops or sometimes paid for *not* producing crops. Certain research-orientated defence contracts proceed on a cost-plus basis rather than on fixed price contract. The subsidy is usually paid on the basis of records kept by the recipient and checked by an official and it is the records which are often adjusted to maximise benefit.

*Hackers and how to deal with them are dealt with on pp 153–8, 258–60 and 324.

A variant of subsidy frauds involves mislabelling and tran-shipping goods across national boundaries. Livestock or crops can be grown under subsidy in one country and then regulations specifying the way in which the meat is sold can be circum-vented. Usually the meat or food is illegally smuggled to a neighbouring country where the regulations are different and where they will fetch more. One particular EEC fraud consisted of barges bearing grain along the canals of Europe without ever unloading. Export subsidies were gathered several times along the route.

Computers can be used to ease the paperwork of the fraudsters.

Impersonation. The computer is a great aid to impersonation. Computers usually recognise identity by means of passwords alone, though there are devices which can read fingerprints or scan a person's appearance. In one rather foolish case, a young 'hacker' acquired someone's password to BT's Prestel and used it to order flowers for his girl-friend. It didn't take anyone very long to discover him and he was convicted of forgery.[14]

Insider trading. Insider trading refers specifically to securities frauds: it occurs when financial professionals – investment and merchant bankers, brokers, professional advisors, financial directors and others who have received confidential information about a company which, if made public, would affect its share price, nevertheless execute a share transaction. A few years ago, insider trading was regarded as no more than a perk of working in the City or on Wall Street. However, it is now considered a fraud on the whole market-place as too much obvious insider trading is thought to deter investors.

This is one of the few frauds which computers have actually made rather harder to carry out. Nowadays the electronic screen-based operations of stock exchanges create journals of price changes; all bargains (buying and selling transactions) are required to be reported to them, usually by the end of the day. Unusual share price movements can be detected by software and all bargains associated with the price movements identified for the benefit of the authorities. Investigating officials will compare the timing of official news releases with those of bargains considered to have been carried out with unusual prescience. Insider traders therefore have had to resort to buying and selling via nominee entities.[15]

Insurance frauds. The usual insurance fraud consists of making a false or exaggerated claim. The two most common methods are to inflate losses incurred in an incident for which insurance cover is held, and to take out insurance and deliberately destroy the asset ('property' in insurance jargon) so that compensation can be obtained. There are also frauds within the insurance community: insurance brokers can over-charge their clients and pocket the difference, or they can claim more in commission from the insurance companies than they have done business to justify.

On a much larger scale are frauds associated with reinsurance. Most insurers seek to spread their risk on any one set of insurances by 'laying off' their commitments either to other insurance companies or Lloyds underwriters or to specialist re-insurance companies. One type of fraud occurs where one insurer misleads another as to the extent or risk. Another variety, which caused scandal at Lloyds of London during the 1980s, was a fraud on lay members of certain Lloyds syndicates. The syndicates are funded by prosperous private investors who, in effect, guarantee the risks of the Lloyds professionals who act as their professional partners. What some of the professionals were doing was to so arrange re-insurance that the private investors took on quite extensive risks whilst the professionals reduced their exposure by being associated with especially privileged re-insurance deals. Computer and computer-related insurances are beginning to become available (see p 336).

Investment frauds. A large number of different frauds are associated with investments. The investment arena is the largest single growth area for fraud now and for the foreseeable future. Increasing numbers of people are coming into quite large sums of money as the result of savings schemes, pensions, redundancy payments, golden hellos, sale of property, and the like. Such people do not always know how to handle money in this quantity. Governments encourage the private individual to invest in new ventures and the financial services industry – both the good and bad element within it – are anxious to help. Some of the schemes are fraudulent from inception, but others become fraudulent because of the incompetence of promoters, who either fail to observe necessary precautions or resort to fraud when their own businesses start to run out of cash. Some frauds involve millions of pounds or dollars in a single case; others consist of lots of small losses, each a terrifying statistic only for the victim, but amounting to large totals. Few of these frauds are 'pure' computer crimes; however nearly all companies promoting investments deploy computers in their activities and can use them either to perpetrate a fraud or disguise what is happening to cash. Investment companies of all sorts turn over huge sums of money and the failure of their computers – complete or partial – for whatever reason can very rapidly put investors' funds at risk.

This is not a book about City fraud and any overview must of necessity be superficial:

Bogus investments. In this group of frauds, members of the public are induced to part with money for investments that are bogus. The simplest form is a strictly short-term operation rather akin to the basic mail-order fraud: an investment company advertises a share, a managed fund, a time-share in a building, etc, collects the cash and disappears.

A variant of this is the issuing of an improperly constituted prospectus. Invitations to subscribe for shares have to follow a number of legal and regulatory requirements – largely to ensure that prospective investors have sufficient information upon which to make a proper decision.

A related fraud is for the investment company to deliver fraudulent certificates for shares or other investment (eg bond, option, commodities future, title to a house, etc): here the underlying investment may exist, it's just that the investor doesn't acquire a legitimate certificate for it. These dangers are particularly great with overseas investments.

Fraudulent investment companies. Companies offering investments may themselves be completely fraudulent: nearly every country in the world requires its investment businesses to operate under some form of licence or registration. Such a licence may be granted either directly by a ministry or specialist entity like the Securities and Exchange Commission or Securities and Investments Board, or by a governing body like an Exchange. However, investment companies have tried to trade without such a licence or, sometimes, after having had their licence withdrawn or, although licensed, have carried out transactions not covered by the terms of their licence.

Some of the worst frauds in this category have arisen across national boundaries: investment companies have been set up in countries with a lax regulatory framework and have sought customers in other countries. Until the end of 1986, Amsterdam in the Netherlands was the site of a number of companies selling aggressively to potential clients in the United Kingdom, Germany and the United States. Netherlands Antilles, Spain and Gibraltar have also provided havens for 'bucket shops'.*

---

*A case which came to a climax on April 1st, 1981, shows how these elements, aided and abetted by several computers, can be combined. An individual with a large East Coast brokerage house developed a reputation as a computer genius based largely on programs which analysed the behaviour of the share market. His speciality was traded options, where investors buy and sell, not the share itself but an option to purchase the share at a future specified time at a specified price. Trading is highly geared so that a relatively small movement in the price of the underlying share results either in big gains or big losses to the holder of the option. By 1980, the computer genius had added another wrinkle to his operations: he exploited differences in the prices of the options on different exchanges, creating a series of instant profits by making large numbers of instantaneous buying and selling deals through electronic trading systems. To satisfy the demand for his services, he formed a series of investment partnerships for private investors – the minimum to join was $100,000 – the funds from which were supposed to be his working capital.

Neither he nor his analytical programs could keep up with the vagaries of stock exchange performance; he now had a large number of clients who had persuaded themselves that large returns could be expected from their investments. Indeed he encouraged them in their beliefs: selected clients would be invited to view the large and impressive computer systems that belonged to his employers; few of his clients were in any position to assess what the software was actually doing. As the performance of all these traded option and arbitrage deals failed to come up to expectation, the genius resorted to two well-known tricks to stave off disaster. First, he generated fake output on a minicomputer so that clients received reports that gave them a misleading impression of how well they were doing. Secondly, when called upon to pay out returns to older-established clients, he used the funds received from his newest clients. $80m passed through his hands in the end, and $53m were never recovered.[16]

A rather separate hazard are investment businesses which do have proper authority to trade but which, for a variety of reasons, are adopting fraudulent practices. Such fraud may not always be deliberate; indeed it is a characteristic of a number of recent collapses among securities businesses that ineptitude on the part of the directors has been the main reason. Among such frauds are:

- trading without the resources to meet commitments – the technical term is insufficient capital adequacy – the danger here is that the investment business becomes insolvent.
- clients' funds not kept separate from those of the investment business; a related fraud which arises from this occurs when an investment company makes an investment (ie buys shares) without being clear whether the investment is for its own benefit or for specific clients: what can happen is that, if the investment is successful, it is deemed to have been for the benefit of the managers and if it is a failure, the client is expected to take the loss.

  If at the same time the investment business is experiencing cash-flow difficulties, clients' money can be misused to shore up the business.
- clients' funds diverted into investments which the client did not authorise: clients usually entrust their money either for a specific investment or class of investments.
- paying dividends from income of subsequent investors: this is the classic fraud that was committed by Equity Funding (see p 49) and also by Bernie Cornfeld's Investor's Overseas Services – 'Do you sincerely want to be rich?' was the famous line in its salesman's manual.

  This fraud is also sometimes called a Ponzi.
- confusing acting as agent and as principal: investment businesses can operate either on their own account, offering the public the right to buy and sell securities direct with them as a principle (eg a market-maker) or as an agent, where the investment business acts *for* the client. In the second case, the business must provide the client with best execution; in the first, the client simply makes a deal. Investment busi-

nesses must never confuse the two, or allow those with whom they deal to become confused.

- over-issuing of contract notes: this occurs when an investment business issues a note to a client that a deal has been executed without being able to deliver a certificate of title to back it up.

- making a false market, or price manipulation, occurs when investors are led to believe that they can buy and sell at certain prices but in fact are unable to do so. Prices can be manipulated by the issuing of bogus 'news' and also if the investment business and its close associates provide the main mechanism by which the securities can be traded.

- churning of managed portfolios. This fraud is very difficult to prove but is widespread. It applies to the situation where the investor has agreed to guidelines with the investment business as to the *sort* of investment and investment targets required, but leaves the specific details to the professional. The professional makes his money not only from fees but also from commissions when buying and selling. 'Churning' consists of sequences of buying and selling in order to secure the commissions at the expense of the client.

Settlement frauds. Most trades in securities are not done for immediate cash; although you can buy and sell instantaneously, in the end, if you are buying, you will want to receive an unambiguous certificate stating what you have bought issued by the company underlying the investment. If you are selling, somewhere there will be an eventual purchaser who will require delivery of the certificates you hold. Settlement of title to the investment, in its very nature, can't be instantaneous. What usually happens is that, immediately after a trade has taken place, a contract note is issued. Within a 'settlement period' (in the case of the London Stock Exchange this proceeds in cycles of two or three weeks), the client has to produce cash (if he has bought) and should receive cash (if he has sold). The physical transfer of shares and adjustments to the registration of the shares follows afterwards. If the trade takes place within the framework of a recognised investment exchange, centralised computer facilities usually speed the matter up. In the not too distant future, some share certificates may become all electronic, but this is not the case at the moment. Outside the recognised exchanges, settlement may be rather more informal.

It is the gaps between the making of the trade and the requirement for cash and the requirement to produce certificates that provides the opportunities for fraud.*

The Eurobond market which, despite the name is completely international, has *two* settlement systems. The market, which is for professional investors only, is in debt instruments created by the world's largest companies – they raise funds rather as governments do, not by issuing shares but by issuing coupons which either pay a guaranteed rate of interest or will be re-deemed at a fixed price at a specified future time (there are other variants). These coupons are then traded in the international Eurobond secondary market. Such regulation as exists comes from a Geneva-based organisation, AIDB. There are two rival settlement systems, the Luxembourg-based Cedel and Euroclear

---

*An investment business trading in London during 1985 and 1986, but run by a US citizen, had most of its clients in Germany and Switzerland. It specialised in issuing and trading small new companies on an over-the-counter basis. The shares were not traded on a formal exchange but between the clients of the investment business. The business had an appropriate licence to trade from the UK authorities and, at the time, there was nothing fundamentally illegal about its modus operandi. Clients usually received contract notes after dealing, but were only given proper share certificates if they specifically so requested. The certificates themselves were supposed to be kept in an escrow account.

Several things went wrong for the company, which expanded at a great rate and had a number of overseas associates. It had invested in a very large computer system which was supposed to provide share trading facilities to the overseas associates as well as generating contract notes and presenting reports to the managers about their stock positions. No existing computer program was identified that could do the required work and one was com-missioned which had to be written from the very beginning. Because the company was expanding so rapidly – its overseas salesmen used high pressure techniques – the computer could never keep up. As a result, the management rapidly lost track of what shares they held, and what deals were being made. Contract notes vastly in excess of the number of shares available were issued. Clients were not paid. So much confusion existed in the accounts that it was not clear which funds belonged to the business and which to the clients. These and rumours of other scandals – that some of the overseas associates had links to organised crime and another that the markets made in some of the shares were false, the prices being ramped up by unjustifiably enthusiastic sales techniques and a reluctance to buy the shares back at a comparable price – brought the company to a spectacular end.

in Brussels. Details of deals are transmitted via the Geisco secure electronic messaging service and payments are sent via SWIFT (see p 76 above). A spectacular case in 1986 involved a former employee of Pru-Bache Securities in London and his friend, a roofer. The employee, Angelo Lamberti was a Eurobond settlement supervisor and he had access to authority codes. John Felinski had a computer terminal at home and tried to move $8.5m worth of bonds to Geneva.[17]

Fraudulent securities. Another form of investment fraud occurs when the certificates themselves are fraudulent: one version is to produce authentic-looking documents for securities which don't exist – either the company doesn't exist at all or it hasn't issued those particular sorts of security; another is to offer forgeries of real securities. In 1983 the London office of Morgan Guaranty discovered between $7m and $10m worth of zero-coupon bonds which were being used as collateral for large bank loans. The forgeries duplicated genuine bonds but had fake serial numbers. Although the bogus bonds had passed through both clearing houses, the bond numbers were not recorded on computer and so the forgeries were not picked up until too late. In another case early in 1987, forged zero coupon notes issued by Exxon and with a face value of $19m were uncovered.[18]

Insider trading. See p 89 above.

Lapping or teaming and lading is similar to cheque cross-firing but does not involve bank accounts: the accounts manipulated are usually all within one company or group of companies. Cash due to be paid out is withheld for a day or so to give the illusion that the account has more wealth than is actually the case; alternatively, accounts can be manipulated to suggest that significant sums are due to the company. Computers can be used both to orchestrate the movement of funds between accounts and to provide plausible output with which to confuse outsiders.

Long-firm fraud is a particular variant on advance-fee fraud. The fraudsters set up in business, typically as wholesalers, place orders with suppliers, the first few of which go through normally in order to build up credibility. Then much larger orders are placed and both the goods and the perpetrators disappear.

Materials frauds tend to arise as a result of deliberate mislabelling. In a typical, small-scale case reported by Ken Wong, the caterer to a large confectionery company had a standing order with a local butcher for a fixed quantity and quality of meat each month. Inferior and underweight meat was supplied and a computer used to disguise the fact from the confectionery company. Approximately £30,000 was misappropriated over twelve months.[19] In another case, this time collected by the Audit Commission, a branch general manager working with other branch executives arranged for customers to quote a misleading description of goods on dispatch documentation so that current goods were shown as obsolete and hence under-priced.[20] This form of fraud is another example of the computer printout being accepted as sufficient evidence of what was happening.

As more and more companies move over to mag-stripe and bar-code methods of data input, the opportunity arises for mislabelling of physical objects to become unreadable to the human eye. A sticky price label can have the proper price printed on it, but a different figure imprinted on the bar-code or mag-stripe that is actually read by a cash-till or warehouse inventory system.

Mistake rectification frauds. Most accounts systems have a fudge facility which allows errors to be corrected. A typical situation where such facilities are needed is where a clerk's keystroking of input has gone beyond the point where the clerk can correct it himself or herself; another is where a customer has made a purchase, which has been properly input into a system and then returns the goods either because they are no longer wanted or are in some way faulty. The mistake rectification facility should be designed so that an individual *in charge* of the clerk who made the faulty input can carry out an authorised correction.

If, however, such a facility has been clumsily added into an established accounts systems, the computer itself may not be keeping proper records of what rectifications have taken place and who has authorised them. Therein lies the opportunity for fraud. The 'spoilt cheque' frauds mentioned on p 76 above also fall into this category.

Payroll frauds share certain features with expenses frauds. The usual fraudster is a payroll clerk who either invents employees whose paycheques can be converted or who boosts the size of their own paycheque. Donn Parker provides an example: a female timekeeping clerk had the responsibility of collecting regular and overtime data for 300 employees; the results were input into a computer which eventually produced payment cheques. The clerk discovered that whilst all human, manual checking and verification of data was based on employee names, the computer appeared to work by employee *number*. The clerk started experimenting: whilst the computer detected if she awarded a worker twice the normal amount of regular hours, it did not pick up if someone appeared to be working large amounts of overtime. So she devised a fraud: on a form bearing the name of a worker who might be expected to work lots of overtime she appended her own employee number. The manual system of checking accepted the form because all the humans involved simply looked at the employee name. The computer paid her the overtime. According to Parker, so far all this had been little more than an experiment but the clerk then decided to embark on a series of repetitions and 'won' herself several thousand dollars before an auditor identified what had been going on as a result of examining income tax returns.[*][21]

POS frauds. The traditional point-of-sale supermarket fraud involves short-changing the customer or 'under-ringing', as it is sometimes called. In non-supermarket retail outlets it is still the most common form. With the arrival of laser and mag-stripe readers and computerised tills this fraud has become more difficult to execute, particularly as the customer increasingly receives an itemised receipt. This reduces the opportunities for

---

[*]This case is also a particularly neat instance of how many datafrauds occur: an employee spots a fault in a computer system and decides to take advantage. There is little computer-related technical skill involved, but the fraudster has knowledge of local procedures, opportunity, and an insufficient sense of moral restraint.

fraud by check-out staff. However new frauds are opening up for local management, either by misuse of the computer-read-able labels (see p 97 above) or by taking advantage of newer forms of payment. Credit-card counterfoils lend themselves to two obvious frauds: altering the amount to be credited to the shop (useful if you are the shop's owner), and using the card number and details to mail-order goods by phone – though this last form of fraud is preventable if the mail-order company says it will only deliver to the address the credit-card company has for the legitimate owner.

As the new debit cards arrive on the scene (where a card is used in place of a cheque and the amount deducted from the owner's account immediately), so new acceptance and authoris-ation terminals are starting to appear in shops. Unlike the older credit-card authorisation terminals which merely give an OK to a particular transaction, the newer machines cause an immediate alteration to an account. These machines are as powerful in their effect as ATMs; however ATMs are nearly always set into walls associated with bank property whilst the debit card machines are small, freestanding and located within retailers' premises. Fraudu-lent tampering with these machines seems almost inevitable.

Public sector corruption. So much money is spent by central and local government that it is not surprising that frauds of all kinds, large- and small-scale, occur. Many of them do not involve computers but consist of bribery of officials by outside contractors. However, in a 1986 case, the DP supremo of West Midlands County Council who controlled a £4m annual budget was discovered to have carried on frauds for a ten-year period amounting to nearly £180,000. His methods relied very little on his knowledge of computers, but he was able to manipulate the invoice-raising procedures, partly by stealing headed notepaper from ICL, the supplier of much of the computer equipment used by the Council, so that companies controlled by him received payment for work that had not been carried out.[22]

Revenue and Customs & Excise frauds. During 1981 a group of about 40 diamond and gold dealers operating from Hatton Garden managed to steal a minimum of £20m from the UK

Customs & Excise authorities. In that year, the price of gold was exceptionally volatile – there was international inflation, fears about interest rates, a falling US dollar and a slump in the US economy – all leading to a flight into gold. Queues of ordinary people bearing gold heirlooms thronged Hatton Garden, hoping for good trade-in prices. In the midst of all of this excitement there was a curious tax loophole. In Britain, gold bullion and jewellery is subject to value-added tax (at 15 per cent); however if you purchased gold *coins*, like the South African krugerrand or Canadian maple leaf, no tax applied. These coins were regarded as normal currency although strictly speaking they did not enjoy normal circulation and the price at which they exchanged hands was not the face value but determined by the existing price for the gold content. An opportunity for fraud – golden in every sense – thus appeared. The coins were removed to quiet, discreet foundries where they were melted down into bullion bars categorised as jeweller's scrap. The bars were then sold to bullion dealers at market prices – plus value-added tax – on invoices which purported to offset their tax liability. The 40 businesses kept two sets of books – the value added tax invoices were 'lost' and 15 per cent of each transaction, amounting to over £20m was retained by the fraudsters. Customs investigators spent six years unravelling the network of deals – the paperwork alone weighed nearly 1 ton – and two extensive lengthy trials, one five months long, ensued. Not all the miscreants were brought before the courts – tax evasion is not an extraditable offence – and a third planned trial will probably never take place. None of the money was ever recovered and the cost to the State of the investigation – called Operation Ernie – and trials was in excess of £3m.[23] If the events of 1981 were repeated today – they won't be precisely because VAT was imposed on gold coin transactions in 1983 – the investigation might be even more fraught, as many of the deals and 'books' would be computerised.

In a rather unusual fraud, a software house offered for sale a package for owners of video rental libraries. It was called 'Movieman' and it had a rather special hidden feature. If the software house had decided to tell, you could automatically run two sets of books, one which gave a proper declaration of value added tax and one which provided a significant, though still not implausible, under-declaration so that the library owner could pocket the difference. The case came to court in 1986, by which time 120 copies had been sold at prices between £5000 and £7000. Nine traders admitted to using the hidden facility and that they had under-declared by a total of £34,487. The software house directors were convicted of conspiracy to defraud.

That the case is a significant development from the traditional 'two sets of books' type of tax fraud can be seen from the comment of the Assistant Chief Investigative Officer of the Customs and Excise: 'This has opened up a whole new interesting area of investigation for us and brings us with a jolt into the computer-age fraud.'[24]

Social security fraud. Certain sections of the public seem to view social security fraud carried out by potential clients of the benefits with unique horror. The anxieties about scroungers on the system is, as we will see later, out of all proportion when compared to frauds committed by tax evasion as well as the business frauds that are being described in this chapter. You need to be pretty badly off before you even qualify to be able to commit social security frauds.

There have, however, been a number of frauds on the social security system committed by those who dispense the benefits. A claims representative in a Social Security office near Palm Springs, California managed to garner $105,000 over two years as a result of his diligence in reading the appropriate operations manuals. He learned how to reactivate a closed account and name a new trustee and worked out that there were no procedures for validating accounts or trustees. In late 1979 he reactivated a closed account and had the cheques sent on to a prepared fictitious identity. Two years later, he was running six such accounts and receiving $3000 a month. He was caught when a puzzled bank teller, recently moved from one office to another, identified a customer with at least two different accounts for different names. A number of similar cases, but involving smaller amounts, are reported by the UK Audit Commission in their 1985 survey. Other cases involve collusion between clerks with access to computer terminals setting up benefits and members of the public.

None of the cases show any great ingenuity beyond the spotting of administrative weaknesses.

Warehouse/inventory frauds. Warehouse frauds are as old as commercial life. They can take various forms: short delivery, mislabelling, relabelling, unauthorised dispatch or theft of inventory, false wastage, misidentified faulty goods, and so on. In computer-aided warehouse fraud, the aim is to use the computer to conceal either that assets are missing, or to obscure the trail leading to the perpetrator. Warehouse frauds are usually collusive, requiring an inside man and an external conspirator, often a legitimate customer or supplier.

Weighbridge frauds. Weighbridge fraud is the generic name for any fraud that relies on a faulty measuring device. If you are selling goods, you adjust the weighbridge to read more than it should. If you are bringing in goods to be weighed, you give your container a heavily-weighted false bottom. The modern equivalents are to interfere either directly with the electronics in a measuring device or give the device the wrong (and suitably doctored) thing to measure. During the boom in illegal CB radio in the UK in the early 1980s, owners of high-powered boosters (amplifiers) discovered that they could freak out the fluid-measuring electronics in petrol pumps on garage forecourts. Modern cash tills and warehouse systems now take their input from laser-read bar codes or magnetic stripes. To arrange a fraud, you simply offer up a bar-code to suit your scheme; the equipment has no means of checking whether it is attached to the right product.

Though there is no suggestion that there was any organised fraud, during 1989 Trading Standards Officers throughout the United Kingdom found themselves taking supermarkets and superstores specialising in discount DIY equipment and materials to court because the bar-encoded pricing on their goods did not agree with the display in human-readable form. In all of the cases there was over-charging rather than under-charging. Increasingly, supermarkets are seeking to avoid having to place human-readable prices on goods, on the grounds that it makes it more difficult to implement short-term discount price schemes.

Classifications of fraud

From these many different forms of fraud a number of themes keep recurring. In his *Corporate Fraud*, Mike Comer produces a five-by-four grid which appears to cover most of the situations and relationships which occur. In terms of *perpetrators*, they are either internal or external to a business, or a collusion between insiders and outsiders. An internal fraudster may be management or operations staff – operations including clerks, check-out and warehouse staff, machine operators and of course computer specialists. An external perpetrator could be a legitimate business contact behaving illegally or it could be an opportunist. In terms of *methods*, Comer suggests a straightforward theft, with no real attempt at concealment; misrepresentation, where reality is falsified; direct manipulation of accounts, and extortion. This gives a theoretical twenty different sorts of fraud:

Concealment Course				
Source & Type	Theft – no concealment	Misrepresentative falsified reality	Manipulative accounts	Extorsive – use force
Internal management				
Internal operations				
External: business contact				
External: opportunist				
Collusive				

Fraud Classification

BY PERPETRATOR

Internal: Management

Larcenous – no concealment
Misrepresentation – falsified reality
Manipulation of accounts
Extortion

Internal: Staff

Larcenous – no concealment
Misrepresentation – falsified reality
Manipulation of accounts
Extortion

External: Business Contact

Larcenous – no concealment
Misrepresentation – falsified reality
Manipulation of accounts
Extortion

External: Opportunist Member of the Public or Criminal

Larcenous – concealment
Misrepresentation – falsified reality
Manipulation of accounts
Extortion

Collusive

Employee and Outsider acting in concert
Larcenous – no concealment
Misrepresentation – falsified reality
Manipulation of accounts
Extortion

BY METHOD

Thefts – no concealment

A theft may not be concealed because:
* the victim's records will not disclose the loss
* although the loss is detected, there is insufficient evidence to point to any single perpetrator
* the victim condones the theft

Some thefts can't be concealed
  internal: management
  internal: staff
  external: business contact
  external: opportunist
  collusion between insider and outsider

Misrepresentation: falsified reality

The aim is to:
* hide or disguise an inventory discrepancy before, during or after a theft
* disguise, confuse or delay, identifying the thief
* enable the thief to obtain, or continue to obtain a dishonest advantage by deception

internal: management
internal: staff
external: business contact
external: opportunist
collusion between insider and outsider

Manipulation of Accounts

This includes:
* misrepresenting the value of physical inventory
* manipulating the company's books

  internal: management
  internal: staff
  external: business contact
  external: opportunist
  collusion between insider and outsider

Extortion and the use of force

internal: management

internal: staff
external: business contact
external: opportunist.
collusion between insider and outsider

Frauds can be either one-off or systematic. A fraud may be fraudulent from inception, it may have only started when a particular opportunity presented itself, or it may be what Dr Michael Levi calls a 'slippery-slope' fraud: actions which arise, not from any greedy intent but as a result of reckless and clumsy trading.

Computer fraud

What the computer does is to concentrate all the factors and risks that assist fraud to occur:

- There is a general absence of human intervention and human accountability
- Increasingly, the main assets of an organisation are measured and managed through the computer systems
- The contents of computer files are invisible until they are requested on a print-out or a vdu
- Administrative controls tend to be poor because those in charge of the organisation tend to expect others to 'look after' the computer systems
- The technology keeps on changing, the demands on each computer system keep on changing, so no version of any software product ever exists long enough for rigorous security controls to be adequately tested
- Considerable reliance is placed on the honesty of data input clerks, programmers and systems maintenance staff
- Computers can be accessed remotely and, in the absence of proper safeguards, without anyone really knowing what has happened
- Top managers do not realise the level of risk to which they are exposed.

From a consideration of fraud, we must now turn to computer-aided industrial espionage.

CHAPTER FIVE

DataSpying: Industrial Espionage

Waterford Glass in the Republic of Ireland had a turnover of £1130m in 1985 and is one of the world's leading producers of crystal glass artifacts. For years unknown quantities of bogus crystalware have been passed off as genuine Waterford in both the US and the UK. In December 1984 a clear plastic box containing 25 computer discs went missing from its plant at Merlyn Park in Galway. The discs held instructions for glass-cutting machines. As with many accounts of industrial espionage, details are sparse and unsatisfactory. The discs were eventually recovered, possibly with the aid of a Dublin-based private investigator, but by then had almost certainly been copied by the thief. Armed with the discs and the appropriate glass-cutting machinery, pirate manufacturers could turn out almost faultless copies. The damage in lost sales and to reputation can't be calculated.

Over fifteen years before, in one of the first-recorded examples of large-scale computer-aided industrial espionage, three computer operators employed by Encyclopaedia Britannica copied tapes containing 2 million customers' names and addresses and sold them to a direct mailing company. The tapes were recovered before they could be used but the loss could, according to contemporary estimates, have been in excess of $3m.[1]

What is unusual about these cases of computer-assisted industrial spying and piracy is not that they happened but that they were fairly fully reported. The noisiest of recent cases have involved the removal of proprietary information from large computer companies; IBM has been reported as spending $50m a year in counter-espionage measures and has been particularly fierce in pursuing through the courts Japanese and other Far Eastern companies that have appeared to have copied its technologies – and in suing former employees. Giants in information technology and the pharmaceutical industry have, for the last thirty years at least, been prime targets for concerted industrial espionage activity, employing considerable teams of prevent- ative agents and lawyers. Industries where marketing effort and strategic advertising campaigns are a large part of the total product sold – detergents and confectionary are good examples – have experienced particular difficulties. Computer companies, together with defence industry concerns, have been the targets not only of spies employed by their rivals, but also those supply- ing the needs of foreign intelligence agencies.[2]

Descriptions of industrial espionage have tended to concen- trate on this high-frontier type of activity; the reader who wishes to know more is referred to *Techno-Bandits* by Nick Anning, Linda Melvern and David Hebditch, Jay Tuck's *Hi-Tech Espion- age*, Brian Freemantle's *The Steal* and, for a view of the role of the Soviets in trying to secure Western technology, *The New Wizard War* by Robyn Shotwell Metcalfe.

What this chapter concentrates on is the less-reported and more mundane sort of activity that can afflict almost any organ- isation.* The fact that such incidents are routine does not mean that they have only minor effects on their victims. The code of ethics that once provided restraint seems to have withered away recently and the techniques now in use have altered beyond the recognition of earlier practitioners. Moreover, most victims lack the resources of multi-national IT and pharmaceutical corpor- ations to take action. The casebooks describe a number of com- puter-related cases from the 1970s – mailing lists or data such as census returns which could be used as the basis of mailing lists were not infrequent quarry together with credit-worthiness data – but into the 1980s there appears to be a falling off of reports, perhaps because they are no longer newsworthy, per- haps because most countries give very little legal protection to victims of industrial espionage. If the information is stored on computer disc there is usually very little advantage for the victim to disclose what has taken place. The most usual situation is

---

*In 1975 the University of Glasgow carried out a survey of information loss among major British corporations. 9 per cent were reported as suffering from industrial espionage and a further 14 per cent had experienced some unexplained information leakage.

that the victim has only slender evidence of datacrime, a mere suspicion of industrial espionage derived from deciding that competitors are just a little too well informed about his activities.

Every business, even the smallest, has secrets which it requires to preserve. Such secrets may be no more than payroll and tax details or lists of customers. Towards the other extreme are companies whose very futures may be tied up in the success of a new product launch, premature knowledge of which by a rival may end its chances; whose innermost financial strengths and weaknesses are being probed by would-be take-over predators; whose market position derives from the ownership of a jealously guarded process or proprietary; whose prosperity depends on an expensively acquired and expansively run set of targeted mailing lists;* who hold confidential information on behalf of others and whose reputation depends on their being able to keep their clients' secrets. There are corporations that have defence contracts and international conglomerates whose activities are the subject of interest to national intelligence agencies.

---

*The importance of mailing lists to the future of retail distribution should never be under-estimated. Direct mail – highly specific mail-shots – are often a vastly more effective way of marketing than using magazine and television advertising where, in the nature of things, most of the people who see your ads aren't actually interested. A well-thought-out and detailed mailing list may record the point at which you bought, say, a washing machine or refrigerator; after five or so years, when you might be considering a replacement, the manufacturer/distributor can write to you with suggestions, taking into account what can be guessed about your level of spending power from where you live, what other big consumer items you have bought recently, and your credit rating. The biggest operators, Sears in the USA, Grattan in the UK, have this information already. Grattan uses the CACI Acord/Pinpoint database which holds details of everyone in the UK based on census data and an area-by-area assessment which can determine social status, wealth and credit status. If you have ever bought from Grattan under any of its many trading names, it will have your buying habits profile. Even in the smallest operation, however, mailing lists are of value to someone.

Company Secrets

All organisations have secrets ... even if they don't appear to be of much interest to anyone outside a very small circle. Data has value, even if it is not secret ... because of the costs of collecting ... and keying it in to a computer database. In so far as this material contains information about individuals, the company may have a statutory obligation to keep it secure under data protection legislation.

Accounts

of interest to
  business rivals
  predators
  financial markets
raw material
  management
  day books
  financial planning
  tax returns

Internal memoranda

of interest to
  business rivals
  predators
  financial markets
raw material
  board minutes
  briefings, presentations
  position papers
  analyses
  correspondence with customers/suppliers
  correspondence with professional advisors

Customers Lists

of interest to business rivals
raw material
  invoice files
  actual customer lists
  potential (ie mailing lists)

Supplier Lists

of interest to
  business rivals
  other suppliers
raw material
  internal accounts

Sales figures

of interest to business rivals

Production costings

of interest to
  business rivals
  financial markets

Payroll & personnel – to be kept confidential both from other employees and from business rivals and head-hunters

pay levels
internal assessments
employee addresses

Research & development

of interest to
  business rivals
  financial markets
raw material
  new products details
  market surveys and analyses
  information held on rivals

Proprietary designs

of interest to business rivals
raw material
  substantive products
  presentation features
  software, data

Marketing plans

of interest to business rivals
raw material
  new products
  new campaigns
  new price lists

Confidential data held on behalf of third parties

of interest to business rivals and those enquiring into the affairs of
the third parties
  eg by professional firms
  eg defence secrets
  eg dealings on behalf of clients by investment business

At the same time, almost every business is anxious to learn its competitors' secrets. Industrial espionage is often portrayed as activity which is completely apart from normal ethical behaviour; it isn't, it's an extension of normal business planning, or R & D, or market research, or corporate financial management, all the things that conventional corporations carry out all the time. Every prudent company that thinks it has competition keeps track in one way or another of its competitors' activities. Essentially, and to paraphrase the politician who explained: 'I brief, you leak' – whilst you carry out market research on your industry peers, they spy on you.

The line between legitimate enquiry into a competitor's strengths and weaknesses and industrial spying, as in so many other areas of business ethics, is not clearly marked out. The title of a guide published at the end of 1985 for company librarians and edited by a former librarian to the European Parliament neatly shows the problem: it's called *Legal Industrial Espionage*. Whilst many businessmen wouldn't carry out an act they would not wish perpetrated on themselves, for others, the critical question is: 'Will I be found out?'

Even if you are found out, the penalty is often relatively small. Many countries still don't have specific offences of industrial espionage; what you get charged with is theft of the medium upon which the information is written or stored. The intrinsic value of disc media for the PC varies from under 60p to £3.50. In England attempts have been made to rely on the law of copyright or, if an employee is involved, undertakings of confidentiality contained in a contract of employment. But these are civil, not criminal remedies. The real penalty of being caught at spying is public opprobrium. However, as we will see, there are ways of creating a wall of deniability.

As 'information' or 'knowledge' or 'data' becomes an increasingly valuable business asset, so the costs of acquiring that material and its importance to the future of the organisation become ever more crucial. The computer has not only made it much easier to collect, generate and process information; it has made it much easier and much more worthwhile to steal. At the moment, we are in something of a transition period where conventional methods of intelligence collection and industrial espionage co-exist with the new computer-based methods. Conventional methods currently predominate over computer-based, but the emphasis is changing rapidly. To understand what is happening it is necessary to get an overview of how organisations secure the external information upon which they base their decisions.

Industrial intelligence

The world's largest companies maintain what amount to internal intelligence agencies, though of course they are seldom called that. These corporate intelligence services often have much more resources than their counterparts maintained by many sovereign nations. This is perhaps less surprising than may at first seem when it is realised how many world companies have annual sales revenues in excess of the gross national product of individual countries. Although it is now widely accepted that the poor countries of Africa have GDPs far below the annual turnover figures of leading industrial corporations, in fact prosperous European countries like Belgium, Austria and Denmark have GDPs below that of General Motors and Mobil Oil. Pakistan's GDP is close to the annual turnover of AT&T (about

$35 bn in 1985); Finland's GDP is close to the annual turnover of IBM (about $50 bn).[3]*

The emphasis of corporate intelligence is in two areas: general information affecting its business interests – mainly economic data and technological developments; and specific – detailed material on the activity of rivals. Depending on the individual conglomerate's interests, attention will be paid to long-range phenomena affecting the commodities markets – crop reports, mining yields, reports from processing factories, from ports and harbours (merchant vessels tend to be designed to carry very specific types of load – the presence of an individual ship in a specific harbour at a particular time gives an excellent indication of how much of a crop or commodity is being dispatched; collect enough data of this type and you can forecast how world prices will move). Good intelligence analysts can frequently draw all sorts of conclusions from the most unlikely beginnings. Recruitment advertisements can indicate expansion – or contraction – in particular areas. The use of head-hunting agencies serves two purposes; not only to locate the best candidates but also to disguise from business competitors that you are recruiting. Similarly news of the acquisition of new sites or new plant and equipment can be a promising indicator of expansion in particular directions.

Open Intelligence
These are sources of information open to organisations by entirely legitimate and ethical means

General Information Affecting Business Interests

Industry-wide market research and analysis
  trade and technical orientated
  collective market research
  reports by securities analysts
Trade & Professional Associations

---

*These global industrial corporations, particularly if they are involved in minerals or soft commodities, or if they are in a position to switch production sites around the world, or if they carry out large currency transactions, are likely to be the object of hostile intelligence from sovereign nations as well as from their obvious commercial rivals.

conferences
association newsletters
association staff

Newspaper, magazine and trade journal reports – note the increase
in specialist newsletter publications – some of these are available
electronically for direct delivery to customers' own computers
trade position
financially-orientated comment
technically-orientated comment
marketing-orientated comment
background on leading personalities in rival concerns
Electronic news services
market prices
news
electronically-distributed newsletters & comment
industry data, eg locations of suppliers, ship and freight
movements
Comments by sales and marketing staff
informal gossip
formal reports
Analysis by advertising agencies
market perceptions
marketing and advertising budgets
Own-commissioned market research into customer attitudes
quantitative
qualitative
Informal contacts with rivals, eg '19th hole'

Specific Information About Competitors

Company accounts of business rivals
Published price lists of rival products
Newspaper, magazine and trade journal reports – note the increase
in specialist newsletter publications
trade position
financially-orientated comment
technically-orientated comment
marketing-orientated comment
background on leading personalities in rival concerns
Comments by sales and marketing staff
Informal contacts
Recruitment advertisements

News of acquisition of property
News of acquisition of production facilities, etc.
Purchase and subsequent analysis of rivals' products>>reverse engineering

---

The actual staff involved in intelligence gathering and analysis may have titles such as 'strategic planning', 'marketing assistant' or 'special assistant' to various directors or vice-presidents, or simply 'research'. Some companies have substantial libraries and company librarians then become the collators and analysts. In *Legal Industrial Espionage*, addressed at this audience, the author says: 'What we have set out to do is to tell those involved how to obtain intelligence without breaking the law.' Like most of the intelligence gathered by nations, at least 90 per cent of what is needed is available from open sources.

One of the more valuable of these sources has been made possible by legislation which is intended to protect individuals whose data is kept on computer. Under Data Protection legislation, all computer-held data (with certain exceptions for government data) must be registered with a central office. Individuals who believe they may be included in a specific database have the right to examine the contents.

Generally speaking, the wealthier (or more aggressive) the corporation, the more extensive the nature of this intelligence material: commercial electronic databank services may be regularly scavenged for relevant news reports, on-line financial services for share and commodity prices watched for untoward movements, analyses will be kept on computer databases and spreadsheets – and hence, incidentally, in turn become objects of interest to the very rivals upon whom the intelligence is being collected.

Over the last few years a number of organisations have sprung up that concentrate specifically in information-gathering for the corporate market. They are in all but name intelligence agencies for hire and include publishers of highly specialised and usually high-priced newsletters, publishers of similar specialised news and comment via electronic means, management consultants – of which more later – and research groups who will accumulate information to a specific brief. I have done this sort of work myself on many occasions. It would be entirely misleading to suggest that all, or even a majority of these organisations behave unethically in the way in which they collect and sell information. But individually their code of ethics is seldom explicit; their arrival in the information market-place marks an important step in blurring still further the differences between legitimate intelligence gathering and spying.

The suppliers to the corporate information market are a diverse group. A number flourish under the umbrella of some of the world's most respected publishers. The *Financial Times*, for example, has a large portfolio of specialist newsletters with a particular emphasis on high technology. Their appearance is similar to that of most such publications: a series of typed pages stapled together, a mixture of long stories and gossipy shorts. Predictions about new industry developments, new product announcements are always high on the list of stories sought. Newsletters offer two things: first, hopefully, news before it appears elsewhere; second, information precisely tailored to the needs of its readership – ideally there's no spare material. The art of the publisher is to identify the specific segments of potential readership and then deliver exactly what that segment requires, no more, no less. Other newsletters are published by very small operations, amounting to little more than a few people with wordprocessors, filing cabinets, long lists of contacts built up in previous careers such as journalists, civil servants, investment analysts or (sometimes) as officers of intelligence agencies – and a willingness to run up large phone bills in pursuit of a good story.

The highest-profile of the research organisations set up in the 1980s was IRIS – International Reporting Information Systems – which established itself in Washington with a cast of international ex-statesmen including former Prime Minister Ted Heath and former Secretary of State Robert McNamara on its board of management, a computer system with an impressive specification and heavy hints at links with the CIA. That operation folded in 1983 but others with more modest claims and overheads appear to be thriving. They include, at varying levels of tariff to their clients and quality of 'connections': Oxford

Analytica, Inter Matrix, Kissinger Associates, Washington Researchers, Global Analysis Systems, Information Data Research and The Dunedin Corporation. Some of these provide services that could only be of interest to the largest of multi-nationals – country-by-country risk analysis (assessments of the problems faced if you seek to do business in particularly volatile countries) and even judgments about the vulnerability of employees of particular multi-nationals to kidnap and ransom demands – but others more mundanely specialise in collecting much-desired market data: how many units of a particular product were shipped in the last few months? talking to potential customers, how many do they think they will be buying in the next year? what new features would they like to see? Yet others publish no regular newsletters but market one-off special reports; these may have a total potential market of fewer than ten readers world-wide but with a break-even of only three copies sold it's not difficult to make ends meet. One of the largest of the operations in the special reports business is Frost & Sullivan who manage to cover a large number of industry areas. Frost & Sullivan is basically a commissioning and market-ing operation; their authors are freelance, often academics and lecturers.

Nearly all of the research organisations are willing to take on consultancy specific to just one customer. What one can only speculate on is where each of them – and the individuals they employ – draw the line between legitimate information gather-ing and full-blown industrial espionage. Brian Freemantle describes how Hitachi, the fourth largest company in Japan and the manufacturer of 'plug compatibles' for IBM mainframes, employed two particular consultancies in 1981 in order to keep abreast with IBM's development of the IBM 308x series machines. The first of these, National Advanced Systems, had recently acquired a recent ex-employee of IBM who had taken with him ten of the twenty-seven volumes of the operational manuals for the series. His boss sold Hitachi not only the 'stra-tegic intelligence' it was seeking, but also the manuals them-selves. The second consultancy, with the same working brief, was asked to acquire further information in terms which made it quite clear that Hitachi already had a number of manuals.

The second consultancy chose to inform IBM rather than help Hitachi.[4]

The range of services available to the world's largest corporations is extensive and growing, but even the smallest companies go in for information-gathering although there will usually be little in the way of a proper department – probably not even a thought-out plan – for the process. The manager in the small company may do no more than subscribe to a few trade papers, collect interesting clippings, have a few lunches, and use his brain as his information retrieval facility. The small scale of this activity does not mean, however, that it is ineffective in terms of the size of operation it is serving, nor that unethical methods are absent.

The industrial spy

The days of the industrial spy with his sub-miniature Minox camera are almost over; the clandestine taking of additional photocopies of vital documents is rapidly losing value. At the most trivial level, the common five-and-a-quarter-inch disc used on the original IBM PC holds 300 to 400 Minox snapshots or the same number of photocopies. It can be copied with a few keystrokes in under a minute and concealed in a briefcase or purse. The newer three-and-a-quarter-inch discs are even more easily hidden, in a pocket. They hold at least twice as much information, often four times. Tape-streamer cartridges, used for back-up, are the size of a hardback book and hold maybe 6000 or more 'pages'. Just around the corner in terms of low-cost availability is CD-ROM and WORM, compact disc technology adapted to data storage. A single 5-inch disc was available in 1986 that held the 9 million words of the Academic American Encyclopaedia, more conventionally published as 20 large paper-and-print volumes; in fact the disc could have held four or five times as much data. The benefits of computer-assisted industrial espionage don't end there, but first we must look at who the spies are, their armoury of techniques and the disciplines to which they subject themselves.

The spies

Popular articles about industrial espionage tend to build up the picture of professional agents using sophisticated technology to siphon away secrets. Most actual industrial espionage agents look like ordinary employees, because that is what they often are. Industrial spies who call themselves by that name are as rare as con-men who announce the fact on their business cards. Generally speaking, they fall into one of the following categories:

- *employees*, motivated by the possibility of employment with a rival to their present employer; or by resentment and spite; or for sexual favours; or for drugs; or for cash
- *sub-contractors*, and other temporary workers. Such people often work first in one company and then with its most obvious rival. They may be motivated by the desire for more work, or cash, or spite
- *amateur agents*, employees of rival businesses, who gather information sometimes by gossip, sometimes by eavesdropping, sometimes by the opportunistic filching of paper- and computer-based internal documents
- *journalists*, mostly concerned with stories they can print, but sometimes interested in information they can trade over to rival businesses – usually for yet more stories, occasionally for cash
- *researchers, analysts*, an amorphous group these, which can include market researchers, management consultants, securities analysts; these people may be either paid to survey a whole industry or may be on a specific assignment retained by a business rival. Such activities are of course entirely legitimate, but the opportunities for unethical espionage are there as a simple extension of the above-ground enterprise
- *professionals*, usually enquiry agents, these are the people who are employed to carry out acts that are obviously unethical and often illegal as well, such as infiltrating a fake employee, breaking-and-entering premises, bugging

Industrial intelligence agents, whoever they are, tend to have a definite discipline of identifying targets and selecting methods. In fact there's no difference in methodology between practices in national intelligence agencies and those adopted in the private sector. The value of the information, its time-critical qualities, the difficulties of securing, the risks of discovery and the costs of transcribing raw data into a form in which it can be used by the eventual customer must all be counterbalanced into a costing and plan of action no different from any other managerial endeavour. It is important to understand these disciplines because when in later chapters we come to examine counter-measures and risk assessment, it becomes much easier to determine what threats one should protect oneself against.

Intelligence Methods
All intelligence consists of four processes:

Collection

Collation

Assessment

Distribution

Define information required

define data
calculate value

Select & cost methodology

is information available openly?
what benefits are expected?
cost out – what is cheapest method of acquisition? which is easiest, or runs least risk?
is information time-critical?
if information is not available openly
   are you prepared to use covert methods?
   are you prepared to use methods to break the law?
   what are the consequences of discovery
     in commission?
     afterwards?

Collect raw data

covert/overt
agent/direct
eavesdropping
data capture

Transcribe raw data

technical processing
prepare transcript

Analyse data and prepare report

If necessary, redefine information required, and commence further collection.

Industrial spies have a portfolio of techniques and sources for their information. As already mentioned, 90 per cent of most information required can be secured from openly available materials; failing that:

- obtaining print documents – or copies – via employee or 'walk-in' agent or intermediary such as printer, courier, etc.
- obtaining electronic documents – or copies – via employee or 'walk-in' agent or intermediary
- scavenging is one of the most effective methods, retrieving waste paper, carbon paper (in so far as it is still in use) and typewriter ribbons
- opportunistic eavesdropping of the old-fashioned kind onto private meetings and lunches
- electronic eavesdropping of conversations via bugs and telephone taps are well-publicised; slightly less well-known are the techniques of the piggybacked data line and vdu emissions*
- one of the best techniques is the bogus job offer; a suitably placed employer in the target organisation is led to believe

---

*Electronic eavesdropping, its advantages and limitations are examined in Chapter 9.

that a job exists for which he or she is well qualified; at interview the employee talks widely – and unwisely – about the job he or she is currently doing; an alternative is actually to recruit someone from a competitor and to hope that any covenant not to give away trade secrets will be ignored
- the payment of cash to an employee of the competitor; it's basic but it sometimes works; if the intelligence gatherer is really cynical, he can shop the employee to his employer afterwards
- at the far end of the ethics spectrum is blackmail

One other important technique, unauthorised access to computers, will be examined in later chapters.

Dirty tricks in the city

To show just how many people are in the business of collecting information, by fair means and foul, it is useful to examine what often goes on during a big hostile take-over bid. On the overt front, the war is conducted by means of announcements by the parties and their professional advisors stating what their intentions are. The aim is to win over a parcel of shares to one side or the other. The predators will be prepared to buy these shares and will make a series of offers at steadily increasing prices. The defenders will want the shareholders to stick with them, and keep voting for the policies of the existing management.

In this fight, knowledge is all: the predators need to identify those shareholders who are least content with the old management; they need to determine how much they must offer in order to buy the shares. The predators must be able to value the target company accurately and demonstrate how assets are being underused and the opportunities missed. The defenders must identify weaknesses in the arguments and in the standing of the predators. All these things will go into the various published statements during the battle. However, in many public companies, the number of truly influential shareholders is relatively small; these will nearly always be big institutions. And their representatives can expect to receive personal attention from predator and defendant in the form of background information that can't always be printed.

In what some City and Wall Street specialists refer to as 'the good old days', large amounts of information could be obtained simply by relying on networks of contacts. In the City certain family and school connections provided access to reams of anecdotal material about the 'soundness' of particular individuals. The networks were effective and cheap: to benefit you had to no more than show your willingness to contribute when asked. Shortly after the UK secondary banks crisis of 1973 and 1974, Lord Poole, who ran the merchant bank Lazards, explained how his bank had survived. In a now famous statement he said: 'I only lent money to people who had been at Eton.' On both sides of the Atlantic, the old networks are less reliable than they were: greater equality of opportunity and the increasing internationalisation of finance have seen to that. Lord Poole's successors need to be much more systematic and professional in their means of collecting intelligence.

Very large numbers of professionals will have assembled information prior to any take-over and more will be being collected throughout the process. Considerable amounts of information are gathered on, as well as by, the very large corporations using their in-house resources of specialist staff: periodically they employ *management consultants* both to provide a temporary augmentation to their own employees and to give them an outsider's view of their strategic planning; these consultancies are usually either divisions of the large international accountancy firms or specialist companies. One of the key tools of management consultancies is research; they will review the work carried out internally and augment it from their own resources.

Stockbrokers and investment houses regularly compile and publish large amounts or research. The *investment analyst* has become an increasingly important feature of the securities business. His (or her – this is an area of the financial world where there is less sexual discrimination than most) role is several fold. On a day-to-day basis the team of analysts – they usually specialise in a particular sector of investment activity – will concentrate on advising the firm's teams of dealers on likely trends. Every quarter or so they will publish analyses of individual sectors, together with 'buy' or 'sell' recommendations. These will go out to the firm's institutional clients and also to other institutions which are thought could be persuaded to become clients. Investment houses compete with each other not only by offering better terms (commission rates) for business, but also by the quality of the research. The best analysts are often frequent television commentators. Investment analysts rely not only on the published reports put out by companies but also on visits, presentations and lunches. A judgment, one way or another, by a leading analyst will nearly always directly affect the share price. When a company announces good half-yearly or full-year figures and the share price falls, it is usually because the investment analysts have over-estimated the quality of the figures, the market has bought in anticipation, and the results have fallen below the market's (rather exaggerated) expectations.

Once the take-over period is mooted, other teams of researchers arrive on the scene. There will be the groups from the *merchant or investment banks* retained as advisors. Their research will be similar to that of the investment analyst, but much tougher and more specific. They will be particularly interested in identifying key shareholders whose opinion must be moulded if the bid is to be successful. There will be specialists in *financial public relations* whose job is to ensure that the press regard their take-over the way their clients wish. In addition to the materials generated by the existing research teams, they may also decide to carry out their own research into the qualities of the personalities involved – predator and victim alike – in order to form judgments about their 'real' goals – would a key figure welcome a large gratuity, perhaps in the form of a golden handshake, to prepare for retirement or to relieve personal cash problems, for example? They also need to know how well they will perform on television and before journalists. 'Opposition' personalities can expect to have their previous careers scoured for mistakes and scandals. Some of this work will be contracted out to *private detectives*.

An idea of the range of services available can be gathered from the promotional brochure of Wall Street-based Kroll Associates:

'Specialists in Corporate Intelligence: providing timely, accurate information, with complete discretion, to business and professional leaders facing strategic decisions.' Among their specific service areas are Due Diligence Analysis, Contests for Control, Corporate and Financial Crimes, Litigation Support and Intelligence and Corporate Security.

All of this activity is considered legitimate, but for take-over teams hungry for success, the intelligence thus gathered may not be sufficient. It is at this point that *industrial espionage professionals* are brought in. Such people are almost never employed directly by the principal participants in a take-over; taking a leaf from leading Western intelligence agencies, deniability of dirty tricks is important. It will be one of the teams of advisors – management consultants, financial PR firm, perhaps the investment bank, even firms of lawyers – that first forms a view of the level of 'hunger for success' in its client. Innuendo, rather than a specific instruction, is used to seek permission for what is to follow. An enquiry agent or private detective is employed, initially to carry out 'life-style' or 'status' or 'due intelligence' checks on the principal opposition personalities:

- what houses do they own?
- what is their net worth?
- are there any signs of undue high living, or unmanageable debts?
- the target's published cv: is it accurate in all respects, are there hidden aspects, have achievements been artificially boosted?
- what is the state of the marriage, if any?
- how many children are there?
- what are the children costing in education, are there any other problems or secrets?
- is there a previous marriage, or a mistress, or socially unacceptable liaison?
- are there any expensive hobbies, or anti-social habits?
- are there any friends or acquaintances with a murky past?

This information will be gathered by a series of discreet visits to the target's home and places where he and those closest to him tend to go. Certain slightly illegal acts are considered routine by such enquiry agents. By pretending to be a company that is considering to extend credit to the target, a credit reference from one of the big on-line agencies (TRW in the USA; CCN and UAPT in the UK) can be obtained.* A bit more impersonation might obtain details of bank accounts. Another technique involves ringing up close acquaintances and saying that you are a head-hunter and would the target be interested in – or qualified for – a particular job? Other roles for the creative enquiry agent prepared to do a bit of impersonation include tax inspectors, representatives from the Social Security, loss adjusters from insurance companies, even market researchers. A modest bribe to a police officer will result in a check-out of any criminal record. Policemen and private detectives are regularly charged with misusing information from police computers: one case, in which the conspirators were set up by a tv programme, occurred while this chapter was being written.

The expenditure of more money with a professional will permit the use of a bug; even more, and a walk-in theft can be arranged. At the top end of the expenditure league, the infiltration of a bogus employee can be arranged. Gary Murray, a British enquiry agent who frequently comments on the poor ethical state and lack of regulation of his industry says: 'Nearly all people in this profession will insist, on first meeting you, that they are solely in the counter-espionage business. I guess that at least 50 per cent of them are occupied most of the time in industrial espionage of one sort or another, and 25 per cent are in what I would call aggressive industrial espionage.'

---

*There is one particularly dirty trick that can be employed to ruin someone's reputation: you feed false information about a debt into one of the credit information bureaux. All such bureaux rely on bad debt information being fed into them and although the bulk of their information comes from court judgments, anyone with the password of a store or other credit-giving agency can log on to a credit information bureau and issue a bad report. The report does not, as is often thought, automatically go out to the customers of the bureau, but some bureaux have a higher reputation for checking such information than others. This is the basis of those stories about 'hackers' switching off the credit lines of people whom they dislike. Of course it is open, under consumer credit legislation, for the individual whose credit record is held on computer to request a copy of the current report and demand changes if the information is incorrect.

The information thus gathered may never be published. As well as being used to help make strategic decisions during the take-over battle, the dirtiest of secrets may be used in blackmail to persuade an individual to pursue a course that he or she was previously opposed to. Some weapons in the covert information war are handed over verbally in the form of discreet off-the-record informal briefings to powerful shareholders. Every now and then a journalist will be given a lead which will result in a story actually being printed, but without a direct link to where the information came from.

The booming stock markets of 1985, 1986 and the early part of 1987 created conditions in which there was an audience among institutional investors for the messages of aggressive entrepreneurs with suggestions that such-and-such a corporation was ripe for take-over. That particular take-over boom ended as the insider trading scandals reminded Wall Street and the City that some of their colleagues had become just a little *too* greedy. Less publicised was the parallel boom in the use of industrial spies, electronic technology and dirty tricks in the service of take-over warriors. A number of cases, however, did reach the newspapers.

In March 1986 at the height of the £2.3 bn battle of the Distillers Company between Guinness and Argyll Foods, private investigator Nicholas Vafiadis was accused of offering around 'dirt' about the academic track record of the Argyll chairman, James Gulliver. A leak had been organised by Distillers' PR company to the effect that Gulliver's 'career' at Harvard was a good deal less extensive than had been implied. Accusations of clandestine filming and even break-ins flew between the three protagonists – and writs were issued against a wide range of merchant banks and PR consultancies. When the career of Guinness chief executive Ernest Saunders came to a spectacular end the following November, the accusations and recriminations reappeared. In July 1986 white goods and consumer electronics chain Dixons made an unsuccessful bid for the UK end of W H Woolworth & Co. which included a rival chain to Dixons called Comet. Four of Dixons' executives joined Comet and in the following November a tape recorder hidden in a tin was found attached to the telephone line leading into the home of one of the defecting executives, Peter Hopper. Unknown to Dixons' corporate advisors (who initially issued a formal denial), Dixons' security manager had retained a security consultant who had in turn, in classic fashion, sub-contracted two men to carry out a bugging exercise. The security consultant and the two bugging engineers were convicted in February 1988.[5] Interestingly enough, it was stated in court that none of the fears about their defecting executives that had prompted Dixons' to embark on their investigations were found to be justified. However, these were cases of more-or-less conventional industrial espionage. These days it is illegal access to someone else's computer, the tape from the mainframe and the floppy disc from the corporate PC workstation that is being sought as much as the printed report. In one spectacular case, an individual who had had a summer job at the US Federal Reserve, used the password he had retained after he had left. He went to work for the Wall Street securities house E F Hutton and used 'Fed' data to add punch to his predictions of the way in which US monetary policy was likely to move. In another case, a programmer was recruited to overhaul the accounting systems at the Cigar and Tobacco Co. of Louisiana. While working on the system, the programmer siphoned off large quantities of corporate data, including customer lists which were then sold to competitors for $140,000. The programmer was smart enough to be able to by-pass the computer's journalising facilities – see Chapters 10 and 12 – so that no evidence of his activity remained. He was caught when a competitor warned the authorities what was happening. However, you don't need to be a programmer to steal information from a PC, merely the entirely basic skill of copying files from one disc to another.

Computer-assisted espionage

But to talk about so many hundred 'pages' of internal documents in computer-readable form considerably underestimates their value. For, aside from pure word-processing activities – letters, memoranda, Board minutes, and so forth, the typical contents of a disc from a computer located in a corporate environment will be: spreadsheet calculations, mailing lists, and databases of all kinds. The thief who gets these not only has the information, but also a means of viewing them and manipulating them in a constructive fashion.

The great benefit the computer spy has over his more conventional colleagues is that, having acquired his raw intelligence, he can use his own computer to sort out the relevant from the irrelevant. The thief – or his client – can send out a mailing based on someone else's hard work over several years of building up, but tailored to the specific requirements of the thief's own organisation. The thief's client can look at his competitor's spreadsheet with all his assumptions and predictions – and use that data and those calculations to decide what *he* should do to outwit him. The datathief who purloins someone else's database gets several things simultaneously: he acquires the raw data that might have taken years to accumulate, he doesn't have to pay anyone to input it into a machine (one of the hidden costs of running a database is all that typing and maintenance) and he gets a database management package that will allow him to explore the data in ways which perhaps the original owner hadn't considered. Even bulk raw text files of letters, internal memoranda, electronic mail and board minutes can be quickly searched using a desk-top computer. If the datathief wishes to find all the references to a particular person, event or process, then either a FTR (full-text retrieval) package can be used – it would be a small-scale version of the search facilities found on big on-line databases like Dialog, Lexis/Nexis or Profile – or, at a pinch, the 'string search' facility on most good word-processors can be put to work.

When it comes to the various forms of eavesdropping, a theme that will be explored in Chapter 9, searching for computer-based telephone traffic is far more rewarding than listening to the human voice. Eavesdropping of data, as opposed to voice transmissions has had relatively little publicity until recently. It is in fact, one of the most attractive routes an industrial spy can follow. The table *Intelligence Methods* (page 121) shows how intelligence tasks are costed out. Conventional, voice-based eavesdropping does not score well in this test. Most people mumble, allude to things and people obliquely, their speech lacks precision and is discursive. Quite often they don't even talk business at all. Whilst electronic eavesdropping is cheap and quite easy to set up – though there are practical pitfalls which never seem to bother fictional heroes and villains – the real cost is in the processing and transcription of whatever has been captured. You have only to read the first versions of transcripts of conferences (where presumably the speakers have made some attempt to marshall their thoughts) to see some of the difficulties faced in deriving useful information from a telephone tap.

Even when a transcript is obtained, it still requires a considerable amount of analysts' time to identify useful new information. A number of spook-watchers – investigative journalists and academics – believe that leading national intelligence agencies possess facilities which use computer-aided speech recognition to identify key words and phrases, so as to home in on conversations worth attention. In so far as such apparatus exists, however, it is doubtful whether they are especially useful: such speech recognition devices announced in the commercial world all require to be 'taught' the particular intonations of each speaker and all but the most expensive can only handle one word, enunciated clearly, at a time. In any case, the first thing anyone does if they suspect a lack of privacy on a phone line is to start talking in riddle-like code.

By contrast, eavesdropping of computer data scores very highly in this same test. Computer-based messages are nearly always very precise in expression and content. There's no transcription cost – you simply tell the printer to print-out; and data analysis is easy – at its most basic you use the 'string search' feature referred to above.

If it is not already the case, within the next two or three years, as the ease of use of the technology becomes more obvious, the methods of choice for most industrial espionage operators will nearly all be computer-based.

CHAPTER SIX

DataTheft: Stealing Resources

According to one of the 'computer crime' surveys quoted in Chapter 3, the largest number of incidents do not involve fraud, embezzlement or theft of data, but theft of hardware and software and misuse of computer resources for private benefit. In the study conducted by Mercy College, New York State, during 1985, theft of hardware, at 23.8 per cent of all reported incidents, was the highest single category, followed by misuse of corporate computers for employee benefit at 17.5 per cent and theft of computer software at 14.3 per cent. Embezzlement and fraud amounted to only 13.2 per cent. Destruction or alteration of corporate data came to 10.1 per cent.

These findings are rather different both from the popular perception of computer crime and from many other surveys, perhaps because the questions were not put.*

One of the earliest of the classic computer criminals, Jerry Neil Schneider** both used illegal access/impersonation as his modus operandi and stole physical computer and communications equipment parts.

Many common forms of datafraud are simply an updating of traditional embezzlements, forgeries, deceptions and other swindles. Industrial espionage had a vigorous history long before the arrival of the computer disc. But although the stealing of computer hardware and peripherals like printers, vdus and modems is clearly little different from any other sort of theft, the stealing of a computer's processing facilities or of software or of computer-readable data has very little precedent in the history of crime.

Theft of software goes back at least to the celebrated 1968 case when the airline management software known as BOAD-

*See Chapter 3.
**See Chapter 7.

ICEA was plagiarised and offered out by employees of the developer, the British Overseas Airways Corporation.*[1] But in 1968 nearly all software was written uniquely for each customer. It was two years later, with the arrival of the minicomputer that software piracy started to make commercial sense. The whole idea of minis was low cost: software houses began to try to produce standard solutions to common business problems so that development costs could be shared between a number of customers. So the software, being non-specific, began to have a value on the open market. At the same time, the very quantity in which minis were being installed made the crime more difficult to detect: an individual piece of software could have come from any of a number of sources; there were too many installations for the original suppliers to be able to monitor.

Ten years later, with the establishment of the desk-top PC, the piracy problem for software houses had become acute: for MicroPro, the producer of one of the most successful word-processors of all time, estimates suggested that as many as four out of five computers using WordStar had pirate copies. Software houses attempted to cover themselves by introducing devices which made copying of original discs more difficult – all computers are supplied with a simple utility to copy discs and files, so until 'copy-protection' devices started appearing, software piracy required almost no technical ability whatever. Many of the copy-protection devices were – and are, for they are still with us – a considerable inconvenience. Floppy disc media can be damaged by many of the normal hazards of office life – spilt coffee, being left near heaters or windows – and also by electrical perils associated with computers – magnetic currents from vdus and power supplies, and voltage spikes. Some software houses reckoned that, for your $300 or $400 licence fee, what you were entitled to was one copy-protected disc. If you wanted another, you paid a further $300 or $400. Owners of PCs with hard-discs discovered that they had to use a floppy 'system' or 'master' disc before their favourite program would run. If they used several copy-protected programs, the

---

*There may have been an earlier large-scale case, in 1964: $5m worth of software was offered to Texaco, who declined and reported the perpetrator.[2]

owner of a hard-disc machine found he was having to do almost as much disc manipulation as if he had bought an all-floppy machine.

Special programs to defeat copy-protection became available; the software houses retaliated by devising even more complicated copy-protection schemes; always within a few months, protection-defeat software appears. Some writers believe that the long-term solution to software piracy is for software writers to go for a very low price/very large volume publishing formula so that large-scale piracy becomes as pointless as photocopying a paperback.

Most software stealing takes place by copying discs or tapes. However it is also possible to steal it down a telephone line by downloading the appropriate file from one computer to another. The most famous instance was in 1970 (which appears to have been a vintage year for new types of computer crime). The case was in the courts for twenty months whilst lawyers argued about precisely what offence had been committed. Hugh Jeffrey Ward, the 'criminal', was a programmer based in California engaged on a Computer-Aided Design package; what he currently lacked was a facility to print the results neatly on a plotter. He was aware that a good plotter module was available on a computer, very similar to the one owned by his company, upon which was running a time-share bureau. After a bit of masquerading and exploration, Ward called down a listing of the program from the bureau onto his company's machine. He also asked for punched cards (then the usual method of data input) and this was his downfall as the cards were later spotted in his wastebin. Following what is now a standard procedure in the investigation of computer crime, the computer's activity logs were examined and sufficient evidence was eventually accumulated to get Ward convicted of theft of a trade secret, for which he received three years on probation and a $5000 fine. The bureau got $300,000 damages from the associated civil proceedings.[3]

Theft of data files was covered in the last chapter; its history goes back at least to 1970, when the 2-million name-and-address file of Encyclopaedia Britannica was offered for sale[4] and when two employees of a computer service bureau copied and sold the population data tapes produced by the Swedish census.[4]

Theft of CPU time

But it is theft of the actual resources of the computer for which there is no real parallel in previous criminal history; what is stolen is the processing and storage power of the machine; indeed it is not always possible to show that an offence has been committed. Employees can be dealt with by their employers on the basis of their contracts of employment, but if one wants to rely on the criminal law, one may have to resort to such round-about charges as 'stealing electricity'.

The normal perpetrator is usually someone with existing legitimate access to the computer: an employee, contractor or maintenance engineer. Three motivations stand out: the first is analogous to the abuse of the office telephone or typewriter and, as we will see in the next chapter, many employers would probably be prepared to turn a blind eye to small-scale violations. The second is simply curiosity – internal hacking or exploration of the computer to see what it can do, coupled perhaps with some non-malevolent interest in corporate 'secrets'. The third is financial gain.

A few typical examples: the Audit Commission report a 1978 case at the time of the interest in biorhythm charts. An employee of a regional gas board responded to a newspaper advertisement for a personal computer-generated chart. When he received it, he realised that it had been produced on his departmental computer and suspicion quickly fell on two of his colleagues. The same collection of case-studies mentions how a whole computer department was dismissed for running a private computer bureau on their employer's hardware and software. More amusingly, a systems analyst at an insurance company set up a whole series of private programs on an IBM 3101 during 1980; they included a football pools aid, a household inventory and a picture-printing program that could create images of Raquel Welch and Mickey Mouse. The systems analyst was developing a program for his girl-friend's catering business when his activities were detected.[5]

Another case shows how matters can get out of hand: two programmers wrote a program which automatically re-scored sheet music. They ran it on their employer's machine. After a while, word of their achievements spread through the music publishing business and, as they commenced a modest advertising campaign, work flooded in. The programmers decided that they would soon quit their jobs, purchase their own machine, and progress from there – but not just yet. Their prices assumed they were getting free processing power. By the time a colleague reported them, they were using up nearly three-quarters of the computer's entire storage space and the regular processing work was being held back in long queues.[6]

Some extra-curricular activities, however, almost certainly have a social benefit, even if the owners of the computers might not think so at the time. During the 1970s, the boys of Kettering Grammar School in the English Midlands had a remarkable record in beating the US National Aeronautical and Space Administrations in their announcements of new Soviet satellite launches. Inspired by an enthusiastic science teacher and using second-hand amateur radio and radio-taxi equipment, they eavesdropped on the satellite transmissions, worked out launch sites and predicted orbits. Less well-known is that the teacher relied on the help of a friend with access to his employer's computer to collate all the data.

There are also instances of breach of computers by outsiders in order to use the processing facilities. Although most of today's activities by hackers seem to be primarily aimed at showing that protective measures can be breached, the early hackers of the 1960s were mainly interested in getting time on the machines in order to learn how to use them.* They were mostly university students who were not authorised to use the campus machines but there were cases of complete outsiders managing to gain access. In 1974 a 15–year-old schoolboy broke into a London time-sharing bureau from his school's teletype terminal. Although this case proceeds by a decade the peak of interest in teen hackers, it has all the features of the classic story: the boy apparently had no specialised knowledge, simply curiosity and

*Hacking is dealt with at greater length in the next chapter.

ingenuity; he discovered by trial and error how to read main memory and get a print-out of the operating system. From there he was able to progress to write a data-piggybank program* to read the activities of each terminal and so discover sign-on passwords for each user.[7]

The story of the music scoring program shows why computer owners should be concerned: computers have finite powers to process and store data. Each additional program provides an incremental load on the overhead and tasks which should get completed within a particular time-frame will take longer. Sensible managers will take a pragmatic view of each situation: in one sense, the modest use of a computer for private applications could be considered a perk of many computer-orientated jobs. The additional overhead on computer resources might, in many cases, be quite low; in fact, employees may be careful only to utilise computer resources when the organisation's own demands are at a minimum. Again, some exploratory activity can be seen as a form of self-training by employees and so to the benefit of the company's management. We will be exploring these matters later on, but in general, a mildly permissive attitude towards the private use of cpu time by employees, coupled with threats about large-scale abuse or commercial exploitation, is likely to the best course for most commercial enterprises that do not carry particularly sensitive data or processes on their machines.

Theft of equipment

Nearly all offices routinely expect to lose a percentage of their stationery supplies to their employees; they know that photocopying machines will be used to replicate private correspondence; they assume that part of the mail and phone bills they pay include items completely unconnected with their business. When things get bad, they know that office equipment like typewriters may disappear also.

In factories, the problem can be the disappearance of components, spares and even finished goods. When managers fail

*See Chapter 10.

both in maintaining proper physical security and at employee relations, matters can deteriorate to the point where large percentages of a factory's output can disappear: in the early 1970s there were highly organised conspiracies between employees in a well-known automobile manufacturer based in Oxford and local spares dealers and garages. British Telecom have had to introduce frequent purges to stem the flow of telephone equipment to its own engineers involved in private contract work. (The fact that the BT bureaucracy took so long to attend to the legitimate orders of some of its business customers pushed them into the hands of those engineers willing to moonlight in return for cash-in-hand.)

In the days when computers meant mainframes and minis and the most that would be seen in ordinary offices would be terminals and printers, the opportunities for theft of computer equipment and peripherals were limited to those willing to undertake serious risk. Although throughout the 1970s there are a few cases of whole minis being stolen, on the whole the equipment was large and heavy; some of it couldn't be moved without expert assistance; there was a limited market-place in which it could be sold; those who bought 'second-user' equipment would tend to require maintenance contracts – and these would be available only from those who had supplied the equipment in the first place. Until the early 1980s, thieves of computer hardware were either those possessed of considerable quantities of *chutzpah*, like Jerry Neil Schneider, those who stole with a particular customer* in mind or engineers trading in spares.**

It seems to have been the Apple II that became the first computer around which routine thefts began to make sense. The Apple II had begun as a hobbyist machine but, as we saw in Chapter 1, it was the first contrivance of the micro revolution

---

*In one 1977 case, components for a specialist type-setting machine were stolen. There were only 200 installations of the machine world-wide and only 35 in the UK, where the crime took place. Most people would have regarded this as a risky enterprise, but the perpetrators were never caught.
**This form of activity carries on and on: whilst I was writing this chapter an ex-employee of Wang was jailed for four years for stealing £500,000 worth of Wang spares which he had obtained by corrupting four current Wang employees – he had paid £20 a part, a tiny fraction of the official list price.[8]

to make it into offices. One of the clever features in the Apple's design were the slots for the add-on boards. You could considerably expand the capabilities of the basic device by adding-in cards for further memory, to give an 80-column by 24-line display, to link in printers and modems, to speed the machine up and, even to provide the Apple with a second central processor so that you had two machines almost for the price of one. But, particularly in the United States, you had substantial populations of Apple IIs in homes as well as offices. So you had a perfect recipe for thievery: offices and businesses bought software which was copied for use at home; they bought floppy discs, a percentage of which vanished just as stationery did; they bought add-on boards and other peripherals and these vanished as well. Unlike the minis and mainframes, routine servicing was not concentrated in the hands of the original suppliers. There was a lively and informal market for second-hand equipment via computer clubs, swap meets, and classified advertising in specialist magazines.

The IBM PC, when it appeared in 1981, also featured slots and needed additional boards to bring it up to a reasonable level of specification. As prices fell, and as IBM clones started to appear, the IBM became a home machine. Discount companies set up to supply the needs of the small businesses in search of PC bargains. Larger businesses discarded early models in favour of more recent ones.

But today, desk-top PCs are just another item of office equipment and so are the targets of 'break-in' thieves many of whom have fences ready to give ready cash for their haul. There's considerable evidence of 'shopping-list' burglaries – theft more-or-less to order. The thieves know enough to avoid taking obsolete or unpopular equipment – and to look around for manuals and operating system software, as this enhances the re-sale value.

Not all thefts of computer equipment are successful, however: thieves removed an office micro from an engineer's car and then found they had no place to sell it; they dumped the machine on waste ground where it was discovered by four boys who had seen a report of the loss on a popular tv programme.

Sometimes theft of equipment and of data can be combined:

it was an everyday sort of crime: thieves broke in and stole an IBM PC AT. New, it could have cost between £1500 and £2000 in 1987 when the event happened; a fence might have offered £200. Unfortunately, this particular machine was in the research and teaching block at the Withington Hospital in Manchester where four consultants were collecting data on patients suffering from gastro-enteritis, the better to understand the illness. They hadn't 'got around' to making back-up copies and the research data – and how does one put a price on that? – was lost for ever.[9]

CHAPTER SEVEN

The Datathief

Datathieves who are deranged systems programmers or who are members of organised crime syndicates or terrorist cells are very much in the minority. However little reliance is placed on computer crime statistics and computer crime consultants, there is one point on which all agree: the bulk of computer crimes, like the greater part of other economic crimes, is committed by people who are employed either as supervisors or clerks by the victim or who have a direct relationship to the victim. The details were reviewed in Chapter 3, on p 64. Such statistics do not of course cover industrial espionage, but even here, most anecdotal evidence suggests that employees selling the secrets of their employers play a very significant role.

The popular picture of 'computer criminals' has been appallingly distorted by writers in search of sensational headlines. It does no service to managers of organisations at risk to perpetuate the idea that their greatest hazard comes from a mysterious group of unpredictable computer geniuses who may at any time crash into their systems and remove large quantities of cash, extract vital secrets, cause untold damage and hold the company to ransom. Not only are information criminals likely to be employees of, or be closely connected to, the victim, most crimes do not rely on particular technical skill for their success.★ The most common method of fraud is alteration of input to a computer; that alteration may be simply a forged amendment to a form that a clerk uses as instructions of what to keystroke into a computer. The most common method of computer-related industrial espionage, as far as one can tell, consists of stealing computer tapes or discs. Proper planning for preventing datacrime must start with these facts firmly in mind.

At the end of this chapter we will examine the more exotic

★For those that do, see the first part of Chapter 10.

types of datathief – the hacker, the professional industrial espionage agent, members of organised crime syndicates, terrorists, and national security agencies. But, in terms of the risks that most organisations are likely to face, the person who wishes to understand the range of motivations of datathieves must first comprehend how nice suburban people with jobs that give them access to sensitive information systems and data are able to justify to themselves and their friends the committing of certain types of criminal act.

White collar crime

When criminologists started to develop explanations for white collar crime in the late 1940s they were attempting to do rather more than draw attention to crime among the middle classes. Like other academics before them, they were struck by the differences in attitude towards white collar wrong-doing compared with opinions about offences against the person and property. Not only did society appear to have distinct ways of measuring moral culpability, so did the criminals themselves. What was it about white collar crime, they wondered, that made an employee's embezzlement from an employer less blameworthy than breaking into a home and making off with cash? Or setting up a fake company in order to defraud the public rather than carrying out a smash-and-grab? Evidence that society recognised important differences could be easily assembled by looking at the amount of policing effort that went into investigating the various categories of crime, by comparing penalties for diverse offences, and by looking at the courts' sentencing policies. Was it merely the absence of violence that appeared to make white collar crime more socially acceptable or were there deeper reasons?

Although the first people to pose such questions were academics, these are matters not merely of interest to armchair theoreticians. As an ever greater proportion of society moves from blue collar to white collar occupations, the quota of individuals qualified to become white collar criminals grows. The figures for the United States and Britain are remarkably similar: in the USA in 1970, 51 percent of the population wore notional white collars; by 1982, 63 percent. In the UK in 1971, 53 percent had white collar jobs, moving to 65 per cent by 1984. (Figures from, respectively, the US Bureau of Labor Statistics and the UK Department of Employment.)

Information crimes, like many others in the criminal calendar, are committed mainly as a result of a mixture of opportunity and motive. Where white collar crimes differ most markedly from traditional 'street' or blue collar crimes is that actual motives are much more difficult to identify.

There is very little moral dilemma about traditional crime: the perpetrators, whether novices or professionals, know that what they are doing is wrong and that the only 'issue' is evaluating the chances of not being caught. Society too, in making judgments about this area of crime, similarly has little difficulty in identifying such behaviour as wrong. When it comes to providing explanations there is the well-known political choice: nature or nurture. Is the villain genetically prone to antisocial conduct or responding to poor social conditions? What is interesting about white collar crime is the lack of agreement about what constitutes wrong behaviour. Even breaking well-understood laws can, in some circumstances, be regarded as 'only technical'. In the white collar world there appear to be no definite boundary markings to separate the official from the unofficial perk and from those contexts in which normally moral individuals persuade themselves that criminal or fraudulent acts are ethically justifiable. Even the professional criminal operating in the white collar environment – one who starts out with crooked intentions as opposed to slipping almost unconsciously into crime – is seen to be on this same moral continuum.

To conjugate an appropriate verb: I have a perk, you are on the fiddle, he is committing fraud, they are congenital criminals.

Explanations for this lack of moral clarity have come in two main forms and, since the problems they address are heightened by the introduction of successive generations of computer-based information processing systems, it's important to understand them. The two arguments – covert reward systems and the dissociated individual – are separate, but they work well together.*

Covert reward systems

Almost every form of employment that has ever existed has given its holder no less than four different sorts of remuneration:

- the direct financial package
- the indirect parcel of agreed perks
- the inherent job satisfaction
- the covert rewards

No one has much difficulty in recognising the first three, nor that people are sometimes willing to make a trade-off between them. Thus apprentice actors will endure poverty-level wages and be prepared to scrub the auditorium in exchange for a chance at a glamorous career; poorly-paid assistants in photographic retail stores are there because they have an opportunity to follow their hobby full-time and get good discounts on equipment. Similarly, skilled oil industry workers on overseas assignments in alcohol-free countries expect large daily rates, preferably tax-free. Of course there are plenty of people without the bargaining power to enable them to make this trade-off.

But nearly every job has covert rewards as well. By definition, these are never specified in contracts of employment and nearly always amount – 'technically' – to theft or embezzlement.

*In a variation of this explanation, Edwin Sutherland, the sociologist who exerted a considerable influence on American criminological thinking, spoke of 'differential association'. He held that criminal behaviour is learned in interaction with other persons, usually in very close groups, in a process of communication. The learning process is not only about technique but also about the specific direction of motives, drives, rationalisations and attitudes. 'In some societies,' he says, 'an individual is surrounded by persons who invariably define the legal code as rules to be observed, whereas in others he is surrounded by persons whose definitions are favourable to the violation of the legal codes. A person becomes delinquent because of an excess of definitions favourable to violation of law over definitions unfavourable to violation of law. This is the theory of differential association. . . .' Sutherland believed that the circumstances in which criminal behaviour was learned were identical to those in which other forms of social behaviour were learned.

The typical examples for the office worker is the limited use of the employer's telephone for private calls, access to stationery, photocopying and, increasingly, use of computers and peripherals. For the blue collar worker, the rewards may range from unofficial time off to opportunities for moonlighting and to the collection and sale of 'scrap' materials.

Two British anthropologists, Gerald Mars and Stuart Henry, sometimes working together but more often not, have made a particular study of these covert reward systems. Among the techniques they used to gather their data was to take up work in areas where they thought the hidden economy may be particularly visible. The following table, lightly adapted from one of Gerald Mars's books, shows the relationships between official and unofficial work and legal and illegal activities:

	Official	Unofficial	Alternative
	Formal Rewards	*Informal Rewards*	*Social Economy Rewards*
Legal	Wages, Salaries Commissions Overtime	Perks Tips Extra work Consultancy	Domestic production Barter DIY
	Criminal Rewards	*Hidden Economy Rewards*	*Black Economy Rewards*
Extra-legal, illegal	Loot, etc	Pilfering Short-changing Over-charged expenses, over- and under-load-ing, dropping short	Moonlighting

Throughout their books and articles – and in those of other researchers on both sides of the Atlantic – the evidence builds up that fiddling is endemic to most occupations; what is unusual is the *absence* of fiddling. Gerald Mars has the inelegant-sounding but clearly understandable concept of the fiddle-proneness of particular jobs:

> Some occupations are so fiddle-prone . . . that the workings of whole sectors of the economy cannot be understood unless these aspects of reward are taken into account. It is impossible to explain industrial relations . . . or to understand the real reasons behind some strikes, or why technical changes are blocked . . . where orthodox theories of strike-proneness are all we have to depend on.

He has the following informal categories of Cheats at Work (the title of the book that describes these ideas most clearly):

> Hawks are individualists. They perch unhappily in organisations; when in them they tend to bend the rules to suit themselves. They are the entrepreneurs, the innovative professionals and the small businessmen.
>
> Donkeys are people highly constrained by rules who are also isolated from each other. [Typical examples are supermarket cashiers and machine-minders.] The response of donkeys is to resist often by breaking the rules – to sabotage the systems that constrain them – or to fiddle.
>
> Wolves . . . work – and steal – in packs. Dockwork gangs are good examples: they have hierarchy, order and internal controls. When they pilfer they do so according to agreed rules and through a well-defined division of labour.
>
> Vultures need the support of a group but act on their own when at the feast. Travelling salesmen are vultures – so too are waiters – linked and supported as they are from a common base, depending on information and support from colleagues, but competitive and acting in isolation for much of their work.

Fiddle-proneness has nothing to do with class or education; generally speaking, it is the hawks – the self-employed and senior managers who have the most opportunity. Mars quotes Eugene O'Neill approvingly: 'For de little stealin' dey gits you in jail soon or late. For de big stealin' dey makes you emperor and puts you in de Hall o' Fame when you croaks.'

Fiddle-proneness is 'any work context where a propensity exists for a job to offer regular material rewards that are excluded from formal accounts or which are included under ambiguous or deceptive headings.' The overt payment arrangements for some jobs – the catering trade is an obvious example – make no sense unless it is realised that a substantial proportion of take-home pay is fiddled – tips from customers, back-handers from suppliers, pilfered food and cutlery. Mars identifies a number of situations that are particularly fiddle-prone:

- where there is a formalised system of tipping
- where all or part of the work is carried out on the basis of 'cash in hand'
- in trades where the workforce is self-employed and the employer is not directly responsible for payment of income tax – 'the lump'
- where an individual is selling expertise to an uninformed customer – garages, plumbers and management consultants are in this category
- warehouses, where someone has to agree that the appropriate amount of goods have been delivered, or taken
- where management and workforce can collude to rip off a third party – this can sometimes be customers, but it could also be the tax authorities; management have a lower wage bill, turn a blind eye to employee fiddles and the revenue don't receive all the tax they should
- where the employee has to maintain a 'float' of cash in circumstances which make it difficult and where he or she has to make up losses personally; often the only way to keep ahead is by fiddling; examples include garage forecourt employees and delivery roundsmen
- at check-out tills where there is a fast throughput
- where there are rewards for special efforts in a normally tightly structured payment scheme; for example journalists and staff computer programmers are often paid on a strict scale which allows no special arrangement for outstanding work. Journalists can make up for this by being permitted to

demand extraordinary expenses and computer programmers can claim overtime

Mars says that it is the *situation* which creates the fiddle, not the individual. However, individuals respond with varying degrees of enthusiasm to the opportunities presented. Some jobs depend so much on fiddling that it is disruptive if an individual decides not to participate.

The rules of the fiddle

These fiddles, diverse as they are, have one feature in common: although the activity permitted is illegal, they all take place within a framework of rules agreed between employer and employee. The 'agreement' is seldom mentioned, let alone formally discussed, but for each covert reward, employees know that, provided they keep within certain bounds, their action will not be questioned. Thus, to go back to the 'free telephone call' illustration: in most offices, the unmentioned rule is: it's okay to ring spouses about late arrival home and to fix appointments with doctors and dentists; it's not okay to have long personal calls every day nor to call long-distance too often. The rules work two ways: employees who transgress can expect not only to be disciplined but also to earn the disapproval of their colleagues; employers who are too restrictive should anticipate a resentful workforce.

It is this framework of extra-legal rules which helps to confuse the morality of the situation. Everyone colludes in persuading each other that what is happening is morally acceptable – 'honest dishonesty', as Henry has it. Everyone becomes used to the idea that there is a category of behaviour which is illegal and grounds for dismissal, but not likely to be acted on. It is the first important stage which permits white collar crime to flourish. For no one can spell out the rules precisely and accurately; there is a penumbra of doubt and within its extended shadow, individuals can seek to push the scope of the rules ever further. And the collusion mechanism ensures that, for every individual who transgresses, there will be many more who hesitate to condemn.

The actual rules change with circumstances. When new work practices are introduced, the entire reward system – the direct financial package, the indirect parcel of agreed perks, the inherent job satisfaction, and the covert rewards – come up for review in the minds of both employer and employee. If the new set of rewards fail to meet the standards and expectations set by the old, the employer is in trouble. When garbage collectors were asked to operate a 'sealed bag' system – theoretically very much in their interests as it made the job less filthy – they rebelled because they were denied their unofficial perk of scavenging. Dockers resented the introduction of containerisation because they had become used to pilfering as an income supplement. British firemen are poorly paid but often take extra jobs as handymen and gardeners: a change of work pattern threatened this. Telephone engineers also didn't want a change in hours of work; it reduced their opportunities to carry out 'private' contracts for customers.

The use of computer-based systems arises at several points in this explanation. First, the use of a computer for private work can be regarded as a perk, along with all the others that office employees feel is theirs. And, *up to a point*, why not? Few employers mind the use of the office typewriter, outside proper working hours, to produce a formal letter, so why not a word-processor? Or why not a spreadsheet to maintain a domestic budget? For more advanced users, it can be argued that such private use of computers is a benefit to the company, as the employee is increasing his or her skills in private time, a bit of self-training. Where do the ethical boundaries exist, the equivalent of the sustained long-distance telephone call as opposed to the brief local contact? And if the computer security manager hasn't set up the means to prevent employees from getting into parts of the computer that are supposed to be confidential, whose fault is that?

More important though, is the way in which computers change jobs, particularly for less-skilled workers. The computer has great power to restrict the scope of activity open to the individual – and to monitor in considerable detail the activities of all employees, cash movements, and warehouse inventories. In so doing it disturbs the delicate package of employee remuneration. In particular, it causes employers to abandon the unspoken features of the covert rewards. If, as often happens, the covert rewards involve items which are not disclosed to the tax authorities, particular problems arise: the computer may be too precise and detailed in its working to allow for 'fudge factors'. But the employee doesn't necessarily understand this; he or she may try to make up the losses by inventing new perks or, if that can't be done, by sabotage and other disruptive action.

The dissociated individual

Outside the arena of the acceptable fiddle lie the acts of individuals who know they are acting both illegally and in ways which their colleagues will condemn. However, the acts still seem not so horrendous that it is impossible to justify them. In this respect they are still markedly different from traditional 'street' crime. No one tries to justify burglary, but many white collar criminals are able to soothe their unease about embezzlement.

This is the second area of explanation of white collar crime – the dissociated individual – the phenomenon of *anomie* as one of the pioneers of modern sociology, Emile Durkheim, had it. The theory attempts to show why individuals who might normally be expected to behave in a responsible, moral fashion towards society stop doing so. Codes of ethical behaviour occur because individuals feel part of society; 'society' can mean either in the widest senses of being part of the human race or a particular nation, but also on a narrower basis of belonging to a neighbourhood or within a company. Behaving properly is part of belonging to society. Under special circumstances, however, the sense of belonging can disappear and, when it does, so does the code of ethics. Individuals who persuade themselves that 'society' has let them down feel released from their ethical obligations and licensed to seek revenge or 'get their own back'. This theory is not without its critics, but it does provide some useful explanations.

For example, a long-term employee who has been passed over for promotion may persuade himself or herself that the company has failed to deliver what was promised. Released from the traditional obligations not to steal, the employee feels able to take perks, borrow money, run private enterprise schemes, and so on. This is rationalised with a series of weasel-justifications:

'I am only borrowing and will repay'
'This is really a perk'
'Everyone else does it'
'They owe it me anyway'
'No one is really losing'
'The insurance will pay'
'It serves them right for being so stupid'
'They shouldn't have passed me over'
'Management are corrupt – they are the worst of the lot'

There are other triggers besides failure to achieve promotion that can promote this feeling of dissociation: poor industrial relations in general is an obvious example, but the introduction of new computer-based information systems is easily the most important. As we saw in Chapter one, such facilities have a radical effect on the ways in which decisions are made in organisations. Among the negative effects are:

- a considerable degree of de-skilling; computers can handle many of the routines used by skilled workers on the factory floor and can by-pass certain important forms of middle-management: the computers generate the reports and draw and act on the conclusions that used to be made by humans; middle-management's main function becomes the managing of the unskilled workforce; again the pall of unemployment hangs heavy
- less manual work is available, leading both to actual unemployment but also inducing a fear of unemployment among those with jobs but without the adaptability to find new ones
- regular workers become threatened by part-timers who are willing to accept lower wages
- top management makes all the important decisions; workers on the shop floor become relegated to tasks that robots can't at present handle, but may one day be able to

All of these trends lead to a widespread feeling of alienation, of not being involved in the commercial process. Employees feel less constrained in seizing what opportunities present themselves. Size too, is an important element. One American academic rather ponderously observed: 'As soon as the owner becomes too large or too impersonal to permit an imaginative interchange with [the employee] then his property rights are likely to be negated.' (E. Cahn in *The Moral Decision* in 1955). In other words, the bigger the company, the more remote the boss, the greater the likelihood of employee ripoffs.

Other theories

It's a matter of taste, or experience, to decide how far you accept such theories. What is beyond doubt is that relatively few information crimes are committed by individuals who set out with criminal intentions: they see opportunities and they find themselves in circumstances in which their normal sense of ethics can become warped. Pressure from an individual's private life may be the trigger: not only problems arising from unexpected unemployment but also the failure to handle personal finance properly. Alcoholism and the effects of drug dependence can reduce moral sensibilities and induce the need to find cash to support the habits. Crises in marriage and sexual life can affect self-image; embezzled cash is often seen as the instant remedy. In two cases from the end of the 1970s, both involving branches of large UK clearing banks, young women clerks manipulated accounts in order to siphon off cash. In one case, the money was to support the drug habit of a violent boy-friend,[1] and in the other because her husband was unemployed.[2] In another case in 1981 a 23–year-old male bank clerk became infatuated with a 32–year-old woman with rather expensive tastes. He bought her presents and clothes, took her on holiday and gave her £1000 to help her start up a business. He then lost about £10,000 at casinos trying to repay the money. In the end, he stole £23,000 and, when he was caught, the woman disappeared.[3] A wife's drinking problem brought about the downfall of a senior clerk in the accounts section of a department store chain – the actual method employed was the old one of the altered computer input form. He finally admitted to stealing over £42,000.[4]

The circumstances of such cases are repeated endlessly throughout the collections of computer crime material. Several years ago they ceased to have much news value and now often go unreported. But these are the typical computer-related crimes and criminals.[5]

The introduction of new computer systems have a crucial effect in muddling what codes of ethics exist. The unspoken treaties at the heart of covert reward systems are a function of precise work relationships; when the computer disturbs these, the code of ethics loses the basis of its validity and, for a while at least, anything goes.

Hackers

From the typical to the colourful: the popular image of the computer criminal is the hacker: the story we are asked to accept is that there are groups of fifteen- to seventeen-year-olds whose skills no computer can resist. They strike almost randomly, are nearly always successful and the only protections against them are heavyweight software and hardware devices.

Elsewhere, I have written extensively about and for hackers* and since that book was published have met and had a considerable correspondence with many actual and would-be practitioners. Hacking, in the sense in which hackers themselves define the term, belongs to the long tradition of playful abuse of technology in order to see 'what happens'. The first people who called themselves hackers appeared in about 1960 around the computer facilities at MIT. They were bright kids who borrowed the mainframes of the age outside regular hours in order to discover what the machines could do. You can follow the same group of people, as Steven Levy does in his book *Hackers*, from these early experiments, through the primitive games writing (often space war games and simulations of lunar landers), past the early days of the mini-computer and through to the heady mid-1970s days when they came together in the

The Hacker's Handbook, Century-Hutchinson, 1985, 1986, 1988, 1989

San Francisco Bay area as the Homebrew Computing Club with the then daring idea that it was possible for a hobbyist to build an affordable personal computer. These first-generation hackers are still around: some of them have run – and left – large corporations and have been multi-millionaires; others have never been rich and continue as consultants and programmers. They were always in revolt against the ideas that bigger computers mean better computers, that regiments of programmers would produce better software than a few mavericks, that computers had to be serious and – though this is one idea that has not survived well – that computer resources ought to be freely available, at least to those qualified to benefit.

Within the ranks of these hackers were the phone-phreaks who explored the long distance lines for interest and challenge; the defrauding of the telephone company was always an incidental, not the purpose of the exercise. Hackers learnt the advantages of long distance computer-to-computer communication early as well; the techniques were interesting in themselves and they put hackers in different parts of the world in touch with each other.

Hacking in the more limited sense of 'people who like to break into computers' appears first in the early 1980s when substantial numbers of personal computers had become available to hobbyists and when, at around the same time, there were beginning to be large numbers of commercial on-line information services. The first well-publicised 'teenage hacker' stories – Ronald Mark Austin[6] who hacked all the way from California to Norway and the Milwaukee 414 gang – occur at this time and were legendised in the movie *War Games* and a tv spin-off/rip-off called *Whiz Kids*. As we have already seen, there is at least one well-documented teenage hacker story from 1974 – the 15–year-old Londoner who broke into a large time-share bureau, discovered how to read main memory, eavesdropped onto other users and eventually secured a high-privilege password which enabled him to read data.*

Among the people who welcomed the arrival of this breed of hackers were the computer security consultants who at last

*Some of these techniques are explained in more detail in Chapter 10.

identified an immediate image with which to sell their products and services.* The September/October 1983 editorial of the newsletter *Computer Security* was headed: 'Let's Hear it for the Hackers!' and began:

> The summer of 1983 may prove the watershed period for data security. The movie *War Games*, together with the well-publicised activities of the so-called '414 gang' from Milwaukee, have given more credibility to data security concerns in the eyes of the general public than a decade of hypothesising and doom-saying by data security professionals.

Up till then, they had to rely on inciting fear of fraud and terrorism in order to win customers. Products with names like 'hacker-cracker' started to appear. In most cases, the products worked; they simply failed to address actual computer security problems.

It would be a bold person indeed who tried to settle up the balance sheet of good and evil for the hacker community: against the few documented cases of hacker-induced vandalism must be set the growth of the mini and microcomputer and the very idea that people could own and run personal computers. The truth should now be told: even among reported computer incidents, hacking probably accounts for less than one per cent of hostile activity. And most hacking is perpetrated, not by the external genius, but by people who already have legitimate access to a system but are able to wander outside the areas where management had hoped to confine them.

The internal hacker is usually employed as a programmer or computer operator; he has a detailed knowledge of how the computer's operating system works and also of the organisation which the computer serves. Hacking starts by taking the form

---

*In the UK a senior consultant at the National Computing Centre, reviewing two books on hacking, one written by me and the other by Bill Landreth, wrote: 'The computer industry should be grateful to hackers like Hugo Cornwall and Bill Landreth . . . Though they had the opportunity to cause a great deal of trouble to many installations, their high ideals and code of conduct forbade it. Their escapades should be taken as a warning to DP management.'

of exploration: roving outside the limits set by the hacker's superiors, perhaps by by-passing features in the operating system, perhaps by assuming someone else's identity with the aid of a 'borrowed' password. A lot of internal hacking never progresses beyond this point; I would guess from my own contacts that in this form it is extremely widespread – unusual by its absence, in fact – and that most of it is never detected. In a voluntary survey conducted by *Computer Weekly* in May and June 1989 and filled in by 540 readers, over a quarter admitted that they had hacked into systems and 87 per cent of those said they were never found out. Forty-two per cent of all respondents said they were aware of unauthorised access by internal users into their systems, with only 5 per cent claiming attacks by external operators. Only one in twenty incidents of unauthorised access were reported to the police.

The next stage along is to commence using the computer's resources for private purposes: running a few programs, printing a few files. The problem management must face is: at what point does such activity run counter to the organisation's interests? Where does unofficial use of the computer cease to be the equivalent of the occasional local telephone call or valuable self-training in computer skills which from which the employer might benefit? The wise manager would do well to attempt to harness the benefits of the internal hacker.★

However, there are clearly internal hacking activities which no employer wants. Surprisingly common are clumsy internal hacks which go badly wrong, because the hacker has lacked the skill and knowledge to anticipate what might happen. In one case reported to me privately, an organisation had an internal electronic mail system so that employees in its far-flung offices could communicate easily with each other. A data-processing staffer wondered how many simultaneous messages the system could handle within a given short period and wrote a program which artificially generated a large amount of traffic. An original message was sent to four destinations and the supervisory program arranged for each of the recipients to copy the original message and send it on to a further four, and so on and so on.

★I explore these ideas more fully in Chapter 12.

This is in fact a crude form of the so-called computer worm.★ The program worked so well that not only the electronic mail system was brought down but so was the company's main computer which carried out a number of other important but unrelated functions. As the subsequent investigation showed, the internal hacker had merely been curious about technical features of the electronic mail service and completely ignored the possibility that his experiment might cause damage to the mainframe's entire operation. In another case, a twenty-six-year-old computer programmer leaving the UK High Street consumer electronics chain Dixons decided to play what he thought was going to be an amusing practical joke. Every time an operator typed in his leaving date, the programmer intended that a message saying 'Goodbye Folks' would flash onto vdus. Unfortunately the program didn't work as planned and, when someone did type in the triggering date, every screen in Dixons' headquarters went blank.[8]

There are of course malicious attacks by internal hackers: in a case quoted by Ken Wong, a contract programmer had been promised a permanent job at the end of his current assignment. The job never came through and the programmer inserted a small routine into the payroll package which checked to see that his name was present before allowing the monthly payroll to be processed. The first month after the programmer had left, the payroll refused to run. This is an example of a 'logic bomb'.★★

External hackers – the folk who have had all the publicity – are motivated principally by curiosity and the opportunity to demonstrate skill. The computer systems that are most vulnerable to their attentions are the ones that are also the most 'interesting'. The interest may derive from:

- who owns the computer,
- what sort of service it is providing
- what sort of data it holds,
- whether there is anything unusual or novel about the hardware and operating system.

★See Chapter 10.
★★See also Chapter 10.

If a computer system scores poorly in this test, it is likely to be safe from external hacking attempts; the more points it scores, the more extensive the protective measures that ought to be employed.

Most external hacking relies on one simple technique: password acquisition. The hacker uses a password that a legitimate user of the system has treated carelessly. Phone numbers and passwords for computer systems have frequently been circulated via hobbyist bulletin board systems: sometimes, valid numbers have remained on view for months on end. In the first edition of *Hacker's Handbook* I provided a print-out of typical bulletin board material. I had cleaned up some of the material beforehand but relied on the fact that six months at least would elapse between my taking the data from the bulletin board and the publication date of the book. To my alarm, a month after publication, people started telling me that some of the information was still valid. By the time a second edition was due I again assumed that all phone numbers and passwords had changed and I made no further alteration to the published print-outs. I was horrified to discover that, eighteen months after the information had been on a bulletin board and after a crescendo of publicity for the book, some of the phone numbers still worked.

Few even of the successful hackers possess the skills to do much at the system level of a computer (see the next chapter for an explanation of what this means) and to carry out some of the hacking methods so frequently described by theorists. Hackers rely heavily on the exploitation of accidental discoveries: the items in the setting up of computer systems that everyone else has forgotten. But a great deal of hacking endeavour is unsuccessful: the hackers in the Prince Phillip case (see page 324) had to wait six months for the break that gave them the ability to take over the Prestel system.

Professional and organised crime

In the speculative articles about the future of computer crime that appear regularly in management magazines, predictions of the arrival of professional criminals on the scene occur frequently. Considering that one can find such forecasts as far back as 1973 – in Gerald McKnight's *Computer Crime*, for example, it is remarkable how little evidence exists to sustain these fears. Which is not to say that such cases don't exist: when Swedish police swooped on five criminals who had attempted to defraud banks of £57 million via the SWIFT network in June 1989 they seemed fairly convinced that this was the work of organised criminals working with a computer expert.[9]

Overwhelmingly, criminals seem to prefer to stick to activities which they already understand. One favoured method could be computer-related extortion, for example to threaten to cripple a computer facility – and hence the business that depends on it.* Another extorsive method is to pressurise or blackmail an employee. This has been used in order to gain assistance in conventional robberies and it is possible it could be adopted in order to carry out a computer-based robbery. The use of student hackers by professional criminals seems highly unlikely: hackers would be too unpredictable and unmanageable.

Similar conclusions must be drawn about predictions that organised crime, perhaps in the form of the Mafia, is about to become centrally involved in information crimes. One of the problems in tracking down rumours about the involvement of organised crime is that definitions of what it is are rather elastic. The Mafia certainly appear to be interested in acquiring financial institutions through which to launder money acquired through drug trafficking, prostitution, extortion and gaming but in all of these the fraudulent misuse of computer systems is very much an incidental to traditional criminal activities. In his 1983 book, *How to Prevent Computer Crime*, US lawyer August Bequai includes a chapter titled *Infiltration by Organised Crime*. However, what he offers is a series of warnings about what *could* happen, rather than descriptions of what has already taken place. Thus 'Computers can easily be used to facilitate the business of the traditional areas of syndicate involvement . . .' Mike Comer quotes a 'Mafia-linked plot to tap municipal treasuries throughout America of millions of dollars by manipulation of

---

*There are instances of computer-related extortion, but carried out by computer professionals as opposed to traditional criminals, see p 57.

a city computer system' but says that investigators had not yet determined precisely how the plan was to be worked. Shortly after the end of one the UK's biggest Mafia drugs cases where Francesco di Carlo was sentenced for 25 years on a £75m heroin charge, at least two newspapers ran stories to the effect that Scotland Yard had found that some of its critical computer files on the Mafia were mysteriously wiped during the investigation. However, I personally have found few authentic and completely reliable instances of Mafia involvement in information crime;* but there is no doubt that there is fear in some quarters that, despite the considerable cultural gap between typical datacrime activities and those associated typically with organised crime, Bequai's predictions may become true quite soon. One particular scenario put before me quite independently by several City figures is worth recording because it effectively links together two known preoccupations of organised crime: that employees of City firms with an over-fondness for drugs might get set up and pressured by their dealers into executing an EFT or securities fraud.

Terrorism/subversion/anarchists

On the other hand, terrorists have identified computers as 'legitimate targets' of their activities. As far back as 1969, a five-man anti-war group called Beaver 55 attacked the computer centre of Dow Chemical at Midland, Michigan. 1000 tapes were wiped with the aid of hand magnets. Beaver 55 claimed that the tapes included work that was being carried out into nerve gases, napalm and other chemical weapons.[10] In 1972 and again in 1978 the IRA bombed computers in Northern Ireland.[11] In West Germany terrorist groups have attacked computer centres which they believed held data on international terrorism and in November 1986 a group calling itself the Hind Almeh Fighting Unit and thought to be part of the Red Army Faction caused over DM 1m worth of damage to IBM's Heidelberg Network-

---

*One of them, involving forged Diners Club cards, appears on page 193, but interesting enough, it was a non-Mafia member hoping to be admitted who devised and carried out the scheme.

ing Centre. IBM said that the centre was not involved in weapons research.[12] In June 1987 a San Francisco woman caused $750,000 worth of destruction to computer systems at Vandenburg Air Force Base using a crowbar and a drill. She also destroyed a radar dish. She believed that the equipment she attacked was part of the control centre for Navstar, a military program that is part of Star Wars.[13]

It is important to view these occurrences with some sense of proportion.[14] Most organisations will never be under threat from attacks by terrorists or subversives. In the case of terrorism, the motivation is ideological: usually, either the company owning the computer is perceived to be in a distasteful business (perhaps it has links with South Africa or another unpopular regimes, or it is thought to use animals for pharmaceutical experiment, or it is part of the nuclear, chemical or defence industries) or the computer itself is regarded as symbolic (because it is used by the police or intelligence agencies, or it can be seen as evidence of imperialism and oppression).

In the case of subversion the aim is to disable a vital point of the economy in order to make a general political point or to cause disruption. Terrorism is overt in its approach, subversion is clandestine. Many more people appear to worry about subversion than suffer from it. Subversion is rather more than the holding of views which dissent from the political consensus, it is the willingness to take direct action oneself to by-pass the conventional means of seeking change. Subversives form only a tiny proportion among political dissenters. There is some confirmation for the view that trade union activists have sought to target computer staff within large organisations, realising that if they can be persuaded to strike, then in effect the organisation rapidly ceases to function. But many of these instances can be seen as little more than legitimate trade union activity: it is the fact of clandestinity of method which marks subversion. Industrial unrest, in any case, needs the pre-existence of some level of employee unhappiness in order to flourish.

What is interesting about all of the cases is the lack of subtlety in the method: it is always a direct physical attack and little attempt seems to have been made to use hacking, logic bombs or viruses. In practical terms one can see why: an attack of software or data requires a considerable level of skill plus the sort of physical access that can usually only be obtained by an insider. What this means to the terrorist group is that an infiltration is required, which both ties up personnel and runs the risk of discovery. Even then, to be effective, the terrorist has to ensure that all back-ups of software and data are destroyed as well, and some of these may be stored on premises to which he or she has no access. So the physical attack makes good sense.

There appears to be only one well-documented instance of a terrorist group whose main focus is computer technology. It is called Comite de Liberation Ou de Detournement des Ordinateurs or CLODO. 'Clodo' is French slang for tramp. Between 1979 and 1983 it claimed responsibility for a number of sabotage attacks on computer manufacturers in the Toulouse area, including Phillips, CII-Honeywell-Bull, Sperry and ICL. It also wrecked an IBM computer belonging to a local bank.[15] In an interview in 1983, a CLODO representative explained why they were involved in computer sabotage:

> To challenge everyone, programmers and non-programmers, so that we can reflect a little more on this world we live in and which we create and the way in which computerisation transforms society. The truth about computerisation should be revealed from time to time. It should be said that a computer is just a bunch of metal that serves only to do what one wants it to do . . . we are essentially attacking what these tools lead to: files, surveillance by means of badges and cards, instrument of profit maximisation for the bosses and of accelerated pauperisation for those who are rejected . . . though what we do is primarily propaganda through action, we also know that the damage we cause leads to setbacks and substantial delays . . . These actions are only the visible tip of the iceberg! We ourselves and others fight daily in a less ostensible way . . . we'll only say that the art consists of creating bugs that will only appear later on, little time bombs.

International intelligence agencies

In March 1989 newspapers and magazines across the world carried a story to the effect that members of the infamous Chaos Computer Club of Hamburg had been receiving money and drugs from the Russian security and intelligence service, the KGB.[16] The more the story is examined, the less clear the truth becomes. For all that was written about the incident, very few journalists appear to have gone back to primary sources and tested out the accounts of both the West German authorities and Chaos members. What is certain is that most of the accusations were dropped almost immediately, that internal rivalry between various West German agencies played some part in the way in which the story was presented to the press and that the leading figure committed suicide in June 1989, at which point it emerged that he had a long history of mental illness, manifesting itself largely in enormous suspicion of the KGB.[17]

Shortly afterwards stories began to circulate that hackers in other countries had links with the KGB, even to the point, apparently, of giving them training. This preposterous idea was printed in an up-market Sunday newspaper.[18]

Whilst one can safely dismiss the wilder assertions of links between hackers and international espionage agencies there should be every expectation that hacking-type techniques are extensively in use by all the world's intelligence agencies with any level of technical competence. The matter is almost never discussed in public, but the role of the National Security Agency in the USA and its close UK partner GCHQ in computer security defence is widely acknowledged to the point where they are the overt setters of security standards in government. It must be inconceivable that they have no offensive role.

Rather more is known about the aims and methods of 'technical' intelligence gathering by the USSR.[19] Between 1981 and 1982 officials of the French counter-intelligence service, DST, secured a series of documents from a Russian agent called 'Farewell' which provided a highly detailed breakdown of the various organs of the Russian state that were customers for high tech and military technical intelligence, the various intelligence-gathering agencies and the organisational structure that holds them together. Most of what has been written subsequently derives from these documents.

Russian successes in high technology have been patchy and there has been a tradition, going back as far as Peter the Great, of acquiring knowledge by means of industrial espionage. Today the co-ordination of such activity is handled by the Military Industrial Commission – VPK. This sets targets and priorities as between internal customers – the military, research and manufacturing organisations – and the various collecting agencies. In 1980, for example, the VPK was claiming that from the 4,502 samples and 25,453 documents obtained there was a saving of 407.5m roubles, 200 R&D projects were started and 1,458 existing projects were accelerated or shortened.

There are several intelligence-gathering agencies one of whose functions is to supply the VPK. Much of the effort is not clandestine: it consists of reading Western technical journals, accessing Western technical databases (sometimes quite openly), attending trade fairs and the various forms of 'legitimate' commercial trading. The use of illegitimate techniques is an extension, not a substitute for the open means. In computer terms, the pirating of hardware and software designs is well-documented – the Ryad-II mainframe is a copy of the IBM 370, for example, the Agat is a cyrillic version of the Apple II. In terms of data acquisition the prime aim has been to secure wider admission to US specialist on-line databases; as far as one can tell, the task has been quite easy because the US research and academic community have been unwilling to accept strictures from Pentagon hard-liners to limit overseas access to their data.

The most important of the Russian pro-active technical intelligence gathering agencies is Department T of the KGB, and it seems fair to assume that it is they who run any aggressive computer hacking activities, though nothing specific has so far ever been acknowledged.

Interestingly, one of the few examples of government-sponsored hacking that has been properly reported took place between apparent allies. In October 1988 two Israelis successfully penetrated Star Wars (SDI) files at the Lawrence Livermore

National Laboratory in California, having been previously denied formal access.[20]

CHAPTER EIGHT

Computer Systems: An Overview

This book must now take one of the first of a series of transitions in style: up till now we have been concerned with the changing impact of the computer on businesses and on the forms of criminal behaviour. We must now look at computer systems themselves in more detail: it isn't really possible to form a proper appreciation of the security risks to a computer system without some basic understanding of the various constituent elements and how they hang together. This, and the risks that can arise specifically from the hardware and software of a computer, as opposed to the commercial environment which it serves, are our concerns for the next three chapters.

Computer systems analysis is preoccupied with two mutually dependent processes: administrative flow and computer technique. The first addresses the questions:

- what information are you putting into the system?
- what information do you want to get out?
- who is authorised to supply the information?
- who is authorised to retrieve it?
- what intermediate routines are necessary to secure these aims?

These questions interact with each other when identifying aims and means: clearly the results you get from a computer system depend on the quality of the information you put in; but some results may not be worth obtaining, given the expense of acquiring the original raw material and/or processing it. In a sophisticated system, there will be large numbers of administrative flows, some wholly independent of one another, others interconnecting to varying degrees.

The second seeks to identify in terms of available and costjustifiable computer hardware and software products the means to achieve those aims. There is nearly always many more than one possible answer.

Computer security specialists use – or should be using provided that they are more than just salesmen for particular products – the techniques of systems analysis to probe for weaknesses in systems that have already been set up or proposed. They should always start with administrative flows and then move on to examine inherent flaws in specific hardware and software.

Hardware, software, firmware, humanware

Conventional descriptions of computers divide their components into hardware and software. Hardware is all the items you can physically touch: main processor, memory chips, disc and tape drives, displays, printers, and so on. Hardware is the consistent, unchanging element in a computer set-up. Software, collectively, is the various changeable elements, and the ones you can't actually see. Essentially, it consists of the instructions and data upon which the hardware acts.

The more closely you examine a computer and its associated systems, the less satisfactory these definitions become. Nearly all computers contain an intermediate feature called *firmware*. These are sets of program instructions – usually covering some basic house-keeping function – which are permanently available on a chip or series of chips. Software itself divides into three segments: systems software which, like firmware, is principally concerned with house-keeping, applications software which are the actual instructions to make a program 'work' and data, which is what the applications program processes. Software is usually loaded from a disc or tape drive but, confusingly, can sometimes exist on a series of pre-loaded memory chips held in a removable cartridge.

The conventional description falls down in another respect: the final ingredient in any computer system is what might be called *humanware* – the human beings who, as designers, maintainers, data inputters and users have to interact with the system. Overwhelmingly from a security point of view, humanware is where the greatest risks tend to occur.

In the next part of the book we will be looking at the areas of direct threat to a computer system. Hardware first, then software. Some groundwork in how a computer's various parts interact ought to be part of everyone education; to the extent that it is not, this section will try to remedy the deficiency. Understanding the guiding principles is not the same as being able to program or set up a system. The manager should take two essential steps in preparing to understand the organisation's computer resources: ask to be guarded against buzz words and realise that, for each end result that a computer system can be asked to provide, there are nearly always several routes.

The lay appreciation of computers is not always helped by the excessive jargon with which computer manufacturers market their products. The ungainly acronyms – CICS/TSO, VAX VMS, CO_3, SQL, MS–DOS, C/PM, OS/2 and so on – are product names for hardware or operating systems or applications programs – which are selected as carefully as the brand names of new motor vehicles, cosmetics and confectionery bars. The marketing men of the computer world believe that their products will appear more powerful, more mysterious and more credible with labelling that itself requires some level of initiation than if they have say, the animal-like names sometimes favoured by automobile manufacturers. The computer industry, along with manufacturers of cameras and stereo components, prefers to use the 'tech speak' approach – suggestive of a project that has just left the research laboratories – to conceal relatively simple ideas. One of the many revolutionary results of the personal computer explosion of the mid 70s was the switch to friendly names like Apple and Pet and it is a little disappointing to find the products of Apple Corporation of 1986 and 1987 with names like Apple IIGS and Macintosh SE. The lay reader, attempting to understand relatively complex computer systems, should prepare themselves to ask their specialist colleagues to strip away the manufacturer-imposed jargon in providing explanations.

Apologies to those readers who think they know it all already. The present chapter gives an overview, the next two examine risks specifically associated with hardware and then software.

Computer processes

The easiest way to understand the various processes computer systems can perform is to look at the history of how computers grew.

Batch. The earliest generation computers required that all the data that was going to be utilised was ready and waiting before the machine was ever asked to do anything. The data itself, typically in the form of punched cards or tape, had to be stacked up, the computer and its associated program were switched to 'run' and the results appeared either as a further set of punched cards or as a print-out. While the computer was running, the operator couldn't ask it to do anything extra. To perform further calculations, the computer had to be started all over again. The computer program used the entire resources of the machine. It is the case that the very largest calculations that computers in the commercial world execute still operate in this 'batch' mode: the world's biggest retail banks with millions of client accounts, the mail order houses with huge numbers of customers and vast inventories, the leading global weather-forecasting agencies, require processing power and speed which demand the total resources of the most powerful computers available.*

Real time. However, 'batch' mode was clearly fairly useless in a number of commercial applications. In the mid and later 1940s, both military interests and the large civilian airlines required computer-aided 'situation report' machines, a replacement in effect of those scenes from World War II movies where girls receive reports on headphones and use long poles to push blocks of wood representing ships and planes around a large-scale map. What these users wanted was the facility of collecting a considerable amount of information from different sources and presenting it on a consolidated display which could be updated immedi-

---

*Users of MS-DOS may be familiar with the batch commands – this is a facility whereby a series (or 'batch') of instructions to the computer which would normally be typed at the keyboard can be stored in a special file which, when called, sends the instructions automatically to the cpu.

ately and, if necessary, viewed from a number of geographically separated locations. The military needed strategic intelligence and the airlines sought, initially, information about seat reservations and the locations of aircraft. These early real-time machines didn't do much in the way of calculating.

The two sorts of computer – batch and real-time – had very different priorities in design. Batch-mode computers concentrated on arithmetic processes; real-time computers needed large memories which could be accessed and updated easily.

Time-share. The successors to batch computers were designed to handle more than one job at a time. They achieved this by taking advantage of the fact that the processors could operate far more quickly than data could be presented to them or taken from them. Data was read into and printed from computers by electro-mechanical means – punch-card readers and line printers. The processor could be asked to switch from one task to another without any perceptible slowing down of the piles of punch-cards. The technique was called time-slicing. As the quality and speed of processors increased, more and more simultaneous tasks could be carried out.

It was still the case, however, that programmers had little direct contact with the machines themselves. Computers were far too expensive for anyone to contemplate that a single individual might be allowed to have an interactive relationship with a machine. Programming was essentially a paper-based exercise. The programmer had to wait his turn until a space was available for a 'run'. The process was expensive and time-consuming as a single error could only be detected by a full run. However, it would have been even more expensive to permit a solitary programmer exclusive access to a machine. Even at the beginnings of the 1960s, the only interactivity you could expect from non-real-time machines were a few blinks from lights on the operating console in reply to flicking some switches.

As processor and memory costs fell, attempts were made to bring to the batch machine some of the interactivity of real-time machines. Programming techniques were discovered which gave operators some limited immediate interaction with the improved machines so that they could type questions on a teletypewriter – the vdu was still a considerable rarity – and get answers back immediately. Time-slicing was used so that batch-mode programs could continue to run at the same time. Much of this work was carried out unofficially by the first generation of computer hackers at the turn of the 1960s. A few years later the first of the proper 'time-share' machines became available: each user could sit at a teletypewriter, ask the computer to perform and get answers – and have the illusion that they were the only person using the machine.

Multi-user. The time-share machine, as it developed, could be asked to serve a number of purposes. In its simplest form, it would act simply as a *multi-user* computer: the same program, essentially, but with several people using it simultaneously. A typical example would be an information-retrieval service: the computer held a large number of items of information and every user connected to the computer could be making their own enquiry. In this simplest version, there would be no question of any true 'real-time' element: it would not be possible for some users to be creating new items of information or modifying existing ones: all the computer could do was to give more than one person at a time access to what was already there. Creating the database of information was an entirely separate operation. Services of this sort are plentiful in the late 1980s: the big credit-status databases and text-based information-retrieval services (where you can ask for a search of several years of several newspapers and magazines for specific mentions of individuals, events, or products) all tend to operate in this manner.

Multi-tasking. In multi-tasking computers, each individual connected could be running a different program, or different aspects of the same program, and have the illusion that they were the only person using the computer. In a university-based computer, each researcher might be taking up a small portion of the computer's memory resources as well as a small time-slice of the processor's activities in order to calculate the results of an individual experiment. In a commercial situation, multi-tasking can mean that while some members of staff input inventory data and others key in orders, management can be asking for cashflow and financial statements.

Modern multi-user/multi-tasking computers have facilities so that the use of the central processor and of working memory is optimised for each application and each user and can indeed be continuously adjusted so that everyone has the greatest possible share of the computer's resource.*

It is possible to have multi-tasking without having multiple users; the most powerful desk-top micros of the second half of the 1980s can offer the single user the capacity to run several programs simultaneously: a word-processor, a database, graphics presentation and at the same time be connected both to a remote information service and an electronic mail bureau. Not many people feel they need this level of functionality at the moment, but at the time of writing, it can be acquired at less than $2000.

The virtual machine. A stage beyond the multi-user/multi-tasking computer is the virtual machine; here, it is possible to give the user the illusion, not only of being the sole person using an individual program on a computer, but of having a whole computer, capable of running many programs simultaneously at their command. In reality, there is an even bigger computer providing the images of several smaller computers. This is what the biggest commercial mainframes and superminis from IBM and DEC are able to achieve.

Distributed processing. But with the arrival of cheaper, smaller computers – first the minis, then the micros – the economics of the situation began to change the sorts of things

---

*Readers who regularly use IBM PCs may be familiar with a very limited form of multi-tasking called 'memory-resident programs', of which Borland's Sidekick is a well-known example. Here, the user is able to suspend the current application, for example a spreadsheet, and then call up for immediate use a fresh program like a note-maker, or simple calculator or a telephone directory-cum-autodialler. When the user has finished, he or she is then returned to the last position in the original program (in this case the spreadsheet), which has in the meantime remained dormant. This is not true multi-tasking, where all programs remain active and not, as in this case, where only one program at a time is active and the other is suspended.

people expected mainframes to do. One of the most dramatic was the realisation that the original equation about the pre-eminent value of computer time compared with human time had become completely over-turned; it no longer made sense for humans to have to wait for the computer to become available. Equally important was the discovery that there were other routes to improving the services computer technology could offer besides building larger and larger mainframes. The reaction of IBM and its followers had always been: you want more users to be connected? get a bigger mainframe. you want more processes to be carried out? get a bigger mainframe. you want more speed? get a bigger mainframe. But big mainframes are costly to purchase and expensive to maintain; moreover, if you try to expand them beyond a certain point, there may be no easy 'upgrade path'; you have to abandon your expensive hardware and start all over again.

Systems analysts took the smaller and simpler applications and ran them on separate small machines. The small machines may have been designed for use in the sort of small business that had never been able to afford mainframes, but there was no reason why larger companies shouldn't have *both* mainframes and smaller machines to provide satellite services such as word-processing or payroll. The mainframe was used for number crunching and the maintenance of very large databases while the small machines were adopted for rapid manageable results.

As the analysts pursued these ideas, they tried providing some way of connecting mainframes and smaller machines so that, while they weren't necessarily talking to each other all the time, computer reports generated on the one machine could be fed as data input into the other, saving manual re-keying.

But the cheaper, smaller systems also pointed the way to other methods of achieving the sort of results associated with large mainframes. Why not use several smaller computers, all interacting with each other? Such an approach can have extensive savings in costs and development time and can more readily allow for a gradual growth in the size of a system. This thinking is at the heart of *distributed processing:* the total effect is achieved by spreading computer power over different machines.

Distributed processing can work both when the separate constituents are widely distanced from each other or when they are tightly coupled as in a *cluster*, as it is often called. In a cluster, several smaller computers, typically super-minis, operate together to deliver the level of performance that used to require a full-blown mainframe. Clustering can also be used to provide a degree of *fault-tolerance*★, so that if one machine within the cluster fails for some reason, the remaining machines can detect what has happened and can step in and take over.

Networks. When distributed processing takes place with machines that are geographically separated, they are usually said to be connected together on a network. Small-scale networks, limited to a particular building, are called LANs, or Local Area Networks; Wide Area Networks, or WANS, cover several different sites and may indeed span many continents. LANs can operate in a number of different designs; the main differences from a security point-of-view is whether the network has some central point, for example a bigger computer, or a file-server (a large-scale storage device together with some controlling software); or if all machines on the network have equal status and can address each other as much or as little as occasion demands.

Hybrid systems. In many typical situations, the actual collection of computers and networks may be quite complex. In fact an organisation's computer system should really be regarded as consisting of all the obvious central facilities, plus every last terminal in every distant office. 'The computer system' consists of all the key-punch stations, all the bar-code readers, all the cash-tills, all the magnetic-stripe readers, all the warehousing and process-control machinery that report back their activities to the centre. It might contain local area networks to service internal office functions; there might be separate autonomous satellite computers to handle the requirements of individual departments. Nearly always there will be individual, stand-alone PCs. Stretching the definition only slightly, 'the computer

★See also below, p 85.

system' also consists of all the leased lines and dial-in facilities that connect branch offices and individual employees with the centre. In a typical banking set-up, there may be a central mainframe for processing customer accounts, working essentially in batch mode, a real-time multi-user system to answer cashier and customer enquiries about the state of an account at the close of business on the previous day and a series of ATMs which have sufficient processing power to decide, on the basis of information on the magnetic stripe of the customer's ATM card, whether to permit a pay-out of cash. Head and branch offices will undoubtedly also have local area networks for word-processing, electronic mail and information for senior management. And of all these will be linked together so that, at the right time, they can communicate with each other. Other sorts of hybrid systems may be found on factory floors – programmable machine tools, materials handling devices, management reporting computers; or in retail chains – electronic tills, credit verification systems, barcode readers, warehouse services, management services, payroll – and so on.

From every perspective except that of security, the increase in the multiple use of computers and the sharing of resources has been good news. However, as we will see later on, effective security cannot be bolted on as an afterthought; it is only possible if security features are designed in from the beginning. From most points of view, the inner functioning of his organisation's computer systems needn't matter to a manager: what count are effectiveness, throughput and cost. However, from a security point-of-view, knowledge of the system's architecture is critical, because it is only in this way that its areas of vulnerability can be identified: where are the points from which control may be exercised? what happens if one part ceases to be reliable – or it compromised? what inner checks exist? how much back-up can be brought into action? And so on.

We must now translate these ideas about computer processes into the ways in which they are realised through hardware and software in practice.

Computer hardware

Stripped of the marketing jargon, the critical differences between various sorts of computers comes down to the following:

Speed the number of instructions that can be processed in a given space of time.

Architecture this can mean two different things. Designers of processors speak of chip architecture, referring to the way in which a chip is structured internally to optimise its efficiency for particular applications and the amount of data that can be handled during each operating cycle. When designers of computers refer to computer architecture they are describing the way in which processor(s), active memory, storage memory, terminals and peripherals are connected together.

Memory the amount of active memory available for programs and work-space. The micros available between 1976 and 1981 could only handle 64 kilobytes of active memory, which had to include the operating system, applications program and data. One of the consequences of this is that spreadsheets and word-processor documents tended to be limited in size or required frequent use of the disc drives. With the IBM PC generation of micros, work-space expanded to 640 k. The one after that can cope with 16 megabytes and more, if necessary. Mini computers of the early and mid 1970s often had only 256 k of active memory and the very early mainframes had only a few tens of kilobytes.

Storage archive memory, for example disc and tape drives. Archive memory can hold programs, sections of programs and data. Material held in archive memory is passed to and from the active memory as required. For most medium-term applications, the disc drive is the usual storage method. Floppy discs hold small amounts of data, hard-discs (Winchester Drives) can hold from thirty times the amount of data a floppy can hold to three hundred times. Soon to be commonplace are optical drives, read by laser, which can hold nearly 2000 times as much data as the floppy disc on, for example, the standard IBM PC.

Peripherals the most familiar peripherals to micros and minis are vdu and keyboards and printers. There can be many others: specialist terminals like cash-tills, bar-code or magnetic stripe readers, links to machine tools, measuring devices and so on. Some peripherals are only unidirectional in operation; in other words, all they do is to collect data which is fed into a system or, in the alternative, all they do is present data from the system. An example of the former would be the bar-code reader used for inventory control, an example of the latter is a printer. (Some printers are very specialised, they are used exclusively for preparing labels, or cheques, etc.) A bi-directional peripheral is one which accepts both input to the system and output from it, for example a vdu (input from the keyboard, output via the vdu) or some machine tools (output from the computer telling a robotic arm how to move but input from sensors telling the computer the effects of the robot's actions so that the next series of instructions can be modified appropriately).

Connections the extent to which the computer can be connected to the outside world and, in particular, to other computers, for example by networking. Most personal computers have no inherent facilities enabling them to be networked, although they can be retrofitted. In a sophisticated computer system, many of the facilities connecting one computer to another or groups of users to particular computers are enclosed in specialist devices like dataswitches and multiplexors which themselves have a certain amount of 'intelligence'. A multiplexor, for example, crams several computer conversations along a single physical path and may use quite complex statistical analysis to optimise the benefits for each conversation.

Tasking the number of apparently simultaneous activities a computer can handle. Most first generation desk-top PCs can only carry out one activity at a time, eg either word-processing *or* a spreadsheet *or* a database *or* external communications, but not two or more. Actually you can fudge most micros to 'multi-task', but the results are unbearably slow. By the beginnings of the 1990s, most office-based desk-top micros will be multi-tasking.

Users the number of simultaneous users that can be handled. There are several ways in which several people can appear to be using a computer simultaneously:

- all terminals using the same program to access similar sorts of data
- most terminals accessing a single class of data whilst a few simultaneously create and modify the data others are examining
- terminals all running different programs and collections of data in apparent ignorance of the activities of others
- a hybrid of all of these

Security if large numbers of users are to be connected simultaneously, security can be most readily established at the hardware level, ideally by limiting individual customers to specific areas of working and storage memory and requiring them to seek 'permission' each time they make a request for the system's resources. This physical approach can be quite costly: unless all customers are using the system all the time, the cost-effective approach would be to allocate resources only when required: having specific physical areas permanently allocated to particular customers, whether they are actually present or not means that the whole system has to be a great deal larger. It is this physical, hardware-bound aspect of security that makes it so difficult to retrofit security facilities where none existed before.

Computer software

We now turn to software. Software falls broadly speaking into three categories:

1 Operating Systems: the computer's house-keeper.
2 Applications: the programs proper – instructions to carry

out such functions as database management, arithmetic calculations, word-processing, etc.

3 Data: the files created and used by the applications programs.

The operating system. The central processing chip at the heart of any computer, removed from its position on the computer's motherboard (principal circuit-board), knows almost nothing about the world outside. At a fundamental level, once powered up, along some of the 'legs' emerging from its casing, it will accept a series of electrical signals, process them according to a set of instructions and then push the results out, again in the form of electrical signals, through another set of legs. The chip knows nothing about keyboards, displays, disc drives, tapes, laser readers, printers, modems and so on.

The operating system provides the glue to link the various input devices (keyboards, vdu, readers etc) and output devices (printers, vdu, etc) and peripheral storage (active memory, archive memory – disc and tape drives etc). When a computer is fired up, more than just the central processor (cpu) must be awakened. The cpu must be made aware of the existence of all the peripheral devices; each one of the separate units and their interconnections must be tested. The disc drive must be set in motion and told to feed instructions into active memory so that the cpu can read them and act in response.

The operating system in all but the simplest of computers usually exists in two physical parts. The first is programmed in a read-only memory (ROM) chip and its functions are as follows:

1 Verify working of central processor, active memory, system clock, keyboard and display of console (console is the name given to the principal terminal controlling a system – on a micro the console is the only 'user' of the system; on a mainframe, the console is where the system manager exercises control).

2 Verify working of main disc drive, set it to read first track for any instructions that might be there

The chip which does this on the IBM PC is called the BIOS – Basic In/Out System, but even the largest machines have some equivalent. Computer engineers refer to this process as 'booting up', as in 'lifting by the bootstraps'.

The second part of the operating system will be on the main disc drive and it will contain proportionately many more instructions than exist on the ROM. The reason for having the operating system in two parts is to give each hardware installation the maximum amount of flexibility: the ordinary, first generation IBM PC usually runs an operating system called MS–DOS (MicroSoft Disk Operating System) but, it can also be made to run under CP/M86, Unix and other operating systems. Operating systems for the same fundamental processor can vary as to how they achieve their effects and can also be optimised for various functions: Unix, for example, is a multi-user/multi-tasking system whereas MS-DOS is for one user at a time running one program at a time. Unix on the original IBM PC is a great disappointment because the chip in that machine is restricted in power, so multitasking runs extremely slowly.

An operating system consists of several functioning parts:

- the *kernel* which controls system hardware and performs various low-level functions
- the *command processor* which accepts instructions from the keyboard (or wherever) and sees that they are carried out – usually by sending requests to the kernel and supervising what emerges

These are always present; in larger systems you will also find:

- the *memory management unit* which decides what physical areas of memory each program, datafile, and user, may occupy
- the *scheduler* which decides on the order in which various tasks are performed

These last two are essential for multi-user/multitasking systems and permit the optimum use at all times of the computer's resources.

Security functions, where they exist, are usually associated with the memory management unit and, as we saw on p 178 above, are much more reliable if specific areas of hardware can be allocated to specific tasks. There will usually be other parts of the operating system allocated to security:

- an *access program* which requires each customer to log on; it will also determine what privileges the customer has (ie what he can see and do). Such a program may also have facilities for recording when the customer signed on and off in each session and may also be able to monitor all activities while logged on*
- a *password file** which allows passwords to be allocated to each customer; these passwords should ideally be stored in an encrypted form.

In addition, associated with the operating system are a series of utility programs to carry out a number of routine functions such as formatting blank discs, copying files, editing files, deleting files, comparing files, maintaining disc directories etc. Some of these utilities are extremely powerful and allow alteration of the operating system itself as well as application programs and datafiles. High-level computer crimes are nearly always carried out by means of abuse of sophisticated utility programs.

Mainframe and minicomputer operating systems usually have many more utilities than those associated with micros. Micro owners will find that they will have to make do with a very rudimentary collection of utilities and are expected to pay if they want anything more sophisticated.

One of the key functions of an operating system is to keep track of the various files that are maintained on disc. When data is archived onto disc drives and tapes, it has to be stored in ways so that it can be easily located and recovered. Data storage has to 'work' both at the level of the operating system and to suit the needs of the particular applications program with which it is associated. Directories often contain quite a lot of information about each file: not only its location, but its size, when

*These and similar functions are examined in more detail in Chapter 15.

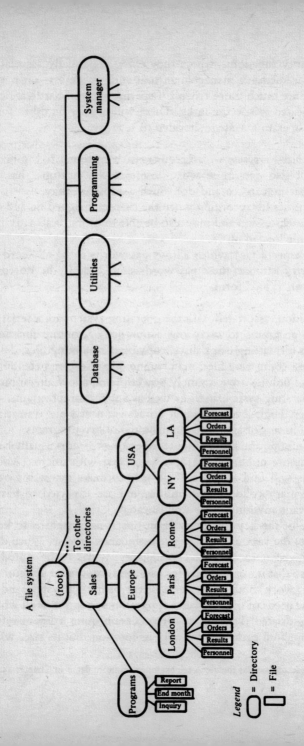

Legend

▢ = Directory

▭ = File

it was last written to, and possibly also various special attributes. Although each computer manufacturer uses this type of solution, the precise methods vary from one to the other, causing extensive problems of incompatibility.

In systems which use lots of disc files, the directory is usually split up into a series of sub-directories, using a hierarchical arrangement. User of MS-DOS and Unix will be quite familiar with the arrangement:

One of the ways in which security within a system can be maintained is by grouping sensitive files into particular sub-directories, and then limiting access to them.*

Applications programs. As far as most lay users of computers are concerned, their experience of computers comes via particular applications programs – word-processors, databases, inventory control, payroll, spreadsheets, and so on. In many cases the existence of the operating system is completely hidden by the applications program which effectively appears to take over the entire computer, though this is not actually the case.

The original philosophy of writing computer programs assumed that each program had to be written uniquely and specifically for the situation in which it was going to be used. It became obvious quite quickly that commercial requirements found in one place tend to be replicated in many others. The modern applications program therefore is an elaborate tool to carry out various functions which can then be customised by each customer for their specific needs. This both lowers the cost of the software and ensures high quality.

Typical applications of software include: word-processing, accounts, payroll, business planning and forecasts, inventory, materials movement, information resources, display presentations, design. Databases require some explanation: essentially they provide facilities for storing and retrieving large quantities of information. There are several types of database application program depending on what is to be stored, sorted and retrieved. Some databases are orientated towards the handling of figures; others assume that there will only ever be a few

*See also Chapter 10.

categories of data that will ever need collecting; yet others consist of large chunks of text. Databases vary also on the extent to which you can sort the data and present special reports based on the results. Each database application program is optimised, in terms of its usage of the resources of the computer, for the particular ways in which customers are likely to want to handle data.

Today, two trends can be seen in the selling of applications software: one concentrates on producing high-quality, keenly priced packages of near-universal appeal. The other is pitched at what are called turnkey markets. Here, the assumption is made that the end-customer wants a complete worked-out solution, including hardware, and not a series of tools that he will have to use himself.

Data files. Data files contain the stored material upon which the applications programs work, for example, files of text generated by word-processing, figures used in payroll and inventory, 'fields' used by databases, and so on.

We have seen how files are stored on a disc; data files, as the computer handles them in active memory, need to have some internal structure so that the applications program knows where each item may be found. In word-processors, a simple pipe or tube format, ie collections of characters in the order in which they are to appear, is quite sufficient. But in an accounts package or spreadsheet much more elaborate arrangements must be made. Even more complicated are the series of data files necessary for databases. The idea of a database is that it can locate a desired item of information very quickly. It may therefore be necessary to create a special intermediate index file which is never seen as such by the user, but which the application program uses in order to find information in the substantive database. In fact, for a application program to run, there may be all sorts of subsidiary files required.

For example, I regularly use a full text retrieval package. This enables me to place complete articles into a computer and then lets me search through my entire collection *for every single occurrence* of particular words. I do not need to have decided, when setting the system up, what sort of information I might want to examine. When the full text retrieval package is running, I have the following files: my original set of documents, a text file which is the data that the program actually searches, an index which is actually 20 per cent larger than the text that is searched because it contains instructions about the location of nearly *every* word in the main data file, and a small file of common words, like 'a', 'the', 'if', 'by', and so on for which there is no point in indexing.

The most common form of computer crime committed by programmers consists of altering data files *outside* the context of the applications program, so that no record is kept. This is usually done by use of the zap utility, a creature we will meet in Chapter 10.

Fault tolerance

Computers that are expected to run continuously need to have the ability to overcome faults. Fault tolerance has four constituents:

- error detection
- damage assessment and confinement
- error recovery
- fault treatment and continued service

The way in which fault tolerance is achieved is by having an excess of computing capacity. It is necessary to have both spare capacity so that if part of a system becomes corrupted there are fresh 'clean' bits that can be used and additional facilities to monitor performance, detect that errors are taking place and decide on an appropriate course of action.

Fault tolerance is one of the ways in which a system's integrity can be protected; however, it is sometimes a description of a solution rather than the solution itself.*

*Fault tolerance is covered in more detail in Chapter 14.

Humanware

The final element in this overview is humanware. It is natural to recoil at the idea of labelling the analysts, programmers, system managers, operators and customers of computer systems as 'humanware'; it sounds as though one is equating sentient human beings on the same level as inanimate hardware and calls up all the old deep-seated visions of humans as mere servants of machines. This is not the intention: so far as this book is concerned, the value of the phrase 'humanware' is strictly as a means of evaluating areas of security risk. Hardware and software may be bug-ridden and fail to perform; only humanware commits crime.

There is no such creature as the complete computer expert; those who earn their living within the computer industry as developers and technicians tend to belong to one of a series of specialisations. Everything apart from one's own area of knowledge is treated as a black box, in other words, the specialist assumes that everything else works, providing he or she gets their own contribution right.

As we have already seen, many computer crimes are committed by non-technical staff. The table gives a list of the people who might be expected to have access to a computer system, in one way or another, and who employs them directly.*

The next chapter examines the way in which hardware can be compromised.

*Further consideration of computer staff as perpetrators appears in Chapter 10.

Job Function	Who employs or controls
Chip Designers	Chip Manufacturers
Hardware designers	Computer Manufacturers
Operating Systems Writers	Computer Manufacturers
High-Level Language and Utilities Writers	& specialist software house
Applications Programmers	Software houses
Systems Analysts	External consultants & DP staff
Systems Managers	DP staff
Maintenance in general:	
Maintenance – hardware	Partly in-house,
Maintenance – peripherals	partly third-party contract
Maintenace – networks	
Maintenance – communications	Communications co & third parties
Maintenance – operating systems services	In-house DP staff
Maintenance – applications programs	Third-party suppliers & in-house DP staff
Computer Services Management	DP staff
Shift operators	DP staff
Librarian	DP staff
Maintenance – end-user help	DP staff
Management Information Services	DP staff or other employees
Key-punch operators	DP staff
Warehouse Staff	General staff
Till operators	General staff
Managers, supervisors	General staff
Financial Control	Managerial
Directors	The Board

CHAPTER NINE

Hardware at Risk

Most of the subtle forms of attack on computer systems consist of manipulating or compromising software. Threats to computer hardware, by contrast, are usually more brutish. They tend to take one of the following forms:

- an all-out attack on hardware with the aim of destroying it or at least causing damage;
- partial destruction of equipment or peripherals in order to create opportunities for overtime;
- total or partial destruction of data and software media with the aims of damaging the owner, extortion or to create overtime opportunities;
- theft of equipment – this subject was covered in Chapter 6;
- theft of media containing valuable data and/or programs – this will be examined in Chapter 12;
- interfering with input or output devices as an aid to fraud or to create overtime opportunities;
- eavesdropping.

Of these, only the interference with input and output devices and eavesdropping involves much sophistication of method; however, as we have seen already, in computer-related crime, there is very little linkage between elegance in the means of execution and damage caused to the victim.

Perpetrators

The instances of spectacular hardware attack best known to the general public are those promoted for ideological reasons by terrorists. In Chapter 7 we met a number of these cases: Beaver 55, the IRA, the German Red Army Faction. In another case, in 1970, five student activists at the University of Wisconsin bombed the Army Mathematics Research Center. A physics researcher was killed and a mainframe computer completely destroyed. The total loss in buildings and equipment was estimated at $2.4m and the research data lost was claimed to represent 1.3 million man hours, an investment perhaps of $16m.[1,2] In the same year a Molotov cocktail was used at a state college in California and an attempt was made to extort $100,000 bail money from New York University by placing petrol bombs near a computer used by the Atomic Energy Commission. The bombs were defused before the ransom was paid.[1] A similar spate of terrorist activities aimed at computers, perhaps ten altogether, occurred five or six years later in Italy.[2]

In quite early cases guns were used: as far back as 1968 someone aimed a pistol at a computer in a state employment office in Washington State; in 1972 a computer in a municipal office in Johannesburg was fired at; in the following year an anti-war demonstrator used a double-barrelled shotgun at an American computer manufacturer's Australian office.[1,2]

Sometimes the aim is unadulterated extortion: shortly after the *Sun* newspaper started to be produced from a new site in Wapping, East London, it received a demand for £50,000 to avoid having an attack mounted on its brand-new computer editing and type-setting installation. Eventually a 31–year-old bricklayer was jailed for eight months.[3]

There are also a number of cases of pure vandalism; pure in the sense that no reason could ever be found for the attack. An example comes from 1970: a vandal broke into an IBM installation and used an iron bar to smash equipment before being overpowered by security guards. In a 1983 case, vandals threw a petrol can followed by a lighted match into a computer room owned by a consultancy. A Hewlett Packard 3000 had to be written off and tapes carefully cleaned before the data could be recovered. About £150,000 of damage was involved.[4]

However, there is a numerically more important type of perpetrator: the employee of the victim. Some of these act out of ideology as well, but more significant are cases where the employee is seeking revenge for a supposed wrong, trying to create opportunities for some overtime, or attempting a fraud. This last includes a series of cases where hardware measuring devices have been modified to give a false reading, and will be dealt with later. Sometimes the offender is not an employee but a contractor, perhaps a freelance, or employee of a maintenance company.

As with ideologues, there are plenty of examples of arson: a 1980 case involving an accounting and inventory control system at a wholesale tobacco distributor; another in the same year reported by Ken Wong where £3m worth of equipment, plus phone exchanges and furniture were lost – quite a lot of the actual damage coming from water that had been used to stop the fire; yet another 1980 case from Ken Wong, and again damage came not directly from the fire but from smoke and water.[4] A gun was used in a 1974 case by a frustrated computer operator at the Charlotte Liberty Mutual Life Insurance Company of North Carolina.[1] Not all anti-computer weapons are obvious: in a 1980 case orange juice was poured into a disc drive. In another, two years before, the damage was caused by manually twisting the read/write head of a disc drive so that it crashed into the surface of the disc media; the culprit had complained of excessive working hours.[2] In the same year, a dismissed tape librarian at a mail order company had, while serving out his notice, cut off the first few feet of a tape of important invoicing data, as a result of which the entire run had to be aborted and the data expensively re-created.[4]

One of the things computers do is threaten to displace human jobs. Fears of this can lead to sabotage, as in a 1978 case involving two computer operators employed near some docks. The company was upgrading from one version of the IBM 370 to a rather larger one and the operators decided to discredit the performance of the new installation by swapping over two printed circuit boards, and changing their labels so that no one noticed. The computer kept failing until IBM engineers were called in.[2,4] There are a whole sequence of cases in which workers have sought attention for themselves or have wanted to maintain or increase their income by creating opportunities for overtime. A typical case occurred in 1972 when Keith Noreen, an operator working for the US National Farmers Union Corporation, used a key to short-circuit a disc drive associated with a Burroughs B3500. He did this 56 times in two years and on each occasion the disc drive became completely unusable. He was eventually caught when a concealed closed circuit television monitor was installed.[2] In a remarkably similar case in 1980, again by coincidence involving a Burroughs machine, a machine operator was caught using a screwdriver to scratch short-circuiting lines across the tracks of printed circuit boards.[4] A couple of years later a 9–volt battery was used by an engineer to cause electrical malfunction. The trouble with these 'overtime-creation' cases is that the perpetrator does not always intend the full extent of the harm that is caused. Computers, particularly at the electrical level, can be extremely complex and a simple scratch to a printed circuit board can result in damage to expensive hard–disc drives and to irreplaceable data.

Hardware damage also occurs in industrial disputes. In 1971 there was a strike at the computer manufacturer Honeywell. One of its big customers was the Metropolitan Life Insurance Company. It had a system for gathering information from remote offices which required the mainframe to make a telephone call to terminals in these offices overnight, exchange identity codes and, in the first instance, collect data. Later in the night, after the mainframe had carried out processing, the remote terminals were again called up and given instructions to print out results and responses. This overnight polling of remote terminals is an extremely common method for central office mainframes to support the requirements of large numbers of out-stations. What the strikers did was to create tape recordings which would confuse the terminals in the remote offices; instructions were sent which effectively emptied the printers of paper. The perpetrators were caught with tape recorders operating from their union offices.[2]

Compromising input and output

As we saw in Chapter 4, most computer frauds consist of deceiving the computer by entering false data, which is then accepted by the system with benefits to the perpetrator. The computer itself, apart from failing to detect the deception, behaves faultlessly.*

In most cases the false data is entered manually by a human being, either the actual fraudster or someone acting under their instruction, as in those cases where a form used by input operators is forged. But computers can obtain information from, among other things, such devices as bar-codes, magnetic stripes and measuring sensors. So one particular line of fraud consists of compromising these devices.

A fairly simple sample appears in a 1979 edition of the *Computer Security and Fraud Bulletin:* a department store chain installed some microchip-controlled cash-tills. The usual arrangements for handling the float and checking takings applied: at the end of trading, the till would be asked to give a print-out of the total of all its takings for the day and this was compared with the amount of cash in the till, less the opening float. The till was thought to be protected both mechanically and electrically against tampering. There was a weakness – you could 'over-wind': once a total of £10,000 was reached, the accumulated total returned to £0.00 and recommenced counting. The fraud carried out by cashiers was quite simple: you kept your own running total of the day's receipts. Before asking the till to print out the total that would be compared with the cash in hand, you rang up non-existent sales until the £10,000 limit was reached and then carried on until the total came up slightly less than the true running total of sales. You took the difference from the cash-tray, asked the till to print-out, checked you hadn't got your sums wrong and asked the branch accounts staff to confirm that everything was as it should be. The department store knew it had losses, but could not attribute them to the cashiers. In fact this is very similar to the second-hand car-dealer's trick of giving cars a spurious low mileage. Most milometers can't be wound back without destroying the gear teeth; nothing prevents you from over-winding. This cash-till fraud is usually prevented these days by maintaining a complete duplicate record of *all* transactions that take place.

---

*There are instances in which the internal workings of software can be induced to misbehave; these are covered in the next chapter.

Forged ATM cards, where the magnetic stripe is over-written* is also an example of compromised input. Here the input device is unable to detect the impersonation. Credit cards can be forged as well: in one of the few computer fraud cases where a Mafia link can be detected, Alfonse Confessore, a repair man was working at a security printing company which had a contract to produce Diners Club cards. In 1967, the key information was embossed on the plastic cards. The security printer received instructions about members and their numbers on punch tape. The printer made provision for 'spoilt' cards and test runs. The repair man was able to get duplicates made of authentic cards and he passed some 500 of these on to mafiosos who set about using them to obtain goods – the bills were sent to the proper card-owners. Following some detective work, the repairman was identified as the perpetrator. After conviction, but before sentencing, the repairman was discovered with three bullet-holes in the back of his head. It is believed that he fell foul of the Colombo Family.[2,5]

Another set of cases involve compromised output. Typically a printer used to create cheques or authorities to issue payments or release goods is persuaded to make a few extra 'runs'. In a fairly early case, a handyman turned up at a data processing centre owned by an insurance company. Over a period of several days he renovated old paintwork, replaced cracked glass and did all manner of useful jobs. After a while he left. Three months later the insurance company discovered it had lost $56,000. The 'handyman' had persuaded the specialist cheque printer to produce some extra cheques. Another case of using a computer to produce cash-cards comes from Norway in 1976.

PROMs

The wide use of EPROMS – Electrically Programmable Read-Only Memory – in a wide range of devices has created new opportunities for fraud. ROMs, or read-only memory, are computer firmware** chips that are neither processors nor banks of

*See page 82.
**See Chapter 8.

memory in which data can be stored while the computer works. The ROM carries permanent instructions, which could be a small program in its own right, or part of a program, or data. As we saw in the last chapter, one of the typical uses of the ROM is when a computer first fires up: one or more ROMs take charge of the preliminary testing and ensure that, as the computer wakes up, it starts to look for the disc drive where more information will be found to complete the 'boot' process. Another use of ROMs is in some calculators, particularly those that can carry out complex conversions between different measurement standards. The PROM is a variant: you can program data or instructions into a ROM yourself, provided you have the appropriate equipment. You can get a suitable accessory for most popular desk-top and hobbyist computers – it consists of a board which can generate the slightly higher than usual electrical voltages necessary to burn the instructions in, and a piece of software. This enables engineers and hobbyists to make highly specific, very fast, very compact and very cheap devices. ROMs and PROMs abound these days in cookers, washing machines, video players, tvs, digital radios, children's toys and so on. ROMs and PROMs are also to be found in the cartridges of some home computer games. The EPROM is one stage further down the line in terms of convenience: it doesn't even require special accessories to be programmed.

A favourite use of both PROMs and EPROMs is the embedded password. First adopted, I think, in some vdus, the idea is that, on sign-on to a computer service, the host computer sends a 'Who are You?' query down the telephone line. (Incidentally, this is often the character ENQ, which is a standard element of the alphabet most computers recognise.) Upon receiving it, the vdu's ROM automatically sends back its embedded password. The process is usually invisible to the user of the vdu. In its simple form, as just described, the practice has fallen into disrepute, as it was obviously easy for anyone to come to the computer terminal and just sign on. If the terminal has important privileges on the main computer, perhaps to order goods or transfer cash, impersonation leading to fraud is easy. Any engineer with a bit of ingenuity can also find out the embedded code (if necessary by connecting the terminal to a home computer which would then issue ENQ to it; the password is then saved on disc file on the home computer and its owner can then call into the host without ever having to use the 'special' terminal). However it is still common to use partial passwords embedded in PROMs or EPROMs, leaving the user to input the last few characters by hand. Many tv sets modified for Prestel work on this basis.

PROMs also appear in most modern telex machines and all fax devices, to supply the automatic answerback and/or owner's address. If you wish to send a message pretending to be someone else, or to receive one, you can alter the identity PROM. There are also opportunities for fraud and impersonation in modern telephone systems. If you are a small–scale user of Mercury, the authorised alternative to British Telecom, you are supplied with telephone equipment that is actually connected to the regular BT dial-up network; you then dial a three digit code which passes you to the nearest Mercury node. To progress further, you must then send your Mercury ID, so that you can be identified; after that you are properly on the Mercury network and can take the benefit of the different tariffs. On much Mercury equipment for the domestic and small business markets, the connecting process is conveniently accomplished by hitting a special **M** button. It really isn't too difficult to get these phones to disgorge their IDs, after which anyone with any tone-phone can access Mercury by hand-dialling their network and sending the ID, which you can send manually. The phone bills get sent to the authorised owner of the ID. You can do a similar trick with cellular telephones. Cellular phones are normally sold by the suppliers with a programmed ID (the same ROM or PROM also determines which network(s) you have paid to be connected to). The PROM can be reprogrammed with someone else's ID and, although you will receive their calls and not be able to get any yourself without fear of detection, you will be able to make calls out – and have the bills sent on elsewhere.[6]

Modified PROMs can also appear as a way of compromising a measuring device. In 1981 two Swedes offered a printed circuit board to replace a similar one in a petrol-vending machine. The usual PROM had been modified so that petrol could be obtained free-of-charge. The fraud spread widely over Sweden.

There are also a series of rumours concerning compromised gaming machines. Program instructions for such machines are usually held in PROM. Nearly all legislatures that permit the use of electronic gambling impose rules to cover fairness and the frequency of payout. The fraud consists of having dual mode programs. The first is the 'legal' version, but the chip contains instructions which enable a second version, more advantageous to the gambling machine owner, to be switched over at will. To make detection of the fraudulent code even more difficult, so the rumours say, such machines had a security device which wiped the PROMs clean in the event of unauthorised disturbance; the wipe out device was justified to gambling inspectors on the grounds that it was there to prevent tampering by *outsiders*.[7]

Hardware bombs

PROMs are also the building blocks with which to make hardware computer viruses. These advanced logic bombs are usually made in software and will be described in more detail in the next chapter, but the idea is to corrupt a computer or the data it holds, preferably in a slow and difficult-to-detect fashion. The idea appears in *SoftWar*, a novel that became a best-seller in France. The authors garnish a formula Cold War story in which an East Coast professor makes renewed contact with a former pupil, a beautiful Russian computer specialist. The Russians want advanced computers, allegedly to improve weather forecasts, but perhaps, so cynical US analysts suggest, for war. The computer, as delivered, appears to go wrong every now and then: what is triggering it to misbehave and, assuming that it is a hardware virus, where exactly is it, how does it work, who put it there – and why? Can the East Coast professor and his Russian former lover (who is now married to an ambitious security official) find out in time and save the world from being blown up by hard-line militarists?

Eavesdropping

Eavesdropping is the one spy technology most people think they know about. In Chapter 5 we showed why bugging computers is such an attractive weapon in the industrial spy's armoury. Eavesdropping can be easy, but not quite as simple as many people imagine. Special effects men in the cinema can make spaceships cruise at faster-than-light speeds, can show dinosaurs gobbling up chunks of Atlantis and can give the leading man more lives than the most charmed of cats. They can also supply on-screen simulations of electronic devices that could never exist – and permit their heroes liberties in their handling that are never given to real people.

What the Bond films and *Mission Impossible* have achieved is a considerable contribution to public illiteracy about the capabilities of surveillance technology. Whilst no one expects the pace of thriller entertainment to be held up while boffins discuss in detail the design of the equipment they propose to deploy, it is difficult to justify the downright absurdity of much of the gadgetry and the way in which it is used. To take one trivial example – why, once a hostile bug is discovered, is it always immediately destroyed? In the real world there are a number of beneficial alternatives: you could leave the bug on, and feed misleading information into it; you could attempt to catch the perpetrator handling it and cause him embarrassment. Here's another example: in movie representations of the use of radio, the operator always finds the exact 'spot on the dial' after a few twiddles of the tuning knob and whistles from the loudspeaker. Now in practice, the whistles – heterodyne 'beat' notes – are uniquely a feature of AM broadcasts and are usually absent in the modes used either for surveillance equipment or for long distance communications; again, the radio frequency spectrum is incredibly crowded in places, and the practical problem faced by the operator of a surveillance receiver is to eliminate all the many *unwanted* signals.

The result of this illiteracy has been first, to make it more difficult for potential victims to form a clear picture of the extent to which they might be at risk and second, to create a none-too-scrupulous service industry of companies purporting to offer James Bond/*Mission Impossible* type merchandise – and, of course, the means to detect and counteract them.

As far as the eavesdropping of data transmissions is concerned, the techniques divide into the following:

1 **tapping** into a telephone line by piggybacking: the data is either carried away by a separate line to a point where it can be captured and then analysed or fed into a tape recorder from which the tapes are gathered at convenient times and then analysed. The technique is easiest to apply on regular analogue telephone lines

2 **bugging** a telephone line – not very different from tapping except that the captured data is converted into an audio-modulated radio signal which is then received remotely and then analysed

3 **detecting** signals direct from computer peripherals such as vdus and printers on suitable equipment

4 **capturing** radio-based transmissions originated by the legitimate users. These could use HF, VHF, or UHF radio or microwave links. Here no bugging or tapping is necessary, the eavesdropper simply has the appropriate receiving equipment and places a suitable antenna in a location where it will capture the signal. The eavesdropper ends up with an audio feed which can then be fed into suitable analytical equipment.

Tapping and bugging use the same sort of device as would be applied to capture ordinary voice conversations on a telephone. Current (1989) prices for suitable bugs (using radio to get the signal out) in London are in the £35 to £75 range.* For this you

---

*By common consent, London is regarded as the bugging capital of the world. There are several reasons. Under English law, whilst it is an offence to *use* taps and bugs – there is an Interception of Communications Act to cover interception and the Wireless Telegraphy Act to cover the use of unlicensed radio transmitters – there is no offence in owning, manufacturing or selling them. (In both of these cases the standards of proof required are rather high so that convictions are very rare.) In addition to the local market of private detectives and paranoid businessmen, there is a considerable business from overseas agencies. Again, the Security Service MI5 appears to be prepared to make regular use of freelance buggers, partly because such men can be conveniently disowned and also to reduce their own staff overheads.[8]

get a small box with a two or three wires protruding, two of which you fasten internally to the phone or better still, inside a junction box where it is less likely to be noticed. Fitting time, less than one minute. No battery is required as power is drawn from the phone line. The lower price ones will radiate a signal for about a quarter of a mile, the more expensive might reach one mile in good conditions. Such devices would be found by a debugging expert, but at those prices you can afford to lose a device every so often.

When data is sent along regular phone lines, dial-up or leased, it is first converted into a series of audio tones in a device called a modem. At the far end of the link, another modem captures the audio tones and reconverts them into the electrical signals required by the computer. What the eavesdropper does is capture the audio signals and then feed them into his own modem and computer. The eavesdropper will face a number of practical, but not insurmountable difficulties:

- bugs in particular are less powerful and reliable than is often imagined, particularly if they are small in physical size. The limiting factors are the amount of power that can be fed into them – 'drop-in' devices that rely on batteries as opposed to mains are particularly limited – and the quality of the antenna. Bugs are also relatively easy to detect; most of the readily-available models on both sides of the Atlantic operate on one frequency-band – 108–136 MHz – chosen because it is easy to adapt regular FM broadcast radios to act as receivers; counter-surveillance equipment can thus also be cheap.

- taps tend to leave physical evidence of their installation; if the data is to be collected on tape, someone has to retrieve the cassettes; a fresh hazard each time.

- the tones that will be heard on the captured tape will vary in frequency, speed and modulation depending on the computer protocols (or standards) in use. Even when the data is properly read into a computer it may be in particular formats. Many programs sent down telephone lines rely on instructions which place bits of information on specific parts of the vdu – to fill in an electronic form, or a spreadsheet or a window – and this is achieved by 'cursor addressing' commands which vary from terminal to terminal. All of these problems require skill and experience on the part of the analyst as well as suitable equipment.

Once captured and decoded, the results can be used either for fraud or industrial espionage. One example of the former occurred in Japan between 1979 and 1982. A technical engineer with Nippon Telegraph and Telephone was responsible for maintaining a leased line used by a bank to transmit cash card information. The engineer developed equipment which enabled him to tap into the leased line and record the results on a cassette recorder. He then printed appropriate information onto mag-stripe cards which he had been given for test purposes. Three out of the four cards he manufactured worked well and he was able to withdraw cash from various dispensers around Sapporo and his final 'take' was around Y130m. It did not take the police very long to catch the thirty-eight-year-old engineer, simply because, once the fraud was discovered and the modus operandi worked out, it was evident that very few people had both the opportunity and skill to commit the crime.[9] This is a neat illustration of why technically sophisticated computer crimes are so rare: there are usually simpler ways of achieving the same ends and the chances of identification after the event are considerable.

There are also rumours of large computers having covert modems installed into them so that internal activity can be monitored by criminals. The disadvantage of bugging a data line is that the line must be listened to at analogue level and then decoded. With higher speed transmissions, and with uncertain or noisy signal paths, the chances of good signal recovery by the eavesdropper become more difficult. The advantage of a covert modem is that the wanted data is squirrelled out in pure digital form and, assuming the availability of a covert telephone line, can be transmitted direct to the data thieves own computer on premises anywhere in the world. Matchbox sized modems – and one-third of the internal space is taken up with a battery – are now available for $100, so a covert modem could easily avoid physical detection. To date, however, these are only rumours.[8]

The same techniques used for eavesdropping onto telephone lines handling data traffic can be used equally effectively to capture fax material. Unlike computer-originated traffic, where there are a large number of different protocols, all fax material is encoded in the same way, in one of three standards all of which most fax machines can handle.

Other forms of electronic eavesdropping onto computers and peripherals have had some publicity, in particular those associated with the code-name Tempest. Most computers and peripherals emit a wide range of electro-magnetic radiation – the cpus, vdus and printers. Tempest is the name given by the US government to a set of standards which reduce the amount of this radiation.

The particular radiation of most use to eavesdroppers appears to be that associated with vdus. This particular scare story keeps on being rediscovered by the press.[10] To understand the limits of the threat you need to know a little of how the phenomenon operates: the screen radiates a broadband signal which is at its strongest in the range 200 to 300 Mhz (this is just above broadcast band III television and in a portion of the rf spectrum chiefly used for military purposes). The signal can be picked up on a domestic television with a slightly modified tuner. However in this form you won't see anything apart from a slight intensifying of the usual 'snow' you get when no tv signal is being received. The reason is that the picture needs a series of synchronising pulses so that each tv line aligns with those that precede and follow it. The sync pulses from the original vdu do not radiate out nearly as far as does the video component of the signal. So, to re-assemble the original image on your tv, you must re-create the sync pulses locally. This can be done at very small cost.

There is no doubt that vdu emanation receivers of this kind work after a fashion. What is in dispute is how effective they are as a practical tool of industrial espionage or fraud. I am personally sceptical:

- whilst it is possible to demonstrate the principles of the technology – and do so quite cheaply – the results are difficult to read even in the best of circumstances: the image 'swims' as the sync pulses fight to lock the picture properly; there is a great deal of 'snow' and most domestic tvs can't cope with the detail of 80-character by 25-line text displays even in the best of circumstances. Once you start to add refinements to the basic device, the technology becomes extremely expensive and hence more difficult to cost-justify

- many desk-top PCs are now using much higher-resolution displays than modified televisions can cope with

- it is quite difficult to operate where there is more than one vdu in the vicinity, particularly if they are all of the same make. It may sometimes be possible to tune the receiver to discriminate between vdus, but the only real solution is to use highly directional antennas which can null out the unwanted signals. Such antennas are not inconspicuous: to be effective it would need to have a minimum length of over two metres and have elements over half a metre wide – scarcely the stuff of covert surveillance

- although the defence industry and national government have different priorities, in a commercial environment anxieties about vdu radiation are easily allayed: move sensitive vdus away from near windows where they can be overlooked. In a steel-framed building the signals will be severely attenuated

- even at its best, the most the technology can offer is a window, one screen at a time, on what the computer contains. Unless the computer log-on sequence actually shows the password being put in (most services echo back dashes or stars to prevent over-the-shoulder views of passwords) the eavesdropper never has the opportunity to see more than what the operator is doing at that moment in time

- as we observed in Chapter 5, practically-minded industrial espionage agents impose a costing methodology on their activities; they and their clients want results, not ingenuity. The bugged computer line, the stolen computer disc, the filched print-out or documentation, the password acquired by looking over someone's shoulder or by finding it taped near a terminal, are all much more attractive and cost-effective methods

Less well-publicised are devices which can reconstruct what is being output on a printer. All you need to capture is the sound of the daisy wheel or matrix head striking the paper; a well-placed room bug will do this. As each letter of the alphabet is struck, a slightly different sound is made. These can be recognised and distinguished by quite simple apparatus – it is much easier than trying to understand human speech, for example. Once you have a collection of sounds a computer can build up a table associating each one with a particular character using readily available letter-frequency tables, as employed in decoding – in English text, for example the letter 'e' is the most frequently used. Once a table has been built up for a given printer, the computer can decode with almost total accuracy almost instantaneously.

Perhaps the final caution on eavesdropping hazards should be to remind that the easiest thing to listen in to is that which is broadcast anyway. Increasing amounts of data traffic are being carried via radio signals of all kinds. Sophisticated receiving equipment, able to light on a channel less than 5 kHz wide over a range from d.c to the bottom portions of the microwave spectrum can be bought for around $600. Such equipment can be programmed to search-scan for wanted frequencies, can retain large numbers of different frequencies in memory banks and can be hooked up to personal computers. Lower cost devices, in the $250 range, give a smaller coverage of the radio frequency spectrum, but can be held in the hand and are the size of a walkie-talkie. Guidance on how to look for particular services of this kind can be obtained partly from official publications (the GPO in the United States, HMSO in the UK) and partly from semi-underground publications. 'Scanning' or 'monitoring' is carried out by some radio enthusiasts, but also by private detectives. Voice-based radio-telephone conversations are quite easy to pick up, once the principles are understood, though traffic on cellular telephones is more difficult because, as the mobile phone's owner moves from one cell to another, the frequency changes. In a city area, where the cells are many and small, during a single telephone conversation there may be several frequency changes. Out in a rural district there is a much greater chance that an entire conversation will be overheard.

Data or text transmission over the air has a very long history indeed: before the advent of trans-oceanic cables and satellites, the *normal* method of sending long-distance telegrams was via High Frequency (short-wave) radio and even to day considerable amounts of commercial and diplomatic traffic still use this medium. VHF and UHF radio are also used for data-links in situations where it would be costly to lay cables. Increasingly, use is being made of microwave links and satellite paths. HF, VHF and UHF radio are easy to intercept and the data as easy to interpret as if it were going along a conventional phone line. Radio modems cost little more than telephone line modems and cater for the type of coding and protocols used. With microwave and satellite links, interception is more difficult, partly because the receiving equipment is more esoteric (though becoming less so) and partly because the signal path is more directional than is the case at lower frequencies and the siting of the intercepting antenna is more critical. Decoding is also more difficult as, on the typical microwave or satellite link, many 'conversations' are multiplexed and combined and indeed may be packetised*. However decoding is not impossible.

*More detail on this subject can be found in *The Hacker's Handbook*.

CHAPTER TEN

Software at Risk

Most forms of datacrime happen *around* computers rather than within them. As we have seen, the typical examples involve, in the case of fraud, the inputting of misleading information into computer systems which is then faithfully passed along and handled by the EDP services so as to create a benefit for the fraudster. This is sometimes referred to as data diddling. In the case of industrial espionage and some instances of piracy, it is the output or data storage medium which is stolen. In both of these cases, the computers and their associated peripherals and networks have operated perfectly. As we have also seen, the special knowledge that the perpetrators have required is often less to do with technical computing skills and more with how an organisation functions administratively.

In this chapter we are examining what many writers have traditionally seen as the heart of computer crime – the manipulation of a system's internal processes and the exploitation of weaknesses either in operating systems or applications programs. By definition, these activities can only be carried out by those who are both computer-literate and, in most cases, who have access to a computer system at a fairly fundamental level. Certain types of application program have particular areas of vulnerability, but first we must look at the sort of people specifically capable of carrying out these operations and also the range of general techniques they employ. As with other forms of information crime, it is the technically ingenious *modus operandi* that has attracted most interest; some of the best-publicised are often among the least frequent in occurrence, indeed it is sometimes quite hard to find reliable and authentic case material for some of the techniques that have been widely trumpeted as presenting great risks. It is the rather unexciting methods that are the most common and also the easiest to perpetrate – and get away with, if the potential victim is unprepared.

Who perpetrates?

Apart from the actions of hackers, no unauthorised manipulation of a computer takes place without there being a point to the exercise. No one, other than certain hackers, is interested simply in the technical challenge. It is important in reviewing what is technically possible to maintain a clear vision of the likely attitudes of, and problems faced by, the criminal. The key elements to consider are:

- motive
- opportunity
- level of technical knowledge

Motive. Implies that the perpetrator must have some reasons for what he does. The usual ones are:

- to provide the last link in a fraud by getting the computer to mislead management, or an auditor, about company records, or the way in which a computer has been used
- to cover up the fact that a computer has been accessed in a particular way, for example to conceal that data has been siphoned off for industrial espionage purposes or an unauthorised program copy taken
- to cause damage to the computer-owner by way of revenge, or to put it out of business for commercial reasons, or in support of an industrial claim, or to make an ideological statement
- to create opportunities for maintenance or overtime work
- to explore a system out of curiosity

Opportunity. In order to carry out serious modifications to a system, systems programmers have two principal requirements. First, they must have access to the system at a quite fundamental level, ideally as system manager; or they must be able to manipulate the machine so as to grant themselves the appropriate status. In some large systems, non-trivial alterations can only be carried out from certain identified vdu terminals. Second, they need to have available appropriate software tools so that they can carry out their unauthorised deletions and modifications. In a properly set up system, such software tools should not be readily accessible.

In order to perpetrate a crime, a programmer also needs to have the opportunity to benefit from the manipulation; in the case of fraud, for example, the end aim is to secure cash or assets in a location where they can be safely taken into the possession of the criminal. Further, having obtained the benefit, the fraudster must be sure that he or she won't be found out.

As we will see later on, one of the most important prevent-ative methods that can be adopted is to reduce opportunities to commit crimes, for example by ensuring that computer users are not given access to services they do not require and by designing job specifications so that power is effectively divided and crimes require collusion before they can be attempted.

Level of technical knowledge. Computer programmers vary greatly in their specialisations and ability levels. Those who design processor, memory and peripheral chips are unlikely to know much about applications programming; those who can write in high-level languages such as Basic, Pascal or Fortran will probably want to take both the computer hardware and the operating systems for granted. And so on.

Computer Professionals: Specialisations
Chip designers

employed by chip manufacturers; seldom have contact with end-users, or indeed many other computer professionals. They produce

central processing units
memory chips
specialist peripheral controllers, eg for hard-discs, graphics ter-minals, modems, networks, telecommunications
customised chips – these are hybrid devices which are capable of being programmed to carry out specific functions

Hardware designers

the people who design computer mother- and peripheral boards. Hardly ever employed by end-users

Operating systems writers

as the name implies, those who provide the fundamental connections between the computer hardware and those who type in instructions on keyboards. Hardly ever employed by end-users

High-level language and utilities writers

the providers of the tools and libraries that are needed by programmers. Hardly ever employed by end-users

Applications programmers

those who write databases, word-processors, accounts packages, inventory control, design, manufacture, distribution services, etc. Such people may be employed by third-party suppliers (software houses) or by the end-user. Or the third-party supplier may provide a 'shell' program which is then customised to the specific requirements by the end-user's own staff. Alternatively, specialist freelance programmers may be employed as and when needed.
In a properly managed computer installation, these people should not have access to 'live' data

Systems analysts

those who turn a customer's requirements (in the form of a specification) into a series of tasks that can be executed by specific items of hardware and software. May be employed by end-user, may be an employee of a software house or OEM, may be a consultant without any ties to a specific hardware or software product

In a properly managed computer installation, these people should not have access to 'live' data

Systems managers

those who are in charge of a specific computer system. By definition, a system manager can go anywhere and can do anything on a computer.
The phrase is used in two senses
  a named employee with high level responsibilities

a function of the operating system: the 'system manager' is the identity/account which has the power to set up the system in the first place and then vary and adjust it; the 'system manager' grants all the other users their attributes (what they are allowed to do)

Security manager

the person charged with maintaining system security. This may be the same as the System Manager, or it could be a separate individual solely concerned with administering passwords and permissions.

Maintenance in general:

end-users normally attempt first-line maintenance themselves, if the matter is thought to simple. Thereafter they are likely to have a series of maintenance contracts
    supplied by original manufacturers
    supplied by external professional intermediary – hardware
    supplied by external professional intermediary – software
    supplied from organisation's own in-house resources

Maintenance – hardware

    cpus
    add-on boards
    vdus
    data storage

Maintenance – peripherals

    printers
    modems
    multiplexors, message switches

Maintenance – networks

usually provided by original supplier, though end-user's staff will probably be able to add or remove a few customers
    Local Area
    Wide Area

Maintenance – communications

supplied by PTT or other authorised company
supplied by 'value added' supplier
supplied by specialist intermediary

Maintenance – operating systems services

The core of an operating system should not require maintenance unless it is very new. However, sophisticated operating systems are to an extent modifiable by others, usually to optimise performance for a particular set of functions. Serious modification is likely to be carried out by third parties, but employees of end-users may do so as well

In a properly managed computer installation, these people should not have access to 'live' data

Maintenance – applications programs

Most end-users would be able to carry out minor modifications (or customisations) of applications programs. It is not unusual to have the tools, eg installation routines, utilities, for such alterations available, even if there is little intent to use them

In a properly managed computer installation, these people should not have access to 'live' data

Computer services management

this is the department in the end-user organisation that decides which computer resources are required (subject to agreement from main management), negotiates with suppliers & maintenance contractors and recruits the appropriate specialist staff
These people will have access to the whole system and special controls are necessary to see what they do
Shift operators
End-user staff who maintain the running of the equipment, carry out routine checks, take back-ups etc
These people will have access to the whole system and special controls are necessary to see what they do
Librarian

End-user staff: Custodian of archived data and programs; possibly also manuals
These people may have access to the whole system and special controls are necessary to see what they do
Maintenance – end-user help
Part of the shift operators team with special role of helping users in difficulties
These people may have access to the whole system and special controls are necessary to see what they do

Management information services

End-user staff, though put to different uses in different companies. Sets up new information systems, negotiates between customers and 'pure' computer staff, provides ad hoc facilities via PCs, etc
These people may have access to the whole system and special controls are necessary to see what they do
Customers
ie various end-user staff, or customers of end-user
These people should have access to relevant data, but not system facilities
   key-punch, routine transcription
   other machines, eg ATMs, machine tools
   management
   accounts
   etc

The weakness of many of the technically ingenious crimes that have been described lies in the fact that, in any given situation, only a very small number of people have both the opportunity and skill to commit them – and strong suspicion must fall on these individuals almost immediately. Computer crime investigators, informed that a crime is thought to have taken place, usually focus their minds on the potential criminal from the points of view of: who had the opportunities, who had the associated skills and who might have had a motive. The investigation of the precise method employed tends to follow from suspicion about an individual rather than a close examination of lines of computer code.

Methods

The most common method of fraud by programmers consists of data alteration; the favourite forms of vandalism are data wiping and the stimulated system crash.*

The usual tool for most types of data manipulation is the 'zap' utility. You could think of it as a collection of locksmith's tools, amounting in some cases to a full-scale engineering workshop. Although it varies from operating system to operating system, appears under a variety of proprietary and slang names and is sometimes called a debugger** its purpose is to enable a programmer to view and edit any stored computer file, applications program or data. It is usually possible to examine and alter the operating system also. Some zap tools will give access to parts of the computer that are ordinarily never seen, such as the precise way in which directories of the contents of disc drives are stored – you can alter the information so that what the directory declares is present is different from what is actually the case. You can also read discs sector by sector, and examine data which the legitimate user thinks he has hidden, or has deleted.*** Other zap utilities additionally let the programmer examine chunks of active memory and alter that as well.

There are plenty of legitimate uses for zap utilities – the maintenance of systems, recovery from accidents, and indeed

*In this section we will be referring to a number of techniques by a series of slang names, eg salami, trojan horse, etc. The reader may find that other writers use these terms to mean slightly different things: what is worth concentrating on is the description of method and opportunity, not the name.
**Strictly speaking, a debugger is a full programming aid enabling the manipulation of a cpu's registers while a zap utility is limited to direct editing of discs and memory
***Disc drives, whether floppy, hard or optical (ie using compact disc-like technology), all store information in a similar fashion: the disc is thought of as being divided into a series of concentric bands called tracks. Each track is divided into a series of sectors. The effect is like a group of pigeon-holes in a circular formation. Certain sectors are reserved for directory information, in other words to record what files are located on which sectors. The way most disc-operating systems work is that files can be spread around the disc almost randomly; the disc directory keeps a record of the start sector of each file, and information about the order in which subsequent sectors must be read in order for the file to be properly re-assembled. A zap utility not only enables a skilled practitioner to uncover what is thought to be invisible but also to carry out large alterations without leaving a trace.

the writing of new applications, would be impossible without them. Users of PC-DOS or MS-DOS, as supplied with the IBM PC and its close clones, are supplied with a program called DEBUG; more advanced facilities – and also easier to use – are marketed under such names as the Norton Utilities, PC-Tools, the Ultra Utilities, PC-Zap, and so on. On Unix machines, nearly all files, program and data, are addressable via **ed** and **vi**, the standard editors; other file manipulation utilities included as standard are **grep, awk, dd, tr, newform, od, sd** and **adb**. There are many more sensitive facilities within the **/etc/** directory.* On modern IBM mainframes, the principal utility is called SuperZap. There are equivalents on all machines.

Data alteration. Under normal circumstances, data files are only written to or altered from within an applications program. Thus, details of entries in an accounts or banking system or an inventory package are only viewable and adjusted by first calling up the applications program. The zap utility allows the miscreant to call up the data files directly. Such files will be formatted in particular ways so that the applications program can identify individual items quickly.** However, it is usually not too difficult to identify the particular items that it is wished to alter. Most 'zap' utilities let you search a file, or even an entire disc, to locate a particular 'string', or series of characters. Editing consists of over-writing the letters and figures that are to be altered.

In practice, in order to carry out a successful fraud, it is often necessary to alter several files, or the same files in several locations. In most accounting packages, for example, one event is usually posted to several ledgers and will appear in any number of reports as well as being taken into play in order to perform various calculations. So the miscreant's skill has to extend beyond the mere operation of a zap utility: there has to be knowledge of all the places where evidence of the event is likely to be located. One alternative, to rerun the package with the altered data (you re-input the source data which is then sent

---

*Security on Unix machines depends partly on grouping these facilities in special sub-directories and guarding who has access to them.
**There are more extensive explanations of data files on in Chapter 8, p 184

to the various files by the applications program – in effect, using the computer to help the rewriting of history) may not always be available. You might be able to do this with a micro computer, but it should be almost impossible on a properly set-up mini or mainframe, where the system clock, from which all programs take the date and time information, can only be altered by the system manager. Often also, the computer's operating system will record the time a file was last altered, or may maintain a log of who used what facilities when. The successful fraudster must attend to all of these. The investigator, of course, is looking for evidence of events that should not have happened if alterations had only taken place in the 'proper' fashion. The UK Audit Commission report a case where supplier's records were falsely updated using Job Control Language coding instructions.

Not all data alterations need be quite so complex: at a trivial level (at least technically), anyone can alter a word-processor document – see below for one rather entertaining case and also for limitations on the scope of the method. The usual application of this technique could involve altering key contractual terms or dates in an existing document – computer-aided document forgery.

Applications program weaknesses. Some applications programs, particularly those that have been specifically designed for just one customer, or a small audience, are not as thoroughly tested as they might be. Whilst they may operate effectively in line with their original specification, it turns out that certain transactions are not effectively recorded or passed through, or there is inadequate verification of input, or journals or dates can be altered.

In this class of software-related crime, some member of staff – not necessarily EDP – spots both the weakness and a means of taking advantage of it. In a typical case from 1982, the deputy branch manager of a loan company found flaws in an accounts system and was able to get defraud the company of £10,880. He was eventually charged with forgery and theft.[1]

Applications zapping. Consists of changing an applications program so that it manipulates legitimate data in unexpected and unauthorised ways. The best-known variant is sometimes called The Salami and sometimes 'Zwana'. The aim is to shave off very small amounts from large numbers of accounts within a system – typically the fractions of units of a currency generated while calculating interest and other percentages but which are usually rounded down and ignored – and dump them into a new account for the benefit of the criminal.* In the Zwana case, the new account was given that name because the programmer assumed that this would always be last in an alphabetical sequence (in one version of this story, which is alleged to have happened either to a bank or a mail order company somewhere in the US in the late 1960s, the account name was Zzwicke). The fraud is supposed to have been uncovered when public relations men, eager to demonstrate the power of the computer, called up details of the first and last accounts.[2]

Although nearly every detailed discussion of computer crime methods includes applications zapping as an important feature, there are very few authentic accounts. The reason is that the skills necessary to modify a program in just the right way and to get the new program accepted as bona fide, taken together with the difficulties of creating new accounts which will be to the benefit of the criminal, are quite rare. There are usually easier ways of making a computer misbehave.

Password acquisition/piggybacking. Another extensively written-up technique. The aim is to acquire passwords which will allow the miscreant a suitable level of privileged access to a computer system. The commonest methods are also the least interesting: looking over the shoulder of authorised users, finding scraps of paper with the password scrawled on, ringing up the system manager and pretending that a password has been lost or forgotten, making repeated inspired guesses based on names, initials, associations, or knowing that certain systems tend to have default passwords supplied by the manufacturers which should have been removed at installation-time, but in fact often are not. These are of course the well-known methods

---

*Another way of looting a whole series of accounts is to pretend to be making service charges; anything in fact that is too small an element in each account for anyone to be bothered to complain.

used by external hackers.* Password acquisition can be the route to other crimes: a former company accountant at the Florida-based Golden Eagle Insurance company felt he was owed money by his ex-employer; he coded a secret password into the company's computer and locked access to $400,000's worth of customer accounts. In December 1987 he was found guilty of holding a computer to ransom.[3]

Other techniques are open to staff of the victim computer; if the system is badly set up, it might be possible to access the password file direct; in more advanced operating systems, the password file is encrypted, but this is not always the case.

There are, however, programming tricks which enable the miscreant to capture a password before it has been encrypted. One technique consists of writing a small supervisory program which captures anything typed in at the keyboards of identified terminals and writes them on to a special file. Later, the file is called up by the miscreant and then examined for the keystrokes indicating the password. This method, although quite well-known, was still in use at at least one University in southern England in 1985 and was also used by Edward Austin Singh, the British 'master hacker' who came to public prominence in 1988.[3] Another trick is to prepare a false log-in page which appears on a user's terminal instead of the real thing. The false log-in page requests the user's password and then writes it away to a file the miscreant can examine later; in one variation of the trick, the password is sent straight from the false log-in through for validation, just as it would be in the authentic version; in another, the false log-in *always* replies 'Not correct, try again', or some suitable equivalent and then disappears, so that the authentic log-in program can take over.

However, it is also easy for a miscreant to get into high-privilege parts of a computer simply by taking over a terminal left 'open' (ie not logged out) which has previously been used by a system manager, or some such. The miscreant can then use the high privileges either to change the password so that he can use the account later from another terminal – this would also lock out the 'legal' user; alternatively, the miscreant may

*See *The Hacker's Handbook*, Chapter 6.

be able to use the high privileges to create new accounts for later use, also with high privileges. In some operating systems, it is not necessary for the miscreant to be sitting physically at the same terminal as the high-privilege user; the terminal can be 'captured' remotely.

Much hacking activity, whether internal or external, is rather like climbing a rock-face: the climber finds one crevice and uses that as the foothold from which to reach the next, and so on. This is why computer security specialists urge the 'series of concentric rings' philosophy: a system is insecure if too much reliance is placed merely on one single barrier and there are no further layers of protection within that barrier.

Access control attack. Nearly all multi-user systems have a program which logs customers on by requesting and checking a password. Access control programs are the first line of defence. In Chapter 15 we'll examine them more closely. In some early operating systems it was possible to defeat the access control program and gain entry to the system *without* having a password. One of the best-known techniques consisted of sending a large number of continuous random characters at the point where the password was requested. What happened was this: the program contained a buffer or space in which characters that could be a password were stored. Once a 'return' or 'enter' was sent, the program was supposed to examine what it held in this buffer and compare it with its files of valid passwords. If the password was recognised, then the customer would be admitted. The buffer was only of finite size – it could only accept a limited number of characters. When the buffer was full, the program could no longer cope and it collapsed, leaving the user with complete entry to the entire system. This particular trick should no longer work.

Trapdoors are hidden routes which enable a miscreant to move from one privilege level to another. Some of the password acquisition tricks described above also count as trapdoors: using a low-level privilege which gives access to a password for a higher-level of privilege and then re-logging on in order to use it. Writers on computer security have also suggested that, during the development stage of the design of operating systems, it is not unusual for short cuts, by-passing the intended security facilities, to be programmed in to make testing of the overall system easier. If these trapdoors are not subsequently programmed out before the operating system is offered to the public, then there is always a chance that someone will subsequently discover and use them. Donn Parker produces a couple of examples, one in a FORTRAN programming language compiler and another in a Florida-based time-share bureau.

Trapdoors of this type are almost impossible to detect in advance, for the same reasons that obscure programming bugs, referring to events that are likely to be extremely uncommon in the context of the aims for which a system was set up, are impossible to eliminate. However, they also appear to be very rare.

Trojan horses. At the climax of the ten-year siege of Troy, the Greeks were able to overcome their old adversaries by leaving a large wooden horse outside the city gates. The Trojans hauled it in, only to discover that, concealed within its belly, were Greek soldiers – 'Beware of Greeks bearing gifts'. The computer versions of this are believed to take one of two forms. In the one closest to the classical original, an interesting program or utility is offered to a systems manager. For example, it may provide a simpler way of carrying out some important system function, such as making back-ups. The program actually does what it claims. However, it has some additional instructions, for example creating a new password identity for the benefit of an outsider, who can then, Greek-like, be drawn within the computer's City Gates. However the trojan may do anything.

In an example I have come across, someone placed on a number of hobbyist bulletin boards a 'free' piece of software for the IBM PC which was supposed to be an archive utility: it should have compressed data files so that they occupied less physical storage space on a disc. (Such programs do exist and are very useful.) What in fact happened when you called it up was that it executed a low-level format command on the hard-disc. The effect was to remove everything, irrecoverably, from the disc. In fact, you couldn't even use the computer afterwards without recreating the entire operating system from the original floppy master disc.

The second variant on the Trojan theme consists of a

bastardised version of a program already on the system; the bastardised program contains the extra, damaging instructions. In the ingenious novel by John McNeil, *The Consultant*, a bank has a main system in London and a back-up in Manchester. The principal accounts maintenance program run in London has a hole in it – part of the program consists of instructions which do nothing. The back-up to the program, held in Manchester, contains applications-zapping instructions (in fact a version of Salami/Zwana for the benefit of a corrupt Data Processing Manager). On the London computer is a small trojan which routinely calls the Manchester version down, along a leased line, to London where fraudulent instructions are executed. The Manchester version is then replaced with the London version so that no evidence remains of how the frauds were carried out. In practice there is no reason why you shouldn't have a whole series of programs which call other programs and only at the end of the chain does a malicious trojan appear.

Like trapdoors, trojans are both rare and difficult to detect in advance. In the reported cases it has been the behaviour of the criminal, or the result of some routine check, which has pointed to the existence of a fraud. The trojans were then discovered by backwards-working, checking on opportunities and skills before narrowing down the areas where a trojan might hide. (In *The Consultant*, a detective/programmer found the trojan – or weevil, as he called it – by staring at a print-out of programs, a method which is quite unlikely to achieve worthwhile results.)

Data wiping is an altogether more artless matter: files are simply deleted in such a way that they can't be recovered.* This

---

*In order to wipe a file irrecoverably you must do more than simply use the conventional DELETE command which, in most cases, simply marks a section as deleted rather than removing all the data. The deleted section is usually only over-written sometime later as the disc fills up. Zap utilities, among other things, allow the programmer to UNDELETE in these circumstances. In a £200m heroin smuggling case in 1986, one of the ring-leaders had kept records of his deals and contacts on a hand-held computer called a Psion Organiser. He thought he had deleted all compromising material on it (the Organiser stores data in EPROM chips rather than on disc). The investigating authorities passed the chips on to Psion who quickly managed to recover all the deleted material.[6] If you really wish to destroy material on a disc, you must ensure that you *over-write* the appropriate files, say with zeroes. There are utilities which will do this.

has the effect of erasing the past, rather than rewriting it, and the benefits to the fraudster are a great deal less. The curious will soon know something is wrong, even if they can't identify specifically what. This is usually a tool of the vandal, revenger or ideologue, or an insider in a blind panic to destroy evidence. This is what appears to have happened in the DM480m (£170m, $260m) foreign exchange fraud at Volkswagen which surfaced in 1987.[5] Software can also be wiped, but the effects of this should be extremely limited as, whilst data files are constantly being changed and updated, software is relatively constant and should be available in back-up files. In the 1985 Mercy College survey of Forbes 500 companies, data wiping amounted to 10 per cent of all 'computer crime' incidents – only slightly less than those associated with fraud and embezzlement.

Induced crash is another tool of the vandal, though it can also be employed by programmers or maintenance staff who wish to invent work for themselves – and hence increase their personal earnings. The objective is to instigate a system to stop functioning in an abnormal fashion, preferably in ways which are difficult to predict and correct. This is not very difficult in principle to do, though the real skill is to conceal both the precise method and the identity of the culprit.

A large number of theoretical methods exist, relying either on wiping out files selectively or cutting off the stream of information to vdus, or refusing to accept input from keyboards, or sending the system into a wild goose-chase, asking it to retrieve data from a non-existent disc-drive, or creating a 'deadly embrace' of conflicting but inter-locking commands. Most of these effects can be created by a good systems-programmer using operating systems calls. There are persistent rumours that one well-known package for the IBM PC which had a software device to prevent the copying of master discs (a common feature to limit software piracy) contained, in one version, a 'trashing' routine which was brought into play if anyone attempted to make a copy. The routine was supposed to wipe out the computer's hard-disc.

Networks, where large numbers of 'messages' or 'system requests' are constantly in transit, are particularly vulnerable to induced crashes, especially if the network was added on afterwards to link different computers together.

A logic bomb is a variant on the induced crash idea, except that the crash is postponed until a particular event triggers it. One such trigger could simply be the arrival of a particular date. In a case involving a dispute between a software house and its customer, the promised package was delivered, still only partially functioning very late and way over budget. The customer, with some justification, decided to withhold the final payment until the software had been fully tested as being up to the original specification. The software house installed a new, allegedly improved, version which appeared to run well until April 1st 1981, when the system crashed. The customer could find no obvious fault with the system and eventually someone had the idea of re-setting the system clock to a date prior to April 1st; the system then ran as before. In the end, no less than six separate logic bombs, date-triggered, were found and the systems house was prosecuted. In a couple of cases reported by the *Sunday Telegraph* in 1983, employees who had feared for the future of their jobs, planted logic bombs to protect their positions. One instance concerned a pharmaceutical company whose head programmer was able to amend facilities by using a terminal down a telephone line from home. In the other, the credit controller of a tyre distributor had been sacked and felt dissatisfied with the amount of severance pay. Although he had been asked to return his keys to the premises, he kept a spare set and was able to re-enter the computer area. He arranged for the destruction of over £1m worth of invoices.

One quite common way for software houses to force their customers to purchase regular annual licences for using their products is to include a time-dated logic bomb linked to renewal dates. The logic bomb is also used by programmers who wish to create opportunities for overtime, or to exact revenge when they have been sacked.

A worm is a logic bomb which works, not by deleting data, but by creating so much spurious data that a computer, or computer network, is caused to slow down or clog up. In one simple version, also covered in Chapter 7, an electronic mail facility was reprogrammed so that a 'golden pyramid' was constructed: each authentic message generated four new ones, each of those spawned four more, each of the sixteen thus created begat (to use the Old Testament word) four offspring of their own, and so on. The method works for non-text material as well, of course. This was the basic mechanism in the IBM Christmas Tree incident, often called a virus – which just shows that definitions are a bit fuzzy in this area.[7] The autumn 1988 Internet incident, also referred to by some as a virus, started out as an experiment by a bright student, Robert T. Morris, Jnr, and ended up infecting around 6,000 computers using the Unix operating system.[8]

What distinguishes the true *virus* from other programmers' tricks is its capacity to replicate an exact copy of itself onto other computers. The precise mechanism by which this is achieved varies from computer to computer and indeed part of the technical challenge for virus writers is to find new ways of achieving the self-copying method. Each virus has to be built for a specific purpose – they do not, without skilled human aid, mutate, or leap from one machine type to another. The most publicised are those that infect IBM PCs – Stoned, Brain, Italian, 1701, 1813 (the Friday the 13th virus), and so on. There is even a case of an anti-virus program, TestVac (to be strictly accurate, a program which was supposed to test the effectiveness of certain types of anti-viral precautions), which was sabotaged so that it itself became a Trojan.

Viruses vary considerably in their design and effect. Some really are only jokes and have no permanent harmful effect, others are extremely vicious. The most sophisticated viruses use a combination of several techniques.

Computer viruses usually sit in the background, waiting for a certain trigger to push them into action. At this point they could begin formatting your hard disc, using special techniques so as to make the formatted data irrecoverable, or they might corrupt your working floppy discs. Versions exist for most popular personal computer families – the IBM PC, of course, the Apple Mac, and the Amiga.

To analyse a virus, you need to know:

- the mechanism by which it creates its effects
- the mechanism by which it manages to conceal its existence
- the mechanism by which it is able to replicate
- what on-screen clues (if any) it gives to its existence
- what its effects actually are.

Some of the programs shown on TV as viruses are really only logic bombs – there is no replication. Unlike many real viruses, however, they look good on screen, and that it what tv companies like. It's important to distinguish between malevolent viruses – such as in the Morris case – and benign viruses, where the user's terminal behaves unusually. One case of a benign virus program is the infamous FALL.COM (also called DROP.COM or DRIP.COM) on the IBM PC and close compatibles. Once loaded, the existing program on the PC continues to run for a few minutes, until suddenly all the letters on the screen fall to the bottom. The program data and working text files that the user is using continue to be accessible, however.

In the UK, the placing of a virus on a computer with intent to cause damage, or with a reckless disregard as to whether damage might be caused would give rise to successful charges under the Criminal Damage Act, 1971. (See also p 352.)

The more complicated forms of software attack can seldom be detected in advance: what investigators can do is identify the events immediately preceding the attack to see if they can reconstruct how it was done. By combining these conclusions with knowledge of the required skills, opportunities and motives of potential perpetrators, the investigation can be brought to a result.

Compromising applications

So much for the tricks of the programmer. Many applications programs have generic weaknesses from a security point-of-view. Such weaknesses occur either because the original specification neglected to identify adequate security as one of the aims or because the costs of applying security, both in terms of programming time and of the use of system resources, was considered too great. Although some of these weaknesses can only be exploited by a programmer, others require no special-ised knowledge other than the ability to think a problem through clearly. Nowhere is this more true than in the case of database compromise.

Database compromise. In many database applications, a fre-quent requirement is that particular classes of user are restricted to being able to read only certain types of information. For example, a database containing information about employees would normally be constructed so that only the payroll and personnel departments can read details of individual salaries, although general information about salary bands might be more widely available so that accurate internal costings can be formu-lated. Or in a medical database, a decision may be made to allow researchers access to a wide range of details about health patterns, provided that it is not possible to identify individuals.

In a number of circumstances it may be possible to derive the confidential information simply by asking the right questions. In the case of a targeted employee, by refining the queries about department, skill level, location, age, family, etc to the point where only one employee would fit the profile, the salary of that profile might become disgorged. A similar series of ques-tions about a known patient might soon reduce the number of examples in the profile to one. Knowing that you had then isolated an individual whom you suspected, say, of concealing from you the fact of having AIDS, you could then ask the profile if there were any instances of that disease.

There are refinements on this technique, particularly if the enquirer has partial rights to add information of their own. For example a personnel manager might be allowed to add com-ments on the attitudes of a staff member but could not see exact details of a health check that had been placed there by the company doctor. The personnel manager could, however, ask for statistics looking at overall health problems. In order to identify his target, the personnel manager could add, on his own authority, a unique 'tracer' – an item of information so unusual that it would have to be peculiar to his target, for example that his hobby was dressing up as Superman. The personnel manager could then use this as a basis of identifying the precise health record and ask questions as before.

The technical solution to minimising the risks to confidentiality in this way is by watching carefully the extent of the overlap of the query sets, in other words, checking who needs to see what. Such policies are easier to describe than action, as the very purpose for which the database was installed, namely to share information widely, may become thwarted.

If you like, this is a form of hacking, but it involves no use of unauthorised passwords and no direct programming tricks.

Word-processing. Forging a print-based document so that dates, figures and other details are altered tends to leave traces – awkward blank spaces, traces of chemicals, and so on. Word-processed documents are ridiculously easy to forge. Get hold of the original disc file, call up the applications program and re-edit. If you use the same printer as the original, no one will ever know. In one rather amusing but technically unsophisticated case in March 1986, someone succeeded in entering a word-processor used by Yitzhak Shamir, at the time the Israeli Foreign Minister, and made changes to a speech prepared for him. The sentence 'We shall sometimes act together with our partners and sometimes against them in the national coalition government.' was altered to: 'We shall never act together with our partners and always against them . . .' Mr Shamir spotted the changes just as he was about to give the speech.[9] This form of forgery can be detected. On most computers except micros with pre-1980 operating systems, the disc directory will contain information about the date and time of the last amendment. You'll need to alter that, but it isn't difficult. If the word-processor is running on a IBM compatible, the time and date recorded on the disc is derived from the way the computer's internal clock/calendar is set. In most cases you can reset it, while you execute your forgery, by using the extremely simple commands TIME and DATE. Alternatively you can use a zap utility. On a multi-user system you would have to accept that it is more difficult to change directory information.

Accounts. There are a number of fairly common weaknesses in packaged software for accounts. The first is found in packages that have been specifically written for a single customer and where checking and debugging turns out to have been inadequate. What happens is that events are not properly posted to all the ledgers to which they ought to be applied. The failure is subsequently spotted by an employee who decides to take advantage.

In a case reported by the UK Audit Inspectorate, a payroll supervisor who had been with his employer for more than twenty years had at least three separate schemes to inflate his own pay. One of them involved a fiddle to reduce his incidence of tax and social security payments. He discovered that the payroll package in use would let him adjust his income tax allowance code, the record of his cumulative taxable pay and the record of the tax paid in its master file without being fully checked. The checking only took place at the end of the tax year. There was a variance between the total tax paid by the employer and the year-end figure produced by the computer, but the computer was prepared to accept and ignore it.

From Ken Wong's casebook comes a case from 1978 where a large furniture company had a training facility on its computer to help cashiers learn the procedures for point-of-sale terminals. In 'training' mode, the computer produced invoices and receipts locally but did not update the centrally-held records. The 'training' mode was too easy to switch on whenever anyone wanted it and later the facility was used to steal money from genuine sales – the customer received the goods and the appropriate documentation, the head office records were not updated and the POS operators held on to the cash.

Some people would call these program bugs, but in a sense they are the result of a failure of specification; a 'bug' is more properly regarded as something which either causes the program to crash or hang, or produces an obviously nonsensical result.

Similar failures to post events properly can also occur when using packaged software, ie a generic package which covers most circumstances likely to be found in regular commercial enterprises. Such packages have to be customised to suit the particular requirements of the company to be served. if the customising is inexpertly carried out, the appropriate ledgers may not be set up.

Another area where accounts packages can fail is in journalising functions. The aim of journalising is to ensure that the time and date each event is input is properly and separately recorded. It provides an equivalent of the old-fashioned hand-written ledger: if there are any gaps or pages torn out, dirty work must be suspected. Journals are expensive in terms of processor time and storage media; on very small computers the temptation for the programmer is to omit or underspecify them. The result is that no auditor can be sure that he is seeing an accurate record of what happened when. On micros, even if the journal functions are adequate, it is possible to reset the system clock (see above) and rewrite history with new data.

In packages for larger machines (serving larger businesses) most auditors are likely to want to see that the ability to write new information into the computer is carefully limited and segregated, so that those with the authority to order goods are not the same as those who book them into a warehouse and are different again from those who sell finished items and those who issue cheques in payment. These are administrative decisions as well as to do with the design of an item of software; however, the software must not be capable of thwarting the administrative intent.

The Administrative Link

In fact, most incidents of datafraud appear to occur because of poor linkage between what the software actually does and how the humans who work with it are able to behave. A sophisticated warehouse/inventory package can contain all the checks a prudent consultant can engineer and a company will still lose assets if the physical controls are poor or if data input depends, in the final resort, on the goodwill and honesty of employees. The importance of physical controls are picked up in Chapters 12 and 14.

CHAPTER ELEVEN

Prevention: Assessing the Risks

With this chapter I must again switch writing styles. Up till now I have concentrated on describing and analysing the phenomenon of datacrime, setting it in a social and historic context and identifying the main areas of hazard. But the time has come to produced explicit advice for the manager who wishes to know how to tackle the problems described – and to speak to those individuals directly. So, from a description of the risks we move to prevention and methods. In this chapter we will be describing the ways in which the specific risks facing an individual organisation can be realistically assessed. It is this discipline which provides the person responsible for a computer-dependent organisation with the best defence against the multitude of computer security scare stories. The hazards associated with using computers can be *managed*.

'Sympathetic magic' is the term used by anthropologists and students of religion to describe belief systems which suggest that by associating like with like, supernatural results may be obtained. If a patient's illness turns his complexion red, a cure can be found from a plant with reddish flowers or leaves; if there's someone whom you dislike, making a wax model of them and sticking pins in it will give your enemy severe discomfort, and so on. Unfortunately the planning of security for many information systems seems to place heavy reliance on this discredited theory. Too often DP managers and those to whom they report appear to think that the spending of money on almost *any* device associated with computer security – encryption, dial-back modems, Tempest-protected vdus, access control packages – somehow accomplishes the aim of total protection.

Ask most corporate managers about their computer systems and, nearly always, they will march you down to a well-guarded, air-conditioned and sterile room filled with large metal and glass cabinets and glowing vdus. The first thing that must be understood is that what you are being asked to look at is not the whole of 'the computer system'; what you and your guide may be gazing at is the *heart* of the computer hardware, perhaps where the largest sums of money have been spent, but it is still only a part. The other common fault with the traditional 'computer security survey' is that it tends to concentrate almost exclusively on computer rooms, hardware installations, the weaknesses of operating systems and applications software, data storage and other 'computer' problems. What this approach fails to identify are the actual risks to the business. What you need to do is to understand what your computer system does for the organisation: you must concentrate initially on the extent of your dependence on it and to examine this in the light, not of hardware or software, but in terms of *administrative flows** or processes or tasks through the company.

There is of course no real alternative to making a proper assessment of the risks that a particular organisation and its information systems are likely to be running. The aims of risk assessment are as follows:

- to **identify** risks to which an organisation might be exposed

- to **quantify** those risks that have been identified so that the value of avoidance or reduction is known

- to **avoid** such risks as can be eliminated in a cost-effective way

- to **reduce** those risks that can't be eliminated to acceptable levels

- to identify risks which can be retained because they are **too small** to be significant

- to identify risks that can be covered by insurance, so that the burden of the risks is **transferred**

*See Chapter 8, p 166. Problems specifically associated with hardware and software are examined in subsequent chapters.

Very large corporations, or those that require very individual forms of insurance, can call in the services of specialist risk assessors.* Apart from their inherent skills and experience, what they offer is a degree of detachment from the business that is to be analysed. Here are the main headings under which a risk assessment should be carried out; if you like, the various 'triggers' to indicate that preventative action is calld for. In following chapters we will review the various solutions that are available.

Preparation

Managers who conduct risk assessments on their own business are quite likely to be too biased in their analyses, holding back from judgment in some cases and suffering from unwarranted paranoia in others. However, with risk assessment surveys costing per day at least as much as other forms of top flight management consultancy, many managers will feel they have no alternative but to carry out the work themselves.

A certain amount of mental preparation is essential:

*A number of readers may be familiar with the practice of the computer audit, which is often carried out as an extension of the traditional auditing of assets and financial controls. It is wider in scope than a straight forward security review and aims to identify weakness in administration and control and to supervise the way in which software is developed. Many of the standard works on computer auditing assume that their readers will be working with mainframes carrying software that has been largely written in-house. They also operate on the premise that, since so much has already been spent on hardware and software, a small additional budget on auditors is quite acceptable. The trouble is, today many significant computer operations can be run on hardware you can buy in any shopping precinct for $3000 to $4000 and package software costing from under $50 to about $1000 unless the application is very specialised; the rate for the computer audit function, however, hasn't dropped and, whereas today's prices for computer software are a reflection of the fact that development costs are shared by the many customers for each package, auditing is by definition unique to each customer. $5000 does not buy very many hours of an effective auditor's time. Whilst the $5000 hardware and software combination will almost certainly be doing its job, as advertised, what no one can assess is the care with which the computer has been integrated into the company's (or department's) administrative controls. Self-auditing is distinctly risky, but better than nothing. The particular problems of small computers are examined later.

- you must seek to view your organisation in the way that outsiders, your employees or business rivals do;

- you must try to develop and then maintain an overview of your business and the information systems upon which it depends;

- you must base your judgments on the known statistics of what forms of information crime are common, given your sort of business and facilities;

- you must resist the temptation to give people the benefit of the doubt: taking prudent precaution against datacrime is not the same as accusing someone of a specific crime;

- do not, at the risk assessment stage, get too involved in purely technical, computer-based problems; still less should you worry about computer-based solutions;

- in fact, during risk assessment, don't even think too much about solutions – that ought to be a quite separate phase of decision-making.

Defining The Business

The first step of this risk assessment is to prepare a realistic and dispassionate list of the tangible and intangible assets of the business – not so much in terms of the preparation of an annual report or balance sheet, but to answer the question: what have you got that others might want? The following questions are designed to help you view your business risks objectively.

Let's begin by looking at the assets of businesses in general and who might be interested in them:

The business itself
Who might want to destroy it?
Who might want to own it?
What value can you put on reputation and goodwill?

Assets of the business of interest to employees
These are the main categories of asset likely to be involved if employees try to commit datacrimes:
- payroll
- commissions, etc
- inventory/stock that can be sold on
- information that can be sold to third parties
- petty cash
- equipment that can be used for private purposes
- intangible resources

Assets of the business of interest to trade associates & rivals
These are what your customers and trade rivals might be interested in:
- inventory/stock
- equipment
- R & D
- proprietary designs, etc
- internal sales figures, project costings, lists of suppliers, lists of customers, financial planning documents, tender documents and other sales proposals, advertising schedules
- market research results
- details of staff (in order that the best might be approached)

Assets of the business of interest to criminals
Criminals would tend to go after the following:
- cash
- inventory
- anything which could be used in blackmail

Assets of the business of interest to ideologues
In most businesses, there would be no single asset of interest to most ideologues, but if the business became the hate symbol of some ideological movement, there would be political advantage in stopping the company functioning, and computer systems may be a suitable means of achieving this.

Next we must look at the individual specific business: how

vulnerable is it? The answers to these questions will affect the extent to which the company can survive an unexpected crisis.

- Is it a **private or a public company?** Is there a Stock Exchange quote? How much information about its activities is available publicly?
- What is its state of **financial health?** What are the borrowings? Are there cash reserves? How far are credit-lines strung out?
- What is the business's **main asset base?** Is it property, or machinery, or special supply lines, or legally-protected proprietaries, or the skills of its staff?
- How **vulnerable is the business to competition?** If the company falters, will others quickly step in to take advantage? Is the business run on narrow profit margins? Is it a market leader or market follower?
- How many **operating sites** does the business use? The more sites there are, the more difficult the company is to manage and the more dependent it becomes on its communications facilities.
- How dependent is the business on its **information systems?** Are the computer services a fully integrated feature or are they genuinely ancillary? Could there be a fall-back to manual methods? Is there a back-up system, how good is it, how quickly can it be brought into action? How long is it possible to survive with compromised information facilities?
- How vulnerable is the business to **crises of confidence?** Certain businesses are expected to be able to handle confidential information, or large sums of money, or to manage themselves well. News of a compromised computer or fraudulent employees would have an effect on public and customer confidence long after the substantive problem had been solved.
- How strong are the existing precautions to maintain the physical assets of the business?

Many forms of datacrime are associated with employees. Discontented employees, even if they do not themselves indulge in acts which are fraudulent or against the company's interests, are often willing to condone such activities in others. A number of frauds carried out principally by outsiders require the collusion of staff. It is thus essential to form a view of the business's workforce.

- In general, the larger the work force, the greater proportionately the chances of misbehaviour: unless particular effort is made, employees of large companies tend to feel alienated from the business objectives of the company and are thus more likely to acquiesce in ripping the company off. In larger companies, too, pockets of misplaced or disaffected employees are likely to exist, following management changes.
- Are there more **management tiers** than the business strictly requires? Middle managers who are kept on after they are no longer needed form a prime class of potential fraudsters: they have the knowledge of the company's internal workings, they have time on their hands, and they have little future prospects.
- Are there particular groups of workers whose jobs are especially critical to the functioning of the business? Such people may not be particularly high in the corporate hierarchy or possessed of special skills; however, they will be responsible for the operation of some 'vital point.'*
- How good are **employee/management relations**? Is there a history of industrial unrest – for whatever reason? If the workforce is unionised, how good are the relationships with the trade unions?
- What are **staff turnover rates**? How do they compare with the norms of the industry and the local area? High turnover indicates a workforce that may not feel committed to the company. On the other hand, some of the most insidious frauds have been committed by long-term employees.
- How do **staff remuneration rates** compare? If staff are underpaid they will probably have a low level of loyalty. However, very high rates of payment may indicate particu-

*See below p 238.

larly strong union activity either now or in the recent past. This too can be a pointer to low loyalty levels.

- Is the **organisation expanding or contracting**? Contracting companies tend to have staff that are unsettled. They are more prone to want to look after themselves and may also be more willing to talk about the company's internal affairs to outsiders.
- How far are **freelancers, temps and sub-contractors** used? Do they have access to sensitive information and services?
- How good are the existing **vetting** and **employment review** policy? Are references properly taken up? Are they sufficiently thorough so that enough is known about employees to weed out the dishonest and to spot the growth of personal difficulties?

We now turn to the outside world: to what extent is the business vulnerable to the activities of such trade associates as suppliers and customers? Given the opportunity and a lack of moral scruple, what damage might a trade rival be able to carry out? You should list out both your associates and rivals and identify what they *could* do.

Would they be interested in:
- poaching your existing customers?
- identifying your suppliers?
- reading your internal financial planning documents?
- learning your marketing plans?
- acquiring the results of your R & D?
- acquiring your best staff?
- gathering information so that they can mount a take-over offer?

Could their staff conspire with your staff in a bit of private enterprise to rip you off?

Analysing your information systems and resources

How dependent are you on your information systems – if the systems went down, how quickly could you recover – if you don't recover quickly, how soon will the company be irredeemably damaged?

To answer the questions effectively, you should draw up a list of the principal tasks your computer systems provide, and then calculate the problems associated with failure of each one of these functions, individually and collectively. In effect, you will be carrying out an audit of your resources, listing them and, eventually ascribing degrees of 'sensitivity' for each case. The theme of the information system audit will re-appear in the next few chapters. The resources/tasks could include:

Payroll
Warehouse/Inventory/Stock Control
Distribution Supervision
Accounts
Financial Planning
Word-Processing: Board Minutes, Letters, Internal Memos
Research & Development
Mailing Lists
Materials Handling
Manufacture
Cash Management/EFT
Electronic Mail
Management Information/Decision Support
Specialist Applications, eg
  Securities Trading
  Travel Trade Booking Systems
  Insurance Broking
  Design of all kinds
  Publishing
  Traffic Management

Once these business-orientated questions have been answered, you can then go on to consider what additional hazards or safeguards the computer hardware and software installation provides. For each of these tasks you should ask yourself:

What form of back-up exists:

- for the hardware?
- for the applications software?
- for the datafiles?

Is it possible to resort to a manual system?

How soon can a back-up be brought into full operation and what would be the immediate associated costs?

What would be the consequences of non-availability of processing capacity if it continued for:

- a few hours?
- a single working day?
- three working days?
- two weeks?
- longer?

What would happen if several processes stopped working simultaneously?

How old-established is your system, has it recently been updated or altered? Generally speaking, unless routine maintenance has been neglected, the longer a system has remained substantially unchanged, the greater the chance that errors and gaps have been identified and rectified. Organisations which are having new systems installed are particularly vulnerable at that time: most new software doesn't work perfectly the first time around, operators will make plenty of errors and the previous system will almost certainly be being kept on in parallel. The confusion provides excellent cover for all manner of misdemeanours.

What opportunities exist for fraud?*

If confidential data leaks, could this lead to:

- loss of competitive edge?
- loss of confidence in the company's competence?
- release of material dangerous in the hands of business rivals?
- public criticism?

Among the consequences you must consider are:

*See also Chapter 16.

- the immediate costs of re-instatement
- the irrecoverable loss of live data – and the associated consequences
- interruption to the company's main business and the associated loss of turnover and profit
- the costs of the diversion of management time
- possible loss of market share and competitive edge
- loss of confidence in your reliability by suppliers and customers
- loss of business confidence generally leading to fall in market capitalisation
- cost of increasing security
- cost of increased insurance premiums, etc.

Some of these risks are insurable, provided reasonable standards are maintained; the issue of insurance is examined in Chapter 17.

Even at this stage you are still not asking very technical questions about the capabilities of the precise equipment you own. You should be able to rely on the answers provided by your technical staff or external suppliers.

Vital points

Throughout the next few chapters we will be pre-occupied with first identifying and then protecting the 'vital points'* or 'VPs' of the information system. A vital point is an area in hardware, software, or humanware the loss or compromise of which will have a drastic effect on the whole system and the services it provides. In the set-up of any system there are particular areas of particular and largely unavoidable weakness, where a failure will cause the entire set of facilities – or an important proportion of them – to cease to function. Most mainframe 'computer rooms' and the staff who run them on a daily basis fall into this category. When, as a result of a pay dispute between civil servants and the UK Government, 60 computer operators at the Customs and Excise walked out in June 1987, one of the unions involved claimed that eventually 40 per cent of government income would be involved.

---

*Some military writers prefer 'key' points rather than 'vital' points.

Hardware vital points

where there is no back up

- because the system has to be 'non-stop'
- because back-up takes some time to be put into operation
- because there is no back-up of any kind

where hardware or peripherals are used to generate valuable output, eg
- EFT, cheques, other forms of money, authorisations

hardware needed for supervision of system
- hardware used by system manager, shift supervisors, etc

hardware needed for maintenance
- points in a computer system and its associated networks where engineers must go in order to keep it operating

hardware needed for access to system

- all points at which lots of people can get access to a system via local terminals or remote dial-in terminals without direct personal supervision

Software

operating system utilities
- eg those that can be used to alter files or programs

applications program
- eg those that are unique, irreplaceable or have external commercial value

data
- eg data which is unique, irreplaceable, commercially sensitive, confidential

Humanware

staff and others with unique skills
- eg specialist programmers, machine operators, senior managers

staff with unique authority and hence special opportunities
- eg senior managers, those who can authorise expenditure, payments, release of inventory

staff with strong work-place bargaining position
* eg arising from union agreements

Greater consideration of these technical matters follows in later chapters.

Formal methods of calculating risks

A number of writers have sought to impose more rigour on the process of risk assessment than this chapter has so far proposed. It is useful to examine what they are and why their value must be regarded as limited.

Questionnaires. The questionnaire method usually consists of a work-book listing every hazardous situation the compilers can imagine. The subjects are typically organised around various topics, such as hardware, software, networking, personnel, and so on. The risk analyst is supposed to work through the questions, ignoring those that don't apply and giving 'points' for levels of deficiency for all those that do. At the end of the process, the points are totalled and compared with conclusions about risk exposure. To be a little unkind, the exercise is a little like those articles in women's magazines which claim to assess your personality or attraction to sexual partners.

There are several weaknesses in the method. First, businesses and their use of computers vary enormously; in any all-embracing questionnaire, many questions must be wholly irrelevant. I am aware of work-books which contain over 800 questions. Second, there tends to be bias towards computer hardware and software, rather than the context in which they are used. Third, many of the questions assume that the main problems are likely to be associated with mainframe computers and the staff who use them. As we have seen, datacrime occurs wherever computer systems are in place and can be committed by anyone who uses them. Fourth, the quantitative results of the survey tend to be very crude. Lastly, the end-product of the survey tends to be an assessment of general risk exposure rather than something which leads naturally onward to the location of solutions.

Mathematically-based methods. Clearly, it is possible to associate a level of risk with each hazard identified. Thus, it is argued, it is realistic to calculate with some precision the extent to which preventative action should be taken. Writers and consultants have then gone on to produce some superficially elegant methodologies to put the theories into practice.

Although there are variants, the most common evaluation approach is this: for each category of risk it is possible to calculate the likely damage should the risk become reality. For each category of risk too, it is possible to ascribe a level of probability that it will occur within a given space of time; for example, a disc-read error might be expected once a month, corruption of the working memory due to a blip in the electricity supply might be expected once every 10 days, a fire might occur once every five years, an employee might sell the company's secrets once every ten years. So, for every risk you have both a cost and a probability which you can then express as an Annual Loss Expectancy or ALE:

If the cost of a fire is expected to be $500,000 and a fire is expected to happen every five years, the annualised risk would be $100,000. Anything that you spend to guarantee that there is no fire risk (perhaps halon fire extinguishers, fire-retardant doors and insurance) that costs *under* $100,000 pa makes sense.

There's nothing conceptually wrong with this approach. The weaknesses lie in the aura of spurious accuracy of the method, the costs of accumulating sufficiently reliable data on the hazards being surveyed, and the absence of reliable industry statistics. In fact, computer technology is changed and upgraded so frequently that to say that a specific event might occur every five years is nonsense; the technology involved may not have been in existence for five years and could well be redundant before five years is up. The mathematical approach takes a series of very rough measurements, passes them through a formula, and comes up with what is often mistaken as a precise result.

The result, even if it were accurate, is limited in value: it tells you how much to spend on prevention, not how to spend it.

Computer-based risk assessment methods. Both the questionnaire and mathematical methods have been subjected to attempts to place them on computers. The method favoured by some UK Government departments is called CRAMM for example. Computerising a process makes data collection and subsequent calculations easier; it is possible to hold a database of risk information on a computer so that it interacts with the survey data that is being fed into it. However, if the underlying methods of the survey are suspect, or if the database is incomplete, the results thus obtained won't be any better; it is just that they may become available more quickly. To be used at all effectively, CRAMM must be operated by someone with an appropriate level of training – and this adds to the cost of using it.

Efforts are currently taking place into using Expert Systems techniques for risk assessment. In Expert Systems, the software is able to draw its own conclusions from isolated facts fed into it – the software identifies new 'rules' – linkages between events. It seems possible that the combination of a good Expert Systems engine and a large amount of case material on datacrimes could produce interesting results and the best features of both the questionnaire and mathematical models might be retained. However, the value of the end-product will depend almost wholly on the qualities of the resident database of information and the ability of the surveyor to collect local information accurately.

Another computer technique which could be used for risk analysis are simulation programs in which a business and its computer systems is modelled within the sort of computer program also used to model battlefields. However whilst it is easy to describe such an approach, turning the idea into a package which is both sufficiently rich in detail to give sophisticated results and easy for the non-computer programmer to use is quite another matter.

All of these formal methods have some value, but the 'informed intuitive' or heuristic approach described earlier in the chapter must remain the most useful tool: it forces an analysis based on risks to the business in broad terms, it forces the analyst to keep up to date with changing features in information

Simple Flow-Chart for Risk Assessment and Management

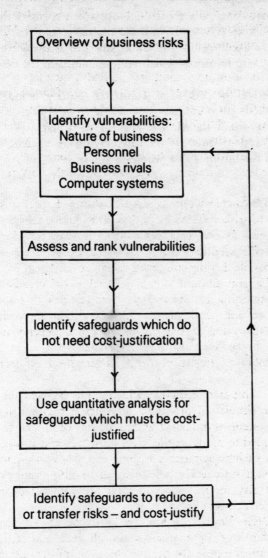

technology systems, it forces an early consideration of solutions to each risk identified.

The chart contains a feedback loop which requires the risk assessor to keep constantly in mind the range and cost of preventative and controlling measures that are available to limit risk. It is these measures which are examained in the next few chapters.

To reiterate: the control of 'computer security' is indivisible from protecting the business as a whole from attack. Initially, all concerns about the vulnerability of particular aspects of a computer system must be mediated by an assessment of the impact on the business as a whole.

CHAPTER TWELVE

Methods I: Controlling Information

The next five chapters are all concerned with methods of controlling or limiting exposure to datacrime. In this chapter we will be examining the ways in which the creation and supply of information around an organisation can be placed under effective management control. In the next, we look at how traditional ideas about personnel management need to be updated to cope with the largest single category of datacriminals, those who are employees of the victim. Chapters 14 and 15 are the most technical in the whole book and cover, respectively, hardware and software aspects of control and prevention. Chapter 16 deals specificially with fraud. These three chapters are more specifically addressd to those managers who have decided to attempt a DIY approach to security.*

Information control

In organisations where the traditional mainframe computing ethos still reigns supreme, software is written in-house, using a library of modules and development tools provided by the computer manufacturer. Rigorous procedures are followed to derive an agreed specification, develop and test, obtain acceptance and finally implement each aspect of the total package. Systems designers involve the 'user' managers at frequent intervals, constantly going back for verification of their actual requirements. Specialist auditors supervise both the development process and ensure that detailed questions are asked about information access and who is authorised to do what, and so on. A company's top management doesn't need to think very

---

* Can I stress that the purpose of this book is to provide an overview of the problems of datacrime and how to tackle it? There are other books, some of them in handbook format, which aim to provide near-exhaustive solutions to typical problems. Some of these can be found in the bibliography.

much about issues of information control because, on the whole, the development process itself tends to throw up the subject automatically. The process is expensive but then so is the hardware upon which everything is to operate. Computer programs which help the supervision of the developement of other computer programs exist – they keep all the many events necessary to prepare a sophisticated package in step with each other and also carry out many standard audit-type checks, but even with these aids, the methodology is costly.

Today, overwhelmingly, apart from the very largest and most specialist applications, companies prefer to buy packaged solutions. These are generic software products for all the standard commercial processes, carefully debugged of programming errors. There are usually facilities to tailor for each separate customer: the customer's name will appear on all the appropriate screens and print-outs, some facilities that an individual customer mightn't need in their business will be suppressed so as to make the program look as uncluttered as possible.

However, whereas the traditional development process of in-house-written software automatically asked the question: who needs to see what, and when; in the package environment, the writer will have made assumptions about what is likely to be convenient in the 'standard' or 'typical' business for which he has been writing. Even if the system specification has not mentioned security, the system designer will have had to reach conclusions about which classes of user will use which items of hardware and which items of data. It will be implicit that order entry clerks have some access to the order processing package – but how much? Do they really need to be able to read all the orders currently being fulfilled, or should they have just sufficient access to be able to enter one order at a time and check that they have done the work correctly? In the absence of clear instructions, the decision made by the system designer may have more to do with the convenience of getting the job done quickly and efficiently than with the long-term security interests of the client. Even if he has allowed in his 'customisation' facilities for special 'information control' routines, he can't guarantee that they are used properly in each case.

As we saw in the last chapter, the people who now buy

computer facilities have become used to software prices that are kept low because development costs are shared between a large number of customers. Once, however, the package is to be implemented in a single customer's work-place, the costs of setting up, customisation and checking of security controls can only be done at the price of the daily rate of a suitably qualified consultant. These costs can very easily exceed those of both the hardware and the basic software combined.★

The normal situation, therefore, for a manager concerned about information security, is that he has to carry out an analysis not of how he would like his computers to handle information around the organisation, but of what they actually do. Many decisions will apparently have already been made. And if the computer user doesn't like what he sees, he has to take after-the-event action. The task is thus to provide the manager with some method for coping with information control himself. In this chapter therefore, we will examine some of the ways in which a suitable 'information control' policy may be formulated and implemented.

Open and closed policies

An organisation can determine who sees what and when, either by taking a series of decisions to *deny* access in particular circumstances or by deciding to *give* access in particular cirumstances. You could call the first, the 'open' approach and the second, the 'closed'. In the open case, the organisation assumes that everything it has should be as widely available as possible and that, where information is identified as being 'sensitive' for one reason or another, exclusions should take place on a case by case basis. In the closed, the organisation says that everything it has and does should be regarded as secret and that information should only be released to employees on a 'need to know' basis.

The open policy has the virtue that employees know what the organisation is up to, and they can use that information

---

★ In a sense, this should not be a deterrent, as the real measure of value is the harm a compromised computer system could inflict on the business as a whole, not the cost of the computer itself.

constructively to further the organisation's interests. The disadvantage is that employees and others may abuse the information thus obtained. In the world of government security, or at least that world as portrayed in popular fiction and non-fiction, 'need to know' is the key policy for limiting the leakage of information; it is the purest example of a 'closed' approach. The problem here is that whilst information remains secure, people may lack the information with which to do their jobs properly.

Most commercial organisations have an 'information control' policy which hovers uneasily between the two extremes. A series of pragmatic decisions are made. In pre-computer days such pragmatism worked well enough. The problem now is this:

- computers handle and generate far more information than manual systems ever could

- the elements that make up the information are more critical to the organisation than they ever used to be

- much of a company's assets – cash, inventory, work-in-progress – and many of its critical activities – the authorising of payments, payroll, are handled *via* computer systems: the company knows what it has and does by what the computer represents to it. If the computer gives a false representation, for whatever reason, the company suffers

- the existence of much of the information is hidden away from the managers who should be determining how it should be controlled

- computers can be persuaded to create information where none existed before, simply by producing new useful representations of raw data they already possess. These new reports can be extremely useful in the formulation of new management plans. The organisation as a whole may not even be aware of the existence, let alone the value, of these new information items

However, the computer has brought some benefits: once the organisation has made its decisions about who sees what, the implementation of those decisions is made much easier:

- computers can segregate users and classify information

- they can enforce 'separation of duties' policies which are at the heart of preventing fraud

- they can provide high quality identification and authentication of individuals

- they can record all the individuals and all the times particular items of information have been accessed

- they provide the possibility of storing information in an encrypted form

- they provide facilities for transmitting date from one place to another securely

What computers can't do, however, is make decisions about who *should* see what and when.

Information elements and datasets

At first sight, 'controlling information' held on a computer system seems to amount to little more than arranging for that system to have an effective password access facility attached to its front. The managerial problem in a commercial situation, of course, is to decide what 'need to know', whether operated from an 'open' or 'closed' posture, should actually mean – and also what mechanism should be used in order to reach that decision. Needing to know is also a function of time and circumstance: you may need to know only if certain conditions become true. A password protection scheme is a means to achieve management objectives about information security, not an end in itself.

'Information' includes **facts** which have value both to the business and to those outside and the **representation of cash or assets** which, through manipulation or deception of a computer system, can be the subject of a fraud. The first step therefore is to identify these information items, to place a value on them, and to decide how they are to be managed.

Aims of Information Control Policy

A: To prevent fraud
B: To retain confidentiality as between sections of the organisation
C: To retain confidentiality & secrets as between the organisation and the outside world

---

The trouble is that many companies, unless they have been using computers for a very long time and so have had the question forced on them by systems analysts and auditors, have never really thought much about the information they use and generate; they have simply taken it for granted.* The first stage in the management of corporate information resources, therefore, is to institute an audit of them. The elements – in computerese, they are often referred to as **datasets**, groups of data which belong to the same family and are found on a database** – can be most easily identified by using the approaches suggested in earlier chapters: look at the administrative flows within the organisation. Essentially there are eight classifications into which information elements may fall – some may be in several categories:

---

* Even large companies often have little idea of the information resources they actually possess. As we saw in Chapter 2, large quantities of useful managerial information are created off the back of sales and inventory packages. Indeed in many many industries, the creation, handling and exploitation of 'marginal' information in this fashion is a key strategy in developing competitive edge. Much information is created on micros, as opposed to mainframes – and neither systems analysts nor computer auditors spend much time examining micros.

**A 'database' is more than simply a way of looking up facts or names and addresses. For example, warehouse management or order processing or payroll or sales prospects packages are all really databases, in that facts are stored in them and are called up during processing. In fact, most software packages used in the commercial world, apart from word-processing and design aids, have a considerable 'database' element.

- cash or the representations of assets
- dynamic information
- historic information
- information which is not yet public
- information that has value to the business and possibly to outsiders
- information which ought to have restricted circulation within the organisation

They could be generated from any of the organisation's main information system components, eg:

Payroll
Warehouse/Inventory/Stock Control
Distribution Supervision
Accounts
Financial Planning
Word-Processing: Board Minutes, Letters, Internal Memos
Research & Development
Mailing Lists
Materials Handling
Manufacture
Cash Management/EFT
Electronic Mail
Management Information/Decision Support
Specialist Applications, eg Securities Trading
Travel Trade Booking Systems
Insurance Broking
Design of all kinds
Publishing
Traffic Management

We looked at this list in the previous chapter but whereas then the idea was to emphasise the identification of processes, here we are interested in the information elements or datasets handled by or generated as a result of those processes. As with the valuation of physical assets, there are several ways in which you can base your estimate of the worth of an information element:

In the case of the transactions that authorise the making of payments, movement of goods, purchases, sales – all the areas where the computer holds representations of the physical assets of the organisation –

- What cash value is being represented?
- What controls are in place to limit the associated authority?

In the case of corporate information –

- What value does it add to the business?
- How much did it cost to collect?
- What would it cost to re-instate?
- What would be the consequences if it were lost:
    - totally?
    - partially?
- What would be the consequences if it fell into 'enemy' hands? (in this case information is not 'lost', it merely ceases to be unique and may remove competitive advantage)

In many cases affecting corporate information, companies will not want to express 'value' in pure monetary terms largely because that is an almost impossible exercise and because for most purposes it isn't absolutely necessary: having asked the questions, it should be possible to grade each information element on a 1 to 5 or 1 to 10 scale in terms of importance or criticality.

The importance of this exercise is that it invites management to think in terms of classifying information in terms of 'sensitivity', a theme that will be picked up later.

Determining access

Having thus identified and valued the information elements, the next step is to determine who needs access to each one. There are several different ways of 'having access' to information held on a computer system: principally, you can read information without having the ability to alter it; you can enter information, for example orders, but without having the ability to read any surrounding data; you may be able to both read and write. You may be able to set up new facilities. You may have access to the information you require at all times, or you may be only able to see it in particular circumstances. And there can be all sorts of hybrid combinations.

Types of Access:

read only
   automatically
   with authorisation
write only
   automatically
   with authorisation
amend only
   automatically
   with authorisation
copy & duplicate only
read and amend/write, etc
authorise others
'dual key'
supervise
eg read dataset
eg under special condition
eg 'data entry', orders etc
eg amend dataset but not create new entries
eg collect from dataset
full authorisation
give permission to others
two people required before dataset can be used
set up and modify aims of dataset, act as administrator (This need not include the right to enter, write, amend or read substantive data, but often it does)

Thus, for each dataset and each computer user, you have a very large number of combinations which you can describe in a grid, of which the one given here is a considerable simplification.

	DS A	DS B	DS C	DS D	DS E	DS F	DS G
Employee 1	–	r	rw	–	–	rw	–
Employee 2	–	–	w	–	–	r	–
Emloyee 3	–	r	aw	–	–	r	–
Employee 4	srw	rw	rw	rw	rw	rw	rw
Employee 6	r	–	rw	rw	–	–	–
Employee 7	–	r	r	r	rw	–	–
Employee 8	–	r	rw	–	rw	–	–
Employee 9	rw	rw	srw	r	rw	rw	–

DS = dataset; r = read; w = write; a = amend; s = supervise

In all but the most basic of situations, working out a complete grid to cover the entire information resource of an organisation is clearly beyond the supervision of any single individual. However, the decisions go to the heart of keeping an organisation secure and techniques have to be found to make them manageable.

There are a number of ways in which the process can be simplified:

1 Divide staff with computer access into those who do line jobs – shop-floor staff, clerks, secretaries, etc – and those who manage. Regard the former as members of a closed system – they see nothing unless they have a specific need. Treat the latter, who should be fewer in number, as being in an open system – they see everything unless they have been specifically excluded.★

2 Start with the processes of greatest vulnerability. In both this chapter and the previous one we have stressed the importance of considering threats to computer systems as part of the larger subject of threats to the business as a whole. Now it is true that fraudsters are able to take

★For this purpose, I am assuming an ordinary commercial organisation; clearly a company with a defence contract or possessed of important commercial secrets would need to be treated as a wholly 'closed' system.

advantage of any loophole anywhere, but obviously areas where payments or the movement of goods can be authorised are the most vulnerable. In terms of valuable information, an in-house classification process (Internal, Confidential, Secret & Confidential) is an obvious first step from which other decisions can flow.

3 Observe the fundamental rules about *separation of functions*: so far as possible, ensure that no significant harm can come to the organisation without widespread collusion; don't allow too much authority to rest with just one individual; if, in a manual system you would want an authorisation to be counter-signed, don't tolerate a computer-based system which allows the event to take place without 'counter-signature'. The traditional areas where separation of functions is particularly important are:

- authority for payment
- authority to move goods
- authority to make purchases
- authority to grant discounts, etc
- payroll
- signing (or production of) cheques, etc

4 Break the overall task into a series of sub-tasks which can be delegated to appropriate department heads. Ask them what they need to be able to do on the computer and why – and for each department get at least one external invigilator to check what is being proposed.

5 You can also ask each department to propose how it would classify its various datasets (Internal, Confidential, Secret & Confidential), electronic and print, from the point of view of:

- information which is not yet public
- information that has value to the business and possibly to outsiders
- information which ought to have restricted circulation within the organisation, for example, payroll/salary, Board minutes

Some writers on Information Resource Management promote the concept of the Information Owner. They suggest that each person or department who creates (or supervises the creation of) information is responsible for, among other things, the quality of that data, as well as its control and security. Thus a sales department is the 'owner' of the sales figures, and so on.

Clearly, if the route is taken to delegate decisions about information access, then the entire process will need supervision from the top. An organisation's top management can be the only body that sets the objectives and standards for the exercise and ensures that they are properly and consistently carried through. Even then, it must be remembered that what is happening is a mere substitute for something which would be extremely costly – a full external audit.

Particular problem areas

There are a number of areas that are especially worth highlighting; they show how 'information control' is also a matter of limiting physical access to computer facilities, a theme picked up in the next chapter:

Paper documents. Although this book is primarily concerned with the effects of computers, 'information security' encompasses material in print, and in people's memories as well as electronically-stored data. Although I believe that within a very few years a great deal of industrial espionage will be carried out by the stealing of electronic storage, the fact is that today overwhelmingly what is sought is paper-based: reports, minutes, computer *print-outs*.

Stationery. Access to authentic stationery is critical in a number of frauds: letterheads are useful in cases of forgery and deception. Most companies have forms which authorise payments or the movement of goods. Many companies even generate cheques via special printers. Stationery supplies should be carefully controlled; wherever possible authorising documents should be pre-printed with serial numbers. A log should be kept on test runs and spoilt stationery.

Corporate data. This is information used by top management and their immediate advisors to plan strategy. Today, this is nearly always maintained on desk-top PCs, using word-processors, spreadsheets like Lotus and SuperCalc, databases and, perhaps, display graphics. Corporate data may also include lists of important contacts. The information held in a single floppy disk could easily be worth millions if it contains details about a take-over strategy or a new product development. PCs are particularly difficult to secure through either hardware or software devices.

Organisations with rival computing facilities. The company with the single centralised computer resource is now a rarity: most organisations have a whole raft of individual computers, sometimes talking to each other, sometimes not. With machines being purchased out of petty cash, information 'control' can become a joke: work is duplicated, or the same job done in slightly different (and incompatible) forms.

Preventing the industrial spy. There are certain circumstances in which businesses are more likely to be vulnerable to the activities of industrial espionage agents; these include:

- during take-overs
- prior to the issue of annual or half-yearly results
- prior to new product launches or ad campaigns

An IE professional is unlikely to be in the direct employ of anyone you know.

The first task is to warn all those who handle 'sensitive' information of the possibility of an attack. All relevant information should be placed within an appropriate security classification. Records of documents and work-discs, together with important modifications should all be placed in a central log kept by one person. Work-discs should not be allowed out of the room in which they are normally used without the fact being recorded in the log. Each print-out of sensitive documents should be individually numbered; if appropriate, subtle changes to each copy, for example word-spacing in a particular paragraph, can be made so that, if photocopies appear, its source can be more readily identified. Procedures for the handling of visitors to corporate headquarters should be strengthened.

Items sought by industrial espionage agents

Internal memoranda
Sales figures
Production costings
Marketing plans
R & D
Consultancy reports
Mailing Lists
Printers' Proofs of Reports, Ads, etc to be published
Any of the above in computer-readable form
Organisation charts
Telephone Directories
Floor Plans
Passes
Keys, metal and magnetic
Contents of waste-paper bins, particularly near photocopiers
Discarded printer ribbons

Discouraging the internal hacker. Most employees with any spark of curiosity will at some stage develop a fascination with the computers and organisation uses. Most employees, used to such perks as 'free' telephone calls, will see nothing wrong in borrowing a little computer time for private purposes.* I am not convinced that, for the majority of commercial organisations, with no requirement to safeguard heavy-duty secrets, a policy seeking totally to suppress internal hacking activity is a good idea.

Rather, the task should be to contain it within limits that the organisation's computer resources can stand and which employees, if asked, would agree was 'fair'. To succeed in this policy, the following elements are necessary:

- any data which the organisation regards as critical must be properly secured so that only the most determined effort by the unauthorised can reach it

*See Chapter 7.

- an employee security awareness policy must be in place which stresses both the requirement of the organisation to safeguard its data and to explain that abuse of a computer can, at the very least, cause considerable degradation of *all* computer services
- encouragement must be given to employee self-training in computer usage, perhaps even a 'play area' with bits of software and hardware to try out
- a warning of strict penalties for abuse of privileges, such as running an independent business using the organisation's resources, taking up too much of the processing and storage power of the machines, and attempting to access data which is plainly confidential.

This approach, if implemented (and it will not suit all environments), sets an explicit standard of behaviour. Most employees will consider they are being awarded a privilege and will resent those who abuse it.

Discouraging the external hacker. If people unconnected with your organisation are able to get into your computer system, the chances are that your level of security is exceptionally low and that you are wide open to many other forms of abuse. Most external hacks do not cause much damage in themselves; the substantive harm usually arises from the publicity because it throws doubt on the competence of the computer owner. So, the first bit of advice about preventing the external hacker is: use the access control facilities you already have. Most external hackers can be discouraged simply by using password facilities properly. Most hackers have just one method of operation: password acquisition. The laziest obtain phone numbers and passwords from friends, sometimes via the informal electronic bulletin board system. More creative hackers rely on knowledge of the way in which systems are set up, and certain default files, passwords and commands.

Some of the more important anti-hacker devices are discussed later, but to anticipate:

- warn your legitimate users to guard their passwords carefully
- don't publish your phone numbers unnecessarily, in fact, if you can avoid it, don't even advertise that you exist
- consider carefully whether you need to have your computer ports available all the time: can they be opened up only by previous request?
- don't have informative log-on pages which tell browsers what the system is
- ensure that, during sign-on, the actual characters of the password are not shown on screen, but that stars or dashes are echoed back
- consider using dial-back modems: these devices are similar to ordinary modems in that they convert tones sent down telephone lines into electrical states that computers can read. A dial-back modem, however, does not admit a user automatically: it provides its own log-on screen and requires a password of its own before deciding to recognise a valid user. Once it has decided to accept someone, it closes the telephone line down and starts to ring up the identified user at a telephone number that has been pre-designated for that person. Only when he has been called back and reidentified himself will the user be able to gain access to the computer itself.

Dial-back modems are not the universal answer to computer security:

- they assume that valid users will always be operating from only one location, and hence one telephone number; they are difficult to operate if the user-base is on the move
- their effectiveness is reduced if non-authorised people can gain physical access to authorised terminals
- they provide only a single-stage protection to computer access; once the user has gained admittance to the computer, it may still be necessary to restrict his ability to see particular files and use certain facilities

Some of the more complex devices available are reviewed in Chapter 15.

The easiest advice a security consultant can give to an organisation about protecting the flow of information is to restrict everything to a 'need to know' basis. Modern commercial organisations, however, thrive and grow partly because of the free flow of information, supplying managers and others with ever more detail of how their business actually works and providing more opportunities for development. In the end, therefore, no one except the organisation's management can decide where to strike the balance. And they can only make the decision if they have carried out the appropriate analysis of how their business actually uses information.

CHAPTER THIRTEEN

Methods II: Personnel

A bluff old computer security consultant, forty years in the data processing business and with a memory stretching back to when significant parts of computers relied on glowing valves, once told me how he set about carrying out a security review on behalf of the insurance brokers that used his services. His job was to give the underwriters a quick overview of the risks faced by particular system installations so that they could determine an appropriate level of premium.

> First of all, I look at the people at the reception desk. Are they alert and friendly? Do they answer the telephone promptly and efficiently? Or are they otherwise pre-occupied? Could I have walked in without being noticed? Then I ask to be taken on a tour of the organisation. Of course, out of the corner of my eye, I am checking the level of the routine precautions for physical security . . . was I signed in properly, what sort of identity badging system is in place – and whether it is being used properly – any key-card systems, locations and ease of access to any vital system and telecommunications components, and so on. I am also checking to see if there are any VDUs that have been left unattended and not properly logged off; or pieces of paper with passwords scrawled on them sticky-taped near keyboards. But usually these days I arrive by prior appointment and memos will have gone round over the previous week warning everyone to smarten up their act.
>
> But what I am really measuring is staff attitude and morale. After a bit you can smell the difference as clearly as you can a new mown lawn from a pile of burning rubber tyres. If the staff appear to be enthusiastic about the organisation for which they work, then I am already almost certain that I'll be giving the underwriter a good report. Next, I'll ask to be

pushed in the direction of the personnel department. I'll want staff turnover statistics, department by department. Are the percentages of those leaving abnormally high for the industry and geographic location, and, if so, do I assume that this is because they don't like the organisation as an employer, or is there a more acceptable reason? Are particular departments over- or under-manned? Are lots of new people being taken on? How many temporary and contract staff are used – and why? How many part-timers? I usually do a spot check on a few files: were CVs and résumés carefully verified for authenticity? What steps were taken to vet temporary and contract staff? I ask for an internal organisation chart – what changes have taken place recently, have there been any signs of employee discontent?

By this time, of course, the organisation's managing director, head of security and EDP manager are all getting rather impatient. Why aren't I questioning them about their new access control software, the banks of dial-back modems, the encryption packages? Why don't I sit down at a VDU and, if I am so clever, break into their host machine at system manager status?

In fact, if the organisation checks out well at the personnel level, given that I may have only a few days for the entire review, I am already fairly confident that I can award them a 'low risk' label. I will have established as much in the first forty-five minutes. And I won't alter that opinion a great deal over the next few days unless I come across some really gross security lapses in the computer set-up. If I don't like what I see in terms of employee morale, staff turnover, personnel checks, and so on, then the organisation moves automatically into my 'high' or 'medium' risk levels and it would take the most outstanding of computer control systems to persuade me to alter my judgment. If the staff don't like their employer it will take more than a few days of even the time of someone of my experience to identify all the ways in which they could be ripping the organisation off.

Of course I adjust my view depending on the nature of the organisation I am surveying; with every one I go to there are always special considerations and I do have to look in some detail at machines and networks and procedures, but if it doesn't check out at the personnel level, then there will always be lots of problems.

The importance of routine personnel considerations in the maintenance of information security stems directly from the facts about who the datathieves actually are and what motivates them that were examined in Chapter 7 and the nature of the various datacrimes that were looked at in Chapters 4, 5 and 6. If you are prepared to accept the dividing up of a computer system into hardware, firmware, software and humanware, then appropriate use of the techniques of personnel management addresses the problem of defective humanware. The 1986 Home Office report on commercial fraud puts it this way: 'The first fraud prevention measure is always take up fully references on anyone who might occupy a post which might give him or her access to fraudulent opportunities and/or to confidential data that might be used for industrial espionage.'

Most decent-minded employers find themselves rebelling against the idea that their employees are dishonest: it is important therefore to emphasise that no one is suggesting more than that employee dishonesty exists and that it is the single largest contributor to white collar crime. It is a matter of simple self-preservation to take protective measures. In particular, steps can be taken to ensure that the individuals selected for employment are who they say they are and to watch benevolently over the welfare of all employees to see what pressures might be developing in their lives. Such measures as are selected should of course be in proportion to the level of potential risk the employer faces: greater than normal intrusions into areas of employee privacy must be justified on the grounds that the individual has particular access to the organisation's secrets, special authority to handle cash and assets, or is in a position to stop the company functioning. There is a further consideration: the clumsy implementation of security policies can have a disastrous effect on morale, turning contented employees into mistrustful enemies of management. Ultimately personnel security and machine security cannot be disentangled.

Personnel management

This book is no place to start a discussion about how managers should motivate staff, but it must be repeated that the introduction of new computer-based information systems can have a strongly disruptive effect on employer/employee relations. It is all too easy for managers to get over-enthused by the benefits of improved information processing and computer-aided decision making – and to neglect the impact on the careers of lower-level workers upon whom the organisation will continue to depend. It's a commonplace among writers on management that organisations tend to have at least three structures: the formal one that is enshrined in charts and reflected in a hierarchy of titles, the informal one which relies on unofficial alliances between individuals who see that things get done, and an establishment of people who are no longer functionally as important as they once were but still have sufficient authority to countermand orders and play internal politics. Again, as we saw in Chapter 7, the remuneration that people receive for working within an organisation is not as straightforward as may at first appear. Their actual reward will consist of: the overt financial package, the agreed perks, the inherent job satisfaction and the covert rewards – the opportunities for fiddling. Every time computers are asked to do something new within an organisation, the delicate balances that make up the power and personal relationships of the staff become disturbed.

Managers have no alternative but to accept that it is up to them to secure the co-operation of employees with the aims of the organisation. Not all employees have the same goals and motives in coming to work – those near the top of the organisational ladder will probably get their pleasures from being entrepreneurs; in the middle there will be individuals whose satisfaction comes from doing a job well but who would not want the uncertainties, pressures and risks of being an entrepreneur, and the shop-floor will look for pleasant working conditions. All will expect an income and rewards package that they perceive as 'appropriate'. Within these limits, management must aim to see that all employees perceive their terms of work as 'fair' and that management, if not overtly benevolent, is even-handed.

In this book we can do no more than to stress the overwhelming importance of employee relations and leave each manager to determine the most appropriate solutions: careful job design, good people management, strong internal communications, high quality staff welfare facilities, employee discounts, bonus schemes, share options. Organisations are nearly always much more in the hands of their employees than they realise:

- however good the inherent security facilities of a computer system, someone has to have access to it at the most fundamental level in order to provide effective maintenance; someone has to act as security manager and unavoidably will have notional access to every single account and terminal. These people have to be trusted and, given the expertise which is necessary to carry out such jobs, there may not be too many other people within the organisation who can oversee them

- employees have one big advantage over systems analysts, computer programmers and experts in information security: their complete familiarity, day after day, with the system they are using and the environment it is meant to serve. Systems are particularly vulnerable to bugs when they have just been installed or when important new features have been added, but even old systems have their problems: fudge accounts and fiddle facilities to cover situations which the organisation needs to function properly but which no one ever told the system designer about. Tricks that appear in no operations or user manual but which 'everyone' knows about. Circumstances in which the computer fails to perform a reconciliation or generate a report properly and which have to adjusted manually. If the employees cease to feel benevolent towards their employer, such fudge facilities will aid them in embezzlement or minor sabotage

- there really is no protection against employee-aided industrial espionage unless the management can institute routine strip searches of all staff; even employees of the most sensitive of national security agencies are likely to rebel against this. The 3½ or 5¼ inch disc is simply too easy to copy and to conceal

- security procedures that are too onerous very quickly prevent organisations from carrying out the business they are supposed to be in: if computers are meant rapidly to supply internal information then over-complicated password access control will slow everything up; over-rigorous physical security will reduce the quality of life of employees and, consciously or not, they will rebel
- computers can be used to provide extensive monitoring of employee activity, but, unless such action can be fully justified and accepted by employees, the facilities will be seen as an intrusion on the individual's privacy and this too will lead to rebellion

The organisation that hopes to rely exclusively on hardware- and software-based security has the odds stacked heavily against it.

There are, however, a number of routine personnel management policies which can be checked out to see if they are being effectively implemented. They are: proper verification of CVs and résumés, the careful use of vetting agencies, annual (or more frequent) reviews of individual employees and, if appropriate justification can be found, an element of employee surveillance. In all of these matters a delicate balance must be struck between the organisation's requirement to know enough to safeguard its assets against its employees and the rights of those employees to privacy and self-respect. It's a point that is stressed throughout this book: managers should not embark on policies which, if revealed, they would be unwilling to justify in public.

Verification of CVs

There can hardly be an employer that doesn't have a procedure which requires that would-be employees supply a curriculum vitae and a couple or more referees. What is surprising is the extent to which organisations fail to follow up references and verify the details. In a wide-ranging survey carried out during 1986 by two UK academics based at UMIST and involving a sample of one-third of all companies in *The Times* 1000 (the UK's biggest companies), they discovered that only 67.3 per cent checked references for all vacancies, 11.2 per cent checked for 'more than half', 2.8 per cent for 'half', 14.0 per cent for 'under a half' and 3.7 per cent never checked references at all. One would expect that smaller companies, with smaller personnel departments, would take even less trouble.

Fraudulent or adulterated curriculum vitae are apparently quite common: academic qualifications are moved up a class, sackings are disguised, the nature of previous posts subtly enhanced. Late in 1985 the British managing director of a US information systems company was convicted of embezzling £36,869 during the eight months in which he was its chief executive. The CV upon which he was appointed was quite bogus, not only was he not a Cambridge-educated accountant, he had a criminal record. In another case, a man who was over retirement age presented his similarly-named (and younger) cousin's birth certificate as evidence, and in yet another, a fake finance director secured his post by assuming the name (and qualifications) of an innocent third party. A former personnel director of the pharmaceuticals giant, Glaxo, Richard Stokes, told the *Guardian*: at least 50 per cent of CVs will be inaccurate in some way and 35 per cent will contain exaggerations.

There's also probably good reason to suppose that, even where CVs are properly checked, insufficient detail is requested in the typical questionnaire: the simple expedient of leaving lots of space for answers to such questions as previous employment history, details of responsibilities, reasons for leaving, and so on, encourages the would-be employee to supply more information. Generally speaking, the greater the detail provided, the more difficult it is to fake. In his *Corporate Fraud*, Michael J Comer advises asking for birth certificate, passport, marriage certificate and driving licence and carefully verifying the information on all of them. He goes on to list other areas for verification: local rating list, school and university, all employers for at least the previous ten years, doctors, banker, credit card companies, checking with neighbours, the electoral roll and the telephone directory. Each employer, he says, should be asked to verify the following: duration of employment, photographic identification, work responsibilities, salary record, reasons for leaving, sickness record, family background, eligibility for re-employment, reputation for work, honesty, reliability, stability, absence of covenants not to compete, prior employment from previous employer's records, educational qualifications as reported to previous employer, and a check with a named manager or supervisor. Some of these suggestions are rather extreme and probably couldn't be justified for ordinary, non-sensitive jobs.

Lapses in the checking of CVs are particularly acute where skills are in short supply and nowhere are the problems greater than in data processing staff of all kinds – analysts, programmers, operators, maintenance men.* In January 1977, both the national and specialist computer press were full of the ICI tapes extortion case, where a computer operations supervisor and a systems analyst attempted to obtain £275,000 as the price for the return of tapes from an IBM 370. They had carefully removed all the back-up tapes but the plan had failed when an attempt was made to collect the ransom. During 1977, the systems analyst was out on bail; he took a number of temporary jobs at computer installations and always used his own name; no one checked on his background or realised who he was until he let on himself.[1]

During the year of the City of London's Big Bang, 1986, the salary levels of relevant staff went up by a minimum of 30 per cent, but the doubling – and more – of some incomes was not unusual. With companies pleased to get apparently qualified staff at all, checking of CVs was being widely ignored.

Large quantities of computer staff are supplied on contract. There are several reasons for this:

- many companies do not have a regular and routine requirement for software and hardware development and

---

*Another of the oft-repeated stories of computer crime is the 'brilliant analyst' who is eventually caught by his management and who, instead of being upset, demands money to leave, plus a good reference for the next job. The company agrees, fearing the anger and ridicule of their sharcholders. The analyst later pulls the same trick on his next employers. The purest account of this story is 'Jim O'Connor' in Gerald McKnight's 1973 *Computer Security*. McKnight's sources appear to be secondary and it is interesting that most subsequent writers on the subject have provided very little detail. Did 'Jim O'Connor' or anyone like him ever exist?

don't want to have to maintain a large staff for occasional use; freelancers are a good solution to augment existing staff as necessary. Some freelancers will be appointed direct, others will come from agencies
- many other companies prefer to let their main computer facility suppliers provide their own staff, who may then be seconded for periods in excess of six months; it will be the facility suppliers who should have carried out the vetting of personnel and it will be their customers who have had to rely on them
- most computer installations require servicing from a variety of specialist companies: not only will the hardware require maintenance, printers, plotters, modems, message switches, telecommunications links, air conditioners, fire alarms and power supplies may each be serviced by different sets of engineers who all will have easy access to 'sensitive' parts of the installation

In 1986, the UK had around 14,500 registered free-lance DP staffers supplied by between 150 and 180 organisations. That would be between 6 and 7 per cent of the UK's entire DP workforce. There is no possibility that vetting in these circumstances can be anything like adequate.

But it's not only computer staff that come into companies as temps; secretarial and clerical functions frequently need augmenting at particular times of year, especially at the peak of the holiday seasons and during times of exceptional customer demand. The temporary secretary is a classic role for the professional industrial espionage agent to adopt. Very few employers carry out their own vetting of such staff and the agencies that supply secretaries and clerks usually limit themselves to checking on their professional competence.

Increasingly, larger companies are using management consultants to help them reshape their strategies. Almost inevitably such people will rapidly become privy to the company's innermost thoughts. Obviously, staff on secondment from the best-known consultancies should have been carefully vetted by their employers, but it's not unknown for some work to be sub-contracted to outside specialists, perhaps market research agencies or technology evaluation consultants. The chain of control over staff with access to important information can get very weak.

Temporary staff of all kinds can acquire a quality of invisibility within the companies where they work: they appear on no personnel records, the costs of their employment disappear in all manner of odd budgets, they tend not to make friends with permanent staff. They are nearly always brought in to cover some emergency when uppermost in the minds of their employers is immediate survival, not longer term security. Often no one, neither employer nor contractor, takes any step in the direction of vetting.

Vetting agencies

For sensitive posts, it is possible to use the services of commercial vetting organisations. There are two sorts of service: one type acts as an extension of a personnel department and is concerned simply with checking information supplied on a CV. By having a streamlined routine and a number of local sub-agents, it is easier to verify addresses, academic records, and previous employment details. A typical US example is Brock International Security. The second variety of service seeks out other relevant information: credit-ratings, criminal records, even political affiliations. It is important to understand what sort of results can be reasonably expected from such operations. They will frequently hint at connections which get them access to police and other law enforcement files, or even those owned by national security agencies. In most countries this type of official data is not normally available to the private sector.

In practice, proper 'positive vetting' is an expensive business because of the amount of legwork and checking involved. Whilst there is a core of important and worthwhile personal data that can be assembled at low cost – credit-ratings, for example, can be obtained from large-scale services like TRW in the USA and CCN in the UK and are derived from information about the failure to complete previous credit transactions – up-to-date and accurate data about political affiliations and friendships is always costly. Even the FBI and MI5 are known to have had substantial inaccuracies in their files. *On the Record* by Duncan Campbell and Steve Connor reports two instances in 1977 where British MPs were the subject of adverse reports from MI5: one was Judith Hart, a Labour Minister for Overseas Development who was confused with a communist called Tudor Hart and the other was Dr David Owen, later to become Foreign Secretary and leader of the Social Democratic Party; he was mixed-up with Will Owen, an MP who had been charged – and acquitted – of an offence under the Official Secrets Acts. The authors quote other more recent cases of mistaken identity, this time involving private individuals. The problem for any agency collecting personal information is this: it takes very little effort to open a file based on a single report – a note from a previous employer, a newspaper clipping, and so on. The cost comes in checking that report, in finding additional supporting evidence, and in keeping the file updated.

No private organisation can afford to check and update information on large numbers of people on spec, yet there are companies and organisations that claim to offer their subscribers instant reports on individuals by phone. Employers that rely too heavily on such services are both gullible and foolish, the information thus gathered can't be complete, it may well be inaccurate, may have been obtained from illegal sources, and worthwhile potential employees may be needlessly excluded from consideration. If the employer is discovered to have used a disreputable vetting agency, there could be bad effects both on public perceptions about the company and in its relationship with its existing employees.

One British agency that has attracted a great deal of criticism over the years is the Economic League which at one stage claimed to have secret files on 250,000 British individuals – that is rather more than 1 per cent of the work-force. The Economic League is no ordinary commercial outfit; it has an annual budget of over £1,000,000 drawn from a number of prominent British companies – according to a Granada Television *World in Action* report in February 1987, some 2000 are known to have contributed to it over the last 15 years – and its aim is to uncover 'subversives in industry'. Unfortunately its definition of subversion appears to be very widely drawn and it will happily mark as 'unsuitable' individuals who are related to those whom they have identified as being involved in politically undesirable activities. In the same programme, a League official claimed that he could supply details on up to ten named individuals over the phone within three minutes, provided they lived locally, and on a nationwide basis, within half-an-hour. A bit of simple arithmetic shows why its files can't be taken seriously: it only spends £4 a year on collecting, verifying and maintaining each file. Even at £150 per 'special investigation' (as quoted to Granada investigators), that would amount to less than one man day's work at the current rate (plus expenses) charged by private investigators. By June 1989 criticism of the League had reached the point where many of its supporting companies had begun to feel embarrassed at being associated with it and were withdrawing their annual fees. Its General Secretary resigned.

If one of the low cost vetting agencies is employed and it produces an adverse report, the sensible course is to use such material as a reason to institute further enquiries, possibly asking the subject for clarification, and not as grounds for regarding such a person as instantly unsuitable.

A handful of private fraud investigators on both sides of the Atlantic offer positive vetting services in association with the employment of top executives or as part of 'due diligence' in financing deals; these will include talking to referees and associates of the subject; however their fees are high – New York-based Kroll Associates expect to bill a minimum of around $5000 per enquiry – and can usually only be justified in the most critical of circumstances. Kroll Associates and Barrick Security Group, which tends to concentrate its operations in the computer-and hitech-related area, also carry out embezzlement and industrial espionage investigations.

Monitoring during employment

In the chapter on fraud, page 105, we pointed to the 1986 Home Office report on commercial fraud where Dr Michael Levi identifies three groups of fraudsters:

1 Pre-planned fraudsters, who start out with the intention of defrauding
2 Intermediate planned fraudsters, who start out honestly but who later devise a fraud
3 Slippery-slope fraudsters, who never have a conscious intent to defraud but slip into it by recklessness.

Paying attention to CVs helps identify the pre-planners, but in-employment monitoring is necessary to detect the others, if they are employees.

Many of the computer fraud surveys comment on the extent to which typical perpertrators have been long-term employees of the victim. In the case of the payroll supervisor with no less than three separate simultaneous schemes to boost his earnings mentioned on page 226, he had been employed by the same firm for 20 years. What typically happens is that some significant change takes place in the circumstances of the individual so that committing a crime becomes an acceptable option. The usual reasons would include: changed career prospects, pressures of personal life, difficulties with personal budgeting, alcohol and drugs.

Good personnel practices suggest the use of, at a minimum, annual reviews of all staff. Normally these would be carried out to decide promotion prospects, but they can also be used to see if the individual has any growing pressures arising either from the job or in private life. There's no need for this to be unduly intrusive; the aim should be to identify the stresses before they become a problem.

No one is likely to object to this form of benevolent employee monitoring. However, from time to time in many organis-ations, it becomes apparent that an outbreak of theft or fraud or leakage of secrets is taking place and it will become necessary to consider forms of surveillance which are more intrusive. Most computer systems above the size of the desk-top micro have facilities for monitoring activity and these will be described in subsequent chapters, but there are some general principles which apply to all forms of employee surveillance, whether using computers, hidden cameras, bugs on telephones, or even rummaging in suspects' desks and lockers. What follows by way of advice is a synthesis of opinions gathered from a variety of private investigators, lawyers and insurers:

- the decision to use such tactics should not be taken lightly. Many managers regard such matters with distaste and give too much discretion to security officers; whilst there are plenty of competent professionals employed in internal security, few of them can see the consequences of a bungled or mishandled investigation in terms of its total impact on a company. There is also a significant minority of security men who have an unhelpful taste for a bit of action and others who derive an unhealthy pleasure from the opportunity to boss others around
- managers should seek to assemble the existing available evidence that wrong-doing is taking place and see how strong it actually is
- advice should be sought from lawyers as to:
  - what offences may be being committed
  - what remedies are likely to be available to management to deal with recalcitrant employees (disciplining, dismissal, civil procedures, criminal procedures)
  - what evidence is likely to be required before the remedies can be effectively used
  - what means can be used to gather evidence
  - what legal risks management run in the event of a faulty accusation (actions for wrongful dismissal, libel etc)
  - what the legal consequences may be in the event of non-action (a suit for negligence from a customer or client, accusations of mismanagement by a shareholder)
- in the absence of the potential of securing strong evidence and if the losses are not too great, management may have to decide that the most effective course is simply to issue warnings of strong action in the future
- an attempt should be made to narrow as far as possible the scope of any enquiry and any associated surveillance; if possible, a limit should be placed on the length of time an investigation should last

- managers should see if there are non-controversial methods of securing the desired evidence; for example, evidence may already exist within the company's own books in the form of invoices and contracts; thereafter, each escalation of surveillance should be the minimum necessary to accumulate the essential material efficiently
- managers should satisfy themselves about the quality of outside investigators employed; the possession of large quantities of exotic electronic surveillance equipment or hints at employment by national security agencies is no substitute for methodical professionalism
- once guilt is established to the point where dismissal is required, the employee(s) should be removed from the work-place forthwith
- managers should pay particular attention to the reactions of innocent staff who may be caught up in the investigation; managers should not embark on a course of action which they would be unable to justify to mainstream employees
- if at the end of an enquiry employees are disciplined, dismissed, or information sent to the police authorities, care should be taken to explain matters as fully as possible to employees and, where appropriate, to shareholders, customers and the press.

Personnel management is usually thought of as the unglamorous, even distasteful, aspect of information security. However, as an advertisement from IBM once pointed out, crimes are committed by people, not computers. The existence of a well-chosen and committed work-force is worth much more than all the access control and surveillance technologies put together. Not only will such employees be less likely to rip off their employers, they are more likely to report transgressions committed by their colleagues. A sound work-force is obtained not only by careful pre-employment vetting procedures; managers must have a genuine commitment to taking care of their employees in every sense.

Security awareness programs

In the remainder of this book are suggestions of suitable hardware- and software-based security precautions. However, if checking out the credentials of staff is the first line of defence for management, then the second line is to persuade and encourage staff themselves to take a pro-active attitude towards security. In other words, to demonstrate how an organisation can be damaged by fraud or information leakage, to invite their co-operation and to explain and justify the measures that have been introduced.

The process, if handled properly, can also address the problems of employee ethics raised in Chapter 7: which covert perks are acceptable, and which are not?

CHAPTER FOURTEEN

Methods III: Physical Controls

Half-way through 1986 I was approached by one of the companies for whom I was then doing consultancy to help them in a security review for an internationally known conglomerate that had recently been involved in take-over bids, both as a predator and as a victim.

The security company had done work for the conglomerate over a period of several years and had advised on the installation of appropriate physical protection. Particular attention had been given to procedures for handling visitors to the corporate headquarters. There was a two-stage welcome: the visitor first identified himself to a commissionaire who telephoned a receptionist on an upper floor. Once the commissionaire was satisfied, the visitor was asked to sign a book and then went up a floor by lift and emerged in front of a remotely-operated glass door through which the receptionist had a clear view. Once the receptionist was satisfied, the visitor was admitted to the reception desk and thence to a waiting area. Individual parts of the corporate headquarters were divided into areas separated by doors that required the use of specially-coded magnetic card-keys. Visitors, basically, needed to be accompanied wherever they went.

What my supervisor at the security company was concerned with, however, was computer security. He had obtained permission from his client's chief executive to attempt a hostile hack into the conglomerate's computers. Would I be interested in doing it? I could think of several reasons for not wanting the job. In the first place, external hacking relies heavily on the mistakes of others; normally people who have just ordered a security review take some trouble to clean up their act before the security consultants arrive. Then, always supposing I had managed to get in, it is often surprisingly easy to cause inadvertent damage. Clearly the point of the exercise was to leave some trace that I had been there, whereas many hackers are simply interested in tourism of the insides of interesting computers, and often leave no evidence of their visitation. What the client manifestly wouldn't want was damage to his computing facilities, even in a good cause. Lastly, as I told my supervisor, it seemed to me that hackers were a fairly low-level risk to his client compared with the chances of a simple walk-in job. If I were an unscrupulous industrial espionage agent, I would want to grab a few discs and perhaps try to bug some critical computer terminals.

Well, why didn't I try that? he asked me. I was both attracted and repelled by the offer. I had no experience in 'black bag' work and I had no wish to develop such skills in my career, and yet here was an interesting experience with a proper safety-net in case I failed. I spent some time on research – rather more, I suspect, than a professional would have done. I checked the building from the outside; I observed the procedures for handling visitors; I delved into the recent history of the conglomerate; I enquired about other tenants of the headquarters building and researched them out as well.

In the event, very little research was necessary. One morning, dressed rather more casually than is my norm and carrying a large item of equipment in the distinctive yellow livery of British Telecom, I went up to the commissionaire and said I wanted to check their data lines. 'You want Mr X,' said the commissionaire, 'I'll get him for you.' Mr X arrived, 'Have you come to move our termination points?' he asked. 'We are moving around internally; I asked for them to be moved weeks ago.' I shook my head and apologised for the disappointment. I brought out my cover story, mentioning one of the other tenants in the building and said, 'They have been getting intermittent interference on some of their data lines and we want to eliminate yours as a possible source, can I have a look?' I took some care not to *say* I was a BT engineer, I let everyone assume it. I had deliberately chosen an intermittent type of fault as this is the most difficult to find; in fact, you often don't find anything. Mr X swept me past the reception area, used his magnetic card identification a couple of times, and took me into the switching room. Here all the telephone lines, voice and data, were terminated. Here were the multiplexors and switches controlling the various terminals about the headquarters building. 'They come in here,' he waved vaguely, 'give me a shout if you need any information.' He then left me alone. The voice lines terminations were in a standard plastic wall box. I opened it up. Inside was a floor plan of the entire headquarters, prepared by one of the most expensive office design companies in the country. By each symbol for a desk were marked details of the telephones each person had. A little further along the wall were the terminations for the data-lines – they connected with other offices, factories and a computer bureau. On the bottom of each termination I left a small bright sticker with the name of the security consultancy that was employing me. I hadn't actually come to bug their lines, but it would have been easy to have done so – there was plenty of spare mains power for the bugs, a mass of wires so that only on a close physical inspection would the bugs have come to light; there was a window nearby through which the radio waves could have been transmitted. I moved out of the telecoms area and looked at the two PCs in the immediate area and decided to 'borrow' a disc or two to see if they contained any useful passwords to bigger computers.

All this had taken a few minutes. 'I can't see anything obvious at the moment,' I told Mr X, 'I hope it isn't necessary, but I may have to come back again.' 'That's okay,' he said. To prove it could be done, I went back a second time and, again, was whisked past all the 'visitor' security procedures. The problem of writing the report for the client's chief executive was to ensure that he didn't think that his telecoms man was uniquely bad, just average. I had simply updated the G K Chesterton story *The Invisible Man* in which Father Brown unmasks the villain disguised as a postman. 'Nobody ever notices postmen, somehow.' Physical security can be breached almost as easily as that.

The aims of physical security

The physical protection of computer equipment and its various peripherals used to be the meat of computer security: that was in the days when the mainframe ruled supreme. Today, when attention is focused on the value of the roles computer systems perform for their owners rather than the intrinsic value of the hardware, and when processing power and access to a computer is spread right through an organisation, protection of the physical incarnation is only a part of the total picture of securing information systems. Its particular concerns are:

- security from the conventional accidental hazards such as fire and flood
- security from theft of equipment and peripherals
- security from wilful damage
- security of magnetic and other storage media
- prevention of unauthorised access to a computer system via an unsecured terminal, or telephone line
- prevention of eavesdropping by any special technologies
- prevention of the introduction to the computer systems of unauthorised software or hardware, especially devices that could be used to compromise its performance

Generally speaking, the sources of these various hazards are:

- **natural events**, acts of God, failures of electricity supply, etc
- **employees**, requiring unauthorised access to a computer in order to execute a fraud or obtain materials for industrial espionage; or wishing to secure equipment which can be used or sold elsewhere; or wishing to induce a breakdown in order to secure some overtime; or wreaking revenge on the employer for some supposed wrong; or as part of an industrial dispute; or as an ideological statement
- **maintenance staff**, for the same reasons as employees might have

- **criminals**, hoping to acquire equipment and peripherals for re-sale★
- **vandals**, seeking to destroy equipment for amusement, in pursuit of an industrial dispute, or for ideological reasons. As we saw earlier, terrorists seem to prefer attacking the physical incarnation of a computer.

The concentric ring principle

In traditional books about computer security, the writer usually describes the problem – and its solution – in terms of the ground-plan of a medieval castle. The castle stands on a hill or open ground, surrounded by a moat full of water which butts on to high walls. Immediately within the walls are the less essential requirements of the community while the holy of holies, where the baron lives, is right in the middle, in the keep. To get to the baron, you must cross the moat, scale the walls, traverse the courtyard and finally storm the keep. The medieval castle is designed on the principle of concentric circles surrounding the elements that are regarded as most precious.

The concentric ring principle is still the foundation of the theory and practice of physical security and can be widely seen in operation on buildings and military establishments all over the world. The task of those who plan and survey physical security measures is to ensure that the levels of protection are adequate to the risks anticipated and that poor design doesn't result in illusory security, because the protective measures can in fact be easily circumvented.

In the days when corporate computing power was concentrated in a central mainframe, controlling physical access to it was relatively easy. You built a computer room complete with

★Although there have been criminals who specialised in stealing mainframe equipment, such as Jerry Neil Schneider (see p 50), the very small number of installations, all of which are known, and the small number of potential customers who could both buy the equipment and use it without going back to the manufacturer for support and service, has meant that theft of mainframes is rare. Most theft is of micros, which these days are just another item of office equipment.

double doors. Indeed physical protection formed a substantial part of the range of measures necessary to achieve security. Today, the computer system is spread all over the buildings owned by an organisation and, thanks to leased lines and dial-in ports, far beyond it as well. To put the problem at its crudest: there is little point in securing the main computer room against terrorist attack if, through any of a number of terminals or personal computers connected via dial-up telephone ports, someone can crash the computer or steal all the company's assets. More, it may well turn out that the most sensitive items of information are not to be found on a central mainframe at all, but on a single PC in the headquarters office, or on a group of PCs loosely linked together via a local area network in the corporate planning suite. There is a considerable temptation to lavish the largest amount of protection on the computer equipment that was the most expensive buy. In so far as you would not want a costly asset to be damaged, this is a reasonable approach; but in terms of protecting the business as a whole, the focus must be on the quality of the information held on each computer. The $2000 corporate PC may need much heavier security than the $1,000,000 warehouse inventory/order processing mainframe. The concentric ring model still holds good, but it needs to be extensively modified if it is to supply a proper recipe for physical security.

The revised principle is this: what really needs protecting are information (in the sense in which it was used in Chapter 12) and administrative processes, the compromise of which would cause immediate harm; although no one would want to see *any* part of a computer compromised or damaged, the emphasis has to be on those physical parts of a computer network that are most 'sensitive'. These might include:

- in a company that has to carry on non-stop operations, the mainframe (but a mainframe that simply processes orders in batch-mode may be rather less crucial)
- any terminals that give the user particularly high privileges on the system
- any terminals left 'open' with access to important system privileges or to critical information

- any terminals that can be abused to perpetrate a fraud
- any PCs that hold important files
- any specialist printers (eg for producing cheques or magnetic stripes or bar codes that can be recognised by machinery), the exploitation of which could lead to a fraud
- dial-in ports where people can attempt to access a computer from outside without being physically observed
- telex links
- fax links
- facilites for staff and service engineers to 'take over' the computer resources during maintenance
- data media containing software, current data and back-up data
- documentation
- print-outs

For each of the areas involved, you must see that they are protected by concentric rings – in other words, more than one independent level of protection with the second and subsequent ones nested inside the first. Physically based and software-based* protection methods often need to work together and support each other. Although you are immediately aiming to limit physical access, some of the barriers could take another form: for example, a vulnerable PC could be kept in a secure office – no one allowed entry without the right card, have a keylock to prevent the keyboard being used or disc drives opened, and have a password protection system. There could be rules that no work files were ever to be kept on a hard-disc and that discs had to be removed from the machine and kept in a special locked cabinet whenever the computer user left the room. Even here, there can be confusion about what must really be protected: if important work-files are always kept on removable media, then it is these that require the concentric rings, rather than the hardware.

Perhaps the most important ring of all is neither hardware

*See the next chapter.

nor software but is provided by the attitudes of employees who have received a proper security awareness program and understand *why* certain procedures are necessary. Essentially the reason I was able to beat the physical controls in the anecdote at the head of this chapter was that, whilst the company had selected the right equipment, the staff lacked sufficient concern for security matters.

Analysing Your Hardware

It is time, yet again, to return to the risk assessment process that was first described in Chapter 11. We have already identified the administrative processes that must be protected and in the chapter on controlling information, we identified the datasets associated with those processes. We must now bring in the last element: the physical locations where those processes take place (which machines, which networks, which terminals, which specialist peripherals) and the physical incarnation of the data and software (disc and tape drives, print-out). We must see how vulnerable these are to direct compromise.

The process is twofold: to obtain an inventory of the hardware and to seek to associate specific sensitive activities with each item. Having done that, one can examine the catalogue of devices able to protect the hardware at a physical level.

To complete the first part it is necessary to return to the overview provided in Chapter 8 and try to make sense of the system one wants to protect. As we saw, one of the most important things to realise is that systems which appear very similar in their outward activities can derive their functionality in very different ways. Superficially, a system based on a single large mainframe looks almost identical to one operating on a network of distributed processors: what you see is lots of vdus (and possibly printers) all performing various services. In the mainframe system, everything is centralised and the vdus are, in the jargon, 'dumb'. In a distributed system, a great deal of the processing is carried out in the machine right next to the operator and communication between various computers (for example to get further data, or to send messages) is done on an 'as necessary' basis. Increasingly, some analysts prefer to say that 'the network is the computer'; in other words, don't worry what is happening inside each piece of hardware, concern yourself with the traffic between them and the overall effects.

Most DP managers or systems installers can be relied upon to produce a diagram of the computer systems in use within an organisation. They should also be able to produce a list of the various information services and other administrative processes that are associated with each piece of equipment.* The security-conscious manager ought to take this away, build up some understanding of how it all fits together and then impose a hostile mind to determine areas of security weakness.

In a large, heavily-computerised organisation, such a diagram can look quite intimidating. The first task is to develop an overview:

1 Has the system got an obvious centre, perhaps in the form of a large mainframe or mini? This is the traditional sort of set-up; you would expect to see this organisation with requirements to keep very large accounts or stock control or a database.

2 If it has, is there simply one actual machine plus a series of supporting disc drives and printers, or is there a *cluster* of processors which work together and back each other up? Such an arrangement is increasingly common, particularly where large minicomputers are used.

3 Or, does the organisation have a series of departments each with their own computer systems?

---

*Many companies still have separate managers for Data Processing and Telecommunications. One of the consequences of this can be that no one has a single set of diagrams to show the inter-relationship of telecommunications and computer facilities. On one survey I was called in to, my colleagues and I spent three days examining a very large IBM installation which had had installed many of the standard security bells and whistles, both hardware and software. It was only at the end of the third day that we realised that the IBM kit was concerned mostly with the processing of internal material and that the company's main business was conducted via telex. The telex was connected by a message switch into the IBM mainframe, but the telex machines, which were under separate management, were completely outside the DP security rings. In fact, until we advised otherwise, they were located adjacent to a loading bay which was often open to passers-by for most of the day.

4 Or perhaps a series of departmental systems which are linked together via some network – this would be a form of *distributed processing*?

5 Or a hybrid system, where there is a mainframe and some satellite computers which are connected to it, and others which are not?

6 Are there small computer systems, perhaps desk-top PCs, which do not appear on the diagram?

For each of the items in the inventory you will require details of their physical location.

Next you must take the list of 'sensitive' processes that were identified during the risk assessment procedure and ask to be told which items of hardware are associated with which processes.*

The other feature to be watchful of are the vital points. In one sense, the whole of a computer system is a vital point for the organisation that uses it, but within the computer itself, some points are more vital than others. The theft or destruction of a single printer or vdu in a largish installation might be comparatively harmless; on the other hand, if someone gets physical access to the master console terminal (which is the location from which the system manager runs the entire operation), then all the services and secrets of the system may be compromised.

Hardware Vital points

```
*   no back-up
            system has to be 'non-stop'
            back-up takes some time to be put into operation
            no back-up of any kind
*   used to generate valuable output, eg
            EFT, cheques, other forms of money
                authorisations
*   needed for supervision of system
*   needed for maintenance
*   needed for access to system
            local
            remote
```

---

*See Chapter 11.

Generic problems: checklists

Although the security analysis approach advocated in this book eschews check-lists, there are certain items which always need careful reviewing:

Back-up facilities. How far is the hardware backed up? Is there a complete duplicate for everything and, in so far as there isn't, on what basis were the decisions made? Are the back-up facilities co-sited with the main services and, if they are, what would happen in the event of arson or some other physical calamity? How far does back-up rely on the performance of third parties? How quickly can the back-up be activated? If storage devices such as disc and tape drives are back-up, how easy is it to load them with up-to-date software and datafiles?

Power supplies. What happens if the power supply fails, for whatever reason? Is there, or should there be, an uninterruptable power supply (a stand-by generator or batteries)? How long before it comes into play and how long will it operate until normal supplies are resumed? Is the stand-by power co-sited with normal power? If deliberate physical action is taken against the usual power supply, what chances are there that the secondary supply will remain functional?

Telecommunications services. What sort of telecommunications services are essential for the information system's operation? Who supplies them? How far are they backed up? What level of non-availability is tolerable? Where do the services enter your building? Are they vulnerable at that point? How are they connected to your computers? Are there long cable runs or termination boxes which are susceptible to outside interference?

Access control facilities. Most access control facilities (for example, a facility for asking passwords) rely on software, but some use hardware methods, for example, magnetic cards, keys, dongles, dial-back modems etc. Do these seem satisfactory – who issues the hardware, how is it managed, what happens if a particular item is lost, or stolen?* Can the hardware device be easily circumvented, has it a 'by-pass' or 'master' facility?

---

*Access control facilities in general are dealt with in the next chapter.

Data and software storage procedures. Assuming that all data and software is properly backed up, how and where are the back-ups stored? Can they be got at to be destroyed? Is it the case that, whilst 'live' data is carefully protected, getting access to back-ups – and the opportunity to copy them – is easy?

PCs. Check out *each* personal computer within the organisation? What does each do? Who is responsible for it? Who uses it? Who sets it up and is first to be called when things go wrong? Is the machine in a physically secure location? Who orders new software? What are the back-up policies? The data storage policies? Is there a scheme for the external review of the way in which it is being used? Are there connections to a mainframe? Or to the outside world?

Networks. Are all or some of the computers linked together in some sort of network? How does this network operate? Is there some central supervisory entity, or is information just passed along as appropriate? Who is responsible for the running and security of the network? How far is it possible for information to be pulled off by by those who should not be seeing it?

Documentation, stationery. Internal documentation, explaining not only the working of software, but also the manual procedures that it supports, is one of the prizes sought by fraudster, industrial spy and hacker alike. How good is the documentation? Where is it kept? What are the issuing procedures? Are all copies individually numbered? What happens to obsolete versions – are they collected up and properly disposed of? What about 'sensitive' stationery supplies? Are they under good physical control? Are they individually numbered? What happens to 'spoils' and 'test runs'? Are appropriate logs kept?

Remote peripherals. Under the heading 'remote peripherals' are included cash-tills, magnetic and laser readers, warehouse monitoring devices, industrial counting and measuring devices, and some intelligent machines – anything, in fact that can send or collect information from a computer. Can any of these be made to read falsely? Can they be by-passed, or over-wound?

External suppliers and maintenance. Who has physical access to your facilities and is not on your permanent staff? Do you have a list? What do all these people do? How much do you know about them – and their employers? How are visits handled? Is there a way of physically limiting the areas into which they can move? Are all visits properly logged?

Physical security. Who in your organisation is charged with the responsibility of maintaining physical security? How far does this extend to computer- and network-related equipment? Do the security staff understand the relative importance of the various devices? Is responsibility divided between a 'physical' security officer and someone who handles just computers? What sort of relationship is supposed to exist between them? If there are disputes, who would resolve them? If there are areas that no one seems to take responsibility for, would you ever know?

The table below provides a series of questions you should have answers for to complete your analysis:

Analysing Your Hardware

Mainframe
     Single site?
     Existing security procedures – who manages?
     Physical access
     Back-up facilities
     Power supply services
     Telecommunications services
     Access control facilities
     Data control procedures
     Software control procedures
     Development procedures
     External contractors/suppliers

Mini
     Single site?
     Distributed processing?
     Existing security procedures – who manages?
     Physical access
     Back-up facilities
     Power supply services
     Telecommunications services
     Access control facilities
     Data control procedures
     Software control procedures
     Development procedures
     External contractors/suppliers

Network
    Wide-area/local area?
    Simple/hybrid?
    External contractors/suppliers
    Distributed processing?
    Existing security procedures – who manages?
    Telecommunications services
    Back-up facilities
    Power supply services
    Access control facilities
    Physical access
    Data control procedures
    Software control procedures
    Development procedures

Micro
    Who uses, who sets up, who manages?
    Existing security procedures – who manages?
    Physical access
    Data discs procedures
    Back-up facilities
    Power supply services
    Telecommunications services
    Access control facilities
    Software control procedures
    External contractors/suppliers

Locations
    central installations
    terminals
    connected PCs
    dial-in ports
    network nodes
    cash-tills, etc
    manufacturing monitoring devices
    warehouse monitoring devices

Measures

Having associated hardware and processes, we can now decide what forms of physical protection should be selected. As we saw in Chapter 11, the cost of a measure must be related to the level of damage that it is supposed to limit:

Visitor procedures. There should, even in the smallest offices and other work locations, be a properly thought-out visitor procedure. You should work out which areas you regard it as safe for visitors to move around in unattended. There should be definite barriers which indicate 'public' and 'private' areas, even if the barriers are only token. A visitor in a private area should immediately cause a query. All computer-related equipment, even of the lowliest status should be inaccessible from public areas, preferably not even in view. In a large office where there can be a proper receptionist, there should be a visitor's book and, if there is any possibility that visitors will move around unaccompanied a system to issue temporary passes should be in place.

The cost of these measures is negligible, but merely requires some planning and ensuring that staff understand the need to follow the laid-down procedures.

Locations. Every place where a computer, terminal, peripheral, telecommunications connection point or power supply is located should have at least one level of protection from the outside world. For each item of equipment there ought to be a list of authorised users or service engineers and it should be made as difficult as possible for anyone else to get near to the equipment without drawing attention to themselves. If it is practical, each item should be kept in a lockable room, which should be locked when empty. There should be a list of those authorised to be there alone.

Where it is not possible to place each item in a separate room, perhaps because the office is open plan or the equipment is located in a retail outlet, or warehouse, or factory, the equipment itself should be capable of being locked. If more than one person is authorised to use the equipment there should be a formal log kept of signing on and signing off, or of opening up and inspecting.

Terminals and PC. Each terminal and PC should have its individual list of authorised users and usages. There should be someone 'responsible' for each terminal or PC. 'Responsibility' means seeing that a terminal is not left 'open' when unattended and that a PC is closed down and its disc media secured (see below) when not in use. In the case of the PC 'responsibility' also implies knowing what the machine is being used for.

Today personal computers are only slightly more expensive than traditional 'dumb' terminals and many companies have installed PCs in traditional mainframe and mini environments because they can both act as terminals and provide, for very little additional cost, local processing. The existence of a disc drive on what used to be a dumb terminal means that files from the mainframe may be extremely easy to copy (see below). In some circumstances it may be wise to replace PCs with a dumb terminal or, as they are sometimes being called, discless workstations, which behave exactly like a PC and enjoy all the flexibility of one, but without having any local storage capacity. Discless workstations can also be used in local area networks where data storage is kept on a central device called a file-server.

Rooms. Equipment which is identified as 'vital point' must be kept in an appropriately guarded room with access controlled by a card-reader or combination-type key. If hostile physical attack is feared, a double-door procedure should be followed: any visitor should be required to pass through *two* doors before being admitted to any vital area.

Closed Circuit Television. Any equipment that is regarded as especially vulnerable and where it is not feasible for it to be under constant supervision can be over-viewed via a closed circuit television system.

Power supplies. Even if an organisation believes it has no enemies in the world, a back-up or uninterruptable power supply is a good idea. At its simplest, this is no more than a set of batteries which are kept charged up by the mains during normal times and which switch over as soon as the mains fail. More elaborate systems use stand-by generators.

Telecommunications. Any vital links should have some proper back-up; many of the professional information services used by the finance industry have duplicate leased lines for all terminals. As an alternative, a leased line can be backed up with dial-up line. However, dial-up lines of any kind are a security risk; whereas the connections on a leased line are permanent – one terminal to one port on a computer system, for example – a dial-up port will accept anyone with the right password.

Disc media. Particular attention must be given to the usage and storage of disc media. In an organisation with mainframes and large minis, regular staff do not have access to disc and tape media and a proper library and archive procedure should be in place. The acute problems are the ones associated with personal and desk-top computers.

Almost any disc or tape can be easily copied. Any file on a hard-disk can be copied onto a floppy disc. There is no way, short of physically searching all staff and visitors as they leave, to prevent the removal of discs from a building. All you can is make it more difficult and increase the moral pressure against copying:

- the issue of software and storage media should be kept in a log. A regular review of the log should indicate if abnormally large numbers of discs are being used up. Although this is a matter which will be covered in the next chapter, for each computer there ought to be a list of authorised software. The use of unauthorised software, even on a personal computer, should be discouraged
- all disc media should all bear some characteristic mark (perhaps a unique label) to indicate that their use is 'official'. The use of unofficial media should be discouraged
- in circumstances where sensitive data files are prepared, such material should not be kept permanently on hard-disc unless the size of each file makes storage on floppies difficult
- if such a procedure is not already in place, separate groups of information should be stored on separate floppies. This makes security classification easier; particularly sensitive material can be isolated and treated with special care
- floppy discs should always be kept in a locked drawer and not in open boxes.

Back-up procedures. The usual way of maintaining back-ups of files in various circumstances is shown in the following diagram:

The three-day rotational back-up scheme

Files	Days 1	2	3	4	5	6	7	8	9	10
Working	A	B	C	A	B	C	A	B	C	A
Off-site b/u		A	B	C	A	B	C	A	B	C
On-site b/u			A	B	C	A	B	C	A	B

Particular attention must be made to the storage and maintenance of back-up material. There is little point in taking elaborate precautions to restrict 'live' data discs if material only one day old can be easily borrowed.

Anti-eavesdropping. Most companies are unlikely to suffer from eavesdropping most of the time, but many may be under threat from time-to-time. There are plenty of precautions that can be taken without recourse to professional help:*

- require all service and maintenance men to provide evidence of who they are
- ensure that visitor procedures (see above) are carefully followed
- double-check that termination points for data lines, telephone lines, etc are not accessible except by authorised personnel
- double-check all modems, telex and fax machines and examine for evidence of physical interference
- taps require lines running away from them to a remote site where a tape-recorder may be located: are there any cables which appear to be recently installed and for which there is no obvious explanation?
- bugs require both a power source (though this may come from a phone line) and an antenna through which to

*These measures relate to devices used by private sector agencies; a rather wider armoury of techniques is available to the police and government.

transmit the captured signal. Radio signals cannot be transmitted through metal and are attenuated by steel-frame buildings. These considerations act as limits on the locations where bugs can be placed if they are to operate effectively

- bugs require a site where a receiver can be operated; can you identify convenient locations for such a receiver?
- the risks of eavesdropping by vdu radiation are at their greatest where there is a single vdu carrying information of great sensitivity. Although there are devices which claim either to restrict the amount of radiation or to mask it, careful siting of terminals away from windows and near the centre of buildings will maximise the benefits of the attenuating qualities of most buildings

'Sweeping' for bugs requires professional equipment and the knowledge how to use it.

This last table relates possible hazards to measures:

HAZARDS	MEASURES
natural events, acts of God, failures of electricity supply, etc	Back-up equipment, back-up sites, Back-up software, back-up data, Duplicated or uninterruptable power supply
employees,	
fraud	Physical location of terminals, Keyboard & equipment locks, Secured data media, Secured stationery supplies, Software controls (Chapter 15)
industrial espionage	Physical location of terminals, Keyboard & equipment locks, Secured data media, Secured stationery supplies, Software controls (Chapter 15)
equipment for re-sale	Physical location of equipment & peripherals
induced breakdown	Physical location of, and limited ac to, equipment
revenge	Physical location of, and limited ac to, equipment
industrial dispute	Physical location of, and limited ac to, equipment
ideological	Physical location of, and limtied ac to, equipment

maintenance staff
fraud
industrial espionage
equipment for re-sale
induced breakdown
revenge
industrial dispute
ideological

criminals,
equipment for re-sale

vandals,
amusement
industrial dispute
ideological

Same measures as for employees

Similar protection that would be used
protect other physical assets, plus
Ensure all data media, including hard
discs are regularly backed up and
stored elsewhere
Physical location of terminals,
Equipment sited to limit
eavesdropping
Keyboard & equipment locks
Secured data media,
Secured stationery supplies,
Software controls (Chapter 15)
Control of dial-in-ports
Sweeps for bugs

Good 'visitor' handling procedures
Careful pre-employment vetting
Careful in-employment monitoring

industrial espionage
professionals

CHAPTER FIFTEEN

Methods IV: Software Controls

Password systems and encryption of various kinds are the two devices that are most frequently associated with computer security. Too many people, alas, believe that they offer a total solution. In Chapter 11 I referred to the process by which people seek to obtain peace of mind about their computer systems by purchasing an item, any item – sometimes quite a costly item – that is somehow associated with computer security. The phenomenon is sometimes called the Magic Talisman Approach. Access control and encryption are the favourites, and often they are bought on the basis of claims about the number of alternative passwords or codes that must be tried before the system can be 'cracked'.

It is not as though these claims are invariably false; it is rather that, by answering what turns out to be the wrong question – 'Can the KGB or NSA or GCHQ break into my computer or read my private mail?', the purchaser is misled as to the level of protection actually obtained. Where computer security is breached at the software level, it is almost always because the existing facilities available to the system owner have not been used properly, or have been set up lazily. The most these devices can do is to support effective decisions that have already been made about the aims of the security program and policies. They won't make them for you. And, unfortunately, they can bring problems all of their own as well as solve the ones you think you already have. Of these the worst is to imbue a false sense of comfort. In previous chapters we have described how to audit an information system both in relation to the processes carried out and the data created and handled. We have also, in the previous chapter, looked at ways of protecting the hardware associated with various processes and forms of data storage. It is now time to look at software devices.

In fact there are four principal forms of protection available at the software level:

- operating system facilities
- access control software (in so far as this is a separate item and not intrinsic to the operating system)
- activity journals
- encryption (which may actually be implemented partly in hardware)

The first two of these are concerned with how individuals are admitted to a computer system and what they can do once they are in. The third is a method of recording events that take place within a computer; it is a tool to enable the reconstruction of history, should that be necessary and is a powerful deterrent to misuse. The last is designed to prevent unauthorised people from reading files in storage or in transit.

As with any form of protection, the methods selected must be related to what it is sought to safeguard:

- Can the devices support the level and complexity of information control required?
- How easy are they to administer?
- Does the administration encourage the taking of false cuts? Is it possible for users to cheat the system in order to save themselves bother?
- Is the expense involved commensurate with the level of risk that it is hoped to avoid?
- Do the methods chosen make significant extra demands on the existing hardware and software in use?

In order to judge the effectiveness of the various devices on offer and decide which are appropriate for a particular application, it is first necessary to see a little of how they work in relation to the more obvious processes that go on within a computer.

When you log on to a multi-user computer or network, you are usually presented with a 'welcome' sign which asks you to sign on and provide a password. If the computer recognises the name and password you are admitted to the machine. You may be aware that you are not seeing the whole of the contents of the machine, that you can only carry out certain processes and see certain types of information. As you go through the menus of choices of things you can be doing, you may find that you are told that certain choices are forbidden. Or, you may discover that the menus you see are more restricted, or different, from those that others see. How is this effect actually achieved? How is it set up? How far does the information protection that appears to exist actually extend?

Operating system facilities

A pick-proof, acetylene-torch-resistant lock is only as good as the door into which it is set. A half-metre-thick door with bolts traversing its length and width is only as good as the frame and wall into which it is set. In terms of computers, the fabric of the frame and wall is provided by the operating system. Some operating systems, particularly those on personal computers, some local area networks and some small minicomputers, are so flimsy in their provision for security that, without extensive modification, no add-on software-based lock is going to be much use.

The operating system provides the essential links between the central processor, the various storage devices, vdus, keyboards, printers, modems and other peripherals; it ensures that software and data can be loaded into memory, that data files can be created, read, modified, and deleted. In the case of multi-user and multi-tasking systems, it provides the first line of facilities to keep individual users separate and to maintain a track of their activities as they call up the various facilities and files the computer has to offer. It decides what happens if two people want to look at the same file, or if one person wants to alter a file while another is reading it.

In an ideal world, computer security ought to operate at a fundamental hardware level so that, no matter what, files are always and only to be found in specific identifiable physical locations on discs and tapes while individual users and individual tasks are only carried out by specific identifiable physical parts of the computer. Now, if you have a personal computer, which is nearly always a single user/single task device, and you keep that PC in a guarded physical place so that only one person ever has access to it, you have a secure computer. The trouble is, most larger-scale computer processes need to operate in a multi-user/multi-tasking way, so that information and processing resources can be shared between several people and departments. And, from a system design point-of-view, once you are sharing resources, it makes sense to try and give each user and each task as much of the total system resource as can at any one time be spared. It is this clash between, on the one hand, the requirements of security and on the other, the importance of sharing, that makes the writing of secure operating systems so difficult. We need to examine how security is obtained both in relation to active memory and to disc storage.

As we saw in Chapter 8, most operating systems break down into the following elements:

- the *kernel* which controls system hardware and performs various low-level functions
- the *command processor* which accepts instructions from the keyboard (or wherever) and sees that they are carried out – usually by sending requests to the kernel and supervising what emerges
- the *memory management unit* which decides what physical areas of memory each program, datafile, and user, may occupy
- the *scheduler* which decides on the order in which various tasks are performed

Single user/single tasking systems, like most of the current generation of desk-top PCs, don't of course require the last two features because, by definition, only one activity is going on at any time. The role of the memory management unit in a multi user/multi tasking system is to allocate chunks of memory to each task and to keep track of what is going on. In nearly all commercial computers, this allocation takes place dynamically; until very recently, computer memory was expensive and designers of operating systems wanted to use every last kilobyte to the greatest effect. As a result a great deal of effort was put into calculating exactly how little memory each user and each task required in order to operate effectively. Under this design philosophy, it was out of the question that a given physical location on a memory board (ie a specific row of memory chips) should ever be uniquely allocated to just one class of activity, or one user. In most operating systems, memory management is largely carried out by special chips: it is one of those computer activities where there is a particularly close interaction between hardware and software. Sometimes particular tasks have to be carried out in contiguous memory (in other words, in memory chips physically next to one another); sometimes the memory management unit allows an individual process to take place in memory chips scattered all over the circuit board. Memory management is an aspect of the operating system that most applications writers and system managers take for granted: the computer manufacturer simply gives them a specification (just as he does for the various functions of the cpu) and they decide to how to use it. In some operating systems it is possible to modify the behaviour of memory management by the use of the *scheduler* which allows the prioritising of certain tasks over others.

Turning now to the way in which data is stored on disc, as we saw in Chapters 8 and 10, space on discs is divided into a series of segments or sectors rather like a series of pigeon-holes arranged in a circular formation. In order to get maximum use of this space, files are very often not located in contiguous sectors but may be allocated to widely separated physical parts of the disc. The problem is this: in the normal course of the operation of applications software, files are constantly being opened, added to, modified, and closed. They keep varying in size. Take the file which contains the text for this chapter: as I write I not only add words so that every time I 'save' the file to disc I require more sectors in which to store the material, but I shift paragraphs around; I delete sections which are repetitive or which displease me. Each time I 'save', a new version of my file has to be written to disc and the old version deleted. (Actually, in the case of this particular word-processor, what really happens is that my previous version is automatically labelled as back-up – in case I want to correct something – so what is deleted is the *previous* back-up.) The same disc contains files for other chapters in the book. The operating system has to have a way of re-using sectors that have been deleted, otherwise there would be a colossal waste. The disc directory is the place where the operating system keeps a record of where all the files are. (In MS-DOS, you only see part of the directory on screen; one of the normally hidden elements is the File Allocation table which relates files to physical segments.) Again, there is conflict between maintaining security at a physical level and using the computer's resources economically.

The way in which multi-user operating systems try to obtain partitioning of users and security of files is by adding a series of concealed 'flags' to both the user name (or 'profile') and to the directory entry of files which can be set on (x) or off ('–'): eg

Files
    x——x–xx ——x–xxx

Users
    x——xxx x——x–xxx

The user's identity acts as a key which, if properly configured in terms of ons and offs, can turn the lock that exists on each file. The user profile must have a flag in an 'on' position to correspond to 'on's which have been set for the file authorisation. Even with only 8 'flags' you have the possibility of 256 combinations of exclusivity. In the case of files, the flagging can cover types of access – read, write, run, and so on. Each flag may be no more than binary digit in a particular position in an 8-bit group. This flagging is necessary not only to provide the obvious security facilities, but also to ensure that users don't find themselves clashing with each other.

Provided that this scheme is built deep into the operating system, then the arrangement has the potential of being reasonably secure.

It is also possible to attach flags to groups of files within a sub-directory.* Used properly, this ensures that there are

*See Chapter 8.

double locks on particularly sensitive files. For example, all computers have a series of files associated with system management and another series of powerful zap utilities which are necessary for system maintenance. Most of the more serious hacks of systems have been accomplished because ordinary users have been able to get access to these powerful facilities. A double lock, one on the individual files and one on the entire directory in which they are located can help stop this happening.

Access control software

In practice, most ordinary managers of computers would not use these flags directly, but would have a program which allowed them to call up the facilities provided and apply them in an easy-to-administer fashion to the particular requirements of a specific organisation. This is the function of access control software.

In Chapter 12 we came across a typical information control problem:

	DS A	DS B	DS C	DS D	DS E	DS F	DS G
Employee 1	–	r	rw	–	–	rw	–
Employee 2	–	–	w	–	–	r	–
Emloyee 3	–	r	aw	–	–	r	–
Employee 4	srw	rw	rw	rw	rw	rw	rw
Employee 6	r	–	rw	rw	–	–	–
Employee 7	–	r	r	r	rw	–	–
Employee 8	–	r	rw	–	rw	–	–
Employee 9	rw	rw	srw	r	rw	rw	–

In reality, an authorisation grid, if set out like this, would be much more complex: not only datasets but programs and entire sub-directories would be covered.

An access control program, which may be part of an operating system or may be an add-on, uses the hooks provided in the kernel and memory management unit of the operating system to allow a system administrator to define profiles for each user by asking him a series of questions about what he would like to happen. To simplify matters, there is often a 'group' facility so that a particular group of employees with similar requirements can be given the same, or almost the same, profile and also that groups of files all associated with similar processes can be given the same types of authorisation.

The access control program, and in particular the way in which the authorisation grid is set up and administered is both the first line of defence and the primary tool in computer security. Whereas there was a period in which the front end of an access control package (the sign-on screen) of some operating systems could be crashed (see page 217), today what counts is:

- The quality of the management thinking behind the authorisation grid of who is to see and use which information
- the quality of the software in responding to the variety of management needs and the ease of achieving them – and how well it locks into the operating system kernel
- the quality and level of authority of the individual(s) who administer the access control package

The process by which an individual is logged on to a system, has their password checked and is then admitted to the machine is a trivial exercise in programming; what counts is the administration of what goes on behind the on-screen activity:

- are passwords of appropriate length and complexity – too difficult to guess but not too difficult to remember?
- are passwords subject to compulsory change at suitably frequent periods?
- how many unsuccessful attempts at logging on are permitted before a line or terminal is disconnected – and how is the system administrator supposed to respond?
- are the facilities for setting up authorisation grids easy to administer? do they encourage the taking of short cuts which mean that some people have facilities they should not have, perhaps by the too-wide use of generic profiles?
- what happens if an authorised user locks themself out

accidentally, or forgets their current password? are there good procedures for re-awarding passwords and recording what has occurred?

Passwords are usually stored in a special file: normally they are in two parts, one defined by the system administrator and one by the user. In most advanced operating systems, the passwords are held in an encrypted form so that even the system manager, who will have the use of zap utilities allowing him to directly read all files on the system, won't be able to find out the complete password for any user.★

Access control facilities on PCs. There are a number of products on the market which aim to give access control facilities on personal computers. Generally speaking, MS-DOS, the standard operating system for the first generation of these machines, has no facilities for supporting security and many of the products can be easily circumvented. One very popular package could be turned off simply by typing in ‹ctrl› C at the right moment as the computer booted itself up. Others work by modifying MS-DOS so that certain standard in-built facili-

---

★Even the encryption of the file of passwords is not an absolute guarantee. One reasonably well-known technique for circumventing this is to write a supervisory program which monitors the keystrokes on all terminals and then writes the results away to a text file. The perpetrator can then examine the file later on to identify the keystrokes corresponding to the password which at that stage, of course, would not be encrypted. An alternative trick to break password encryption is to write a program containing an extensive list of frequently used passwords. The program sends the dummy passwords to the access control package, but also watches the encrypted file of real passwords and associated user identities. The program, as well as giving the 'hacker' a greater chance of obtaining admission, also collects together a series of valid passwords – together with, in each case, their encrypted form. This provides the basis from which, by reverse engineering, to derive entire encryption system. The way to prevent the writing of such programs is to ensure that the facilities to do so are well locked away in a sub-directory only accessible by a very few people who could be readily identified. Zap utilities can also be used, as we have already seen, to read files directly, by-passing both the applications program which is normally used to read them and any authorisation 'flags' that may have been set by an operating system. All the more reason to hide zap utilities in heavily-protected file directories or, better still, not to keep them on the system at all, and only install them each time they are actually required, and after logging their use.

ties, like copying and asking for directories, are removed and altering the kernel (a normally hidden file usually called IO.SYS) to require a password at a fairly early stage of the booting-up process. Most of these can be circumvented by replacing the modified MS-DOS with an ordinary version (of which there are millions of copies, worldwide) and booting up that way. The whole of the computer is then open. Nearly always, PCs can only be effectively secured by the combination of special hardware and software which interact and which also arrange for files to be encrypted (see below). Alternatively, if a hard disc is in use, software can be used to modify the operating system – but if that is done, the resulting files may be unusable on another machine . . . There's no shortage of computer products, you simply have to decide what you wish to protect against – and which essential business facilities you do not want to lose in the process.

Another factor to bear in mind is that with the PC, the security manager is typically the ordinary user, who may have no computer skills other than in one or two applications programs. There is no point in giving such people security packages of such sophistication and complexity that they are unable to use the facilities. In the end, settling for purely physical controls – keeping the PC in an office which is always locked when the authorised user is not present, forbidding the retention of sensitive files on hard disc and the locking away of floppy discs – may provide more achievable practical security than more 'elegant' security solutions.

Local area networks. LANS are usually built up from PCs which are connected together in various configurations. There are two principal forms: one in which all machines have the same status and merely have the capacity to share peripherals and send files to each other; and one where effective control is exercised from a central unit which contains both network supervision hardware and software and mass-storage in the form of large hard discs. Most LANs have some form of password protection but, as with other sorts of operating system, what counts is the availability of in-built software hooks upon which to base a proper protected authorisation grid.

Micro-mainframe links. A PC connected to a mainframe can be operating in a number of different ways:

- if it is simply acting as a replacement for a regular 'dumb' computer terminal, then security will depend entirely on the quality of the security systems implemented on the mainframe
- if it is acting as a simple PC, then there will be little or no security save as can be provided by limiting physical access to it
- if while connected to the mainframe, the PC is allowed to download files from the mainframe and hold them in its own memory and disc drives, then, without proper controls, a serious security loophole could exist. Information which was thought to be secure on the mainframe and subject to stringent authorisation procedures, could now be sitting on an easily removable, easily copyable PC disc. PCs linked to micros in this particular way must be subject to very careful physical control

Activity journals

An activity journal is a sub-program which monitors the movements of a user through a computer system. It can record to almost any level of detail, from simply recording when someone logged on to the system and then logged off, through listing out the files that have been viewed or called up, right down to recording every single key-stroke.

Activity journals have all sorts of functions not directly associated with security:

- they provide the core data for system accounting so that individual customers can be charged for their usage on a time connected or facilities used basis
- they are used by systems installers so that the actual time each process on a computer takes place can be calculated and the system fine-tuned
- they can be used as the basis of determining future computing requirements

- they can be used to measure employee productivity*

Journalising can be built into the computer system in a number of different ways: it may be part of an access control program; it may be part of an applications program, especially accounting-type packages, where it is inherently important to have checks and double-checks on purchases, sales, payments in and payments out; it may be an entirely independent package designed to monitor 'threats' to the computer system.

Journalising is an extremely important weapon in the computer security armoury because it enables events to be reconstructed; it is useful both in detective work after a suspicion of computer abuse and as a deterrent.** In some situations it can act as a substitute for the absence of other types of security protection. As we have already seen, much packaged software makes assumptions about who should see what, and in which circumstances. Often companies who use the software are unwilling to take the trouble to check that the assumptions suit their particular situation. Especially full journalising will provide a record of who had been using information and when. It may be cheaper to use full journalising than to carry out highly detailed analytic work to determine a proper information authorisation grid.

There is however, a substantial drawback to activity journalising: it is extremely resource-intensive. If a computer, in addition to running the program and handling the data that

*The fact that it is easy to monitor employee activity does not mean that it is necessarily a good idea to do so without considering the broader effects on staff/management relations.

**A striking example of the value of journalising occurred during the early investigations of the 1987 Irangate Affair in which officials of the US National Security Council deflected profits made from covert sales of arms to Iran into funding for the 'Contra' rebels of Nicaragua. Both the trading with Iran and the support for the Contras was in defiance of the expressed views of the US Congress. Operational memoranda about these activities had been maintained at the White House on an IBM office automation product called Profs. The senior officials most closely involved in Irangate shredded as much paper documentation as they could and also deleted files on Profs. However, they did not appreciate that Profs had a back-up procedure and as a result, the Tower Commission, the first of many bodies that were to investigate what happened, were able to examine much evidence that might otherwise have disappeared for ever.

is seen on-screen or that comes from a printer, has to record all activity, processing power may need to be doubled – or the substantive program could run at half-speed, which may be commercially unacceptable. The demands on storage media can, depending on the level of detail, be phenomenal.

In practice, therefore, judgments must be made about how far to use journalising. If, for example, it is being used as a substitute for other forms of security then it is possible to carry out rough calculations about the balance of advantage. In the case of a generic accounting package, it may cost £7000 in consultancy fees to check that the information control parameters are as they should be and to customise the package appropriately. £5000, however, may be more than adequate to purchase the additional hardware required to run activity journalising without slowing down the expected speed of the substantive program. Again, it may be only necessary to switch activity journalising on selectively, to supervise particularly sensitive activities or where there is a suspicion that malfeasance is taking place.*

There are specialist *threat monitoring* packages for large mainframes and minis; these are, in essence, specially tailored and tailorable activity journalising programs used by computer crime investigators. Once set up, they enable the monitoring of particular terminals or watch out for the use of particular passwords, or attempts to access particular files. They allow for supervisors to be alerted to unusual activity. Some of them can draw attention to the fact that a significant number of failed attempts to gain access to part of the computer seem to be occurring, and so on.

---

*Evidence obtained from activity journals may not necessarily be admissible as evidence in legal proceedings, particularly if the datacrime has taken the form in some way of tampering with the normal running of the computer. Some activity journals are maintained by separate computers the sole purpose of which are to monitor what goes on in the main system and, providing that these have not be interfered with, their output would be admissible. See Chapter 19, page 348 and 351.

Encryption

Nearly all advertisements for data encryption packages have sought to sell their product on the strength of the quality of the encryption algorithm. In an ordinary commercial situation, this is almost the least important feature. What counts is how easy the total system is to use effectively.

Encryption is worth using in two main situations:

- to ensure that data, if intercepted during transmission, cannot be read and understood
- to ensure that data stored on a disc to which several people may have access can only be read by those whom the original author intends should see the material

The encryption system, considered as a whole, is thus rather wider than the mere software or hardware product. These are the technical elements of the system:

the algorithm, the mathematical process or method used for processing the original plaintext into ciphertext
the key, which determines how the algorithm is to operate on the plaintext in each case. Usually the key that is used to encipher is the same as the one required to decipher but some systems have enciphering and deciphering keys which are completely different

Generally speaking, the more complex the algorithm and the longer the key, the more secure the encryption becomes, unless, that is, the encryption designer has committed some mathematical flaw and part of the algorithm is in fact redundant.*

Now for the human elements:

*Encryption can be achieved either in software of hardware. Hardware encryption is achieved through special chips. Software gives more flexibility in that keys and even algorithms can be changed more easily; hardware gives greater speed which can be important in situations like banking, where large amounts of information may need to be processed and transmitted. If it is desired to keep data on a computer stored in an encrypted form and decrypted only on demand, then, unless the whole process is to become unbearably slow, hardware encryption is essential.

the originator is the person who prepares the original plaintext, specifies the algorithm to be used in general and selects the key for each transmission or storage. The originator must see to it that the group of people who are to be *recipients* has a copy of the algorithm and some way of knowing what the key is to be in each case

At the originator end, the message or file must first exist in unenciphered form and, because of its sensitivity (or no one would be bothering with encryption anyway), access to it must be carefully guarded. This plaintext must then be enciphered. Again, particular care must be taken to guard physical access both to the algorithm, but also especially the key. The encrypted file, of course, requires very little physical security.

At the recipient end the ciphertext is processed and eventually comes out as plaintext.

The system is thus vulnerable at a number of points:

- the algorithm may end up in hostile hands or may be publicly available
- through slipshod procedures, the key, or range of possible keys, may become known to the enemy
- the plaintext or key may be acquired at the originator end, possibly as a result of carelessness
- the plaintext or key may be acquired at the recipient end, possibly as a result of carelessness

Viewed from this point-of-view, what a good encryption package should do is to *prevent* users from leaving around clues that may be helpful to an enemy. A greal deal of this can be done by the way in which the supervisory software prompts the user, eg:

Do you wish to destroy your plaintext? (Y/N)
Please do not use this particular key again

and so on. Unfortunately, too many encryption packages

encourage the writing of plaintext and ciphertext on the same disc, or allow keys to be stored next to algorithms.

There is another whole area where the use of encryption can be largely rendered pointless by lack of thought. Historically, most successful decrypts have been possible because the deciphering analysts had some clue as to the content of the material they were handling. They knew, for example, that the message must contain the name of an addressee, an originator and often locations for both. They might assume that particular words would be likely to recur. They might deduce content simply from length, or from the location of origination, or the time at which it was transmitted. Thus Gordon Welchman, one of the team that breached the Enigma machines during World War II: (*The Hut Six Story*, 1982):

> The machine as it was would have been impregnable if it had been used properly . . . at any time during the war, enforcement of a few minor security measures could have defeated us completely . . . That we managed to stay in the game until the end of the war was made possible only by a comedy of errors committed by the Germans, who failed in many ways to do what could and should have been done to protect the security of their communications.

Where encryption is used to encrypt files on a computer in order to ensure that unauthorised users don't read what they shouldn't, particular care has to be taken to see that algorithms and keys are not inadvertently left on the machine in places where they can be used.

But special problems attend the would-be user of computer systems that encrypt and decrypt files only when they are specifically asked for, in real-time. Encryption is a resource-intensive process and a word-processor or database that kept most of its files in encrypted form and decrypted on demand would be significantly slower than regular machines. Usually it is necessary to have additional hardware specifically for the encryption function.

HAZARDS	MEASURES
employees,	
fraud	Access control software
	Separation of duties
	Full journalising
	Secured data media
	Secured stationery supplies
	Limited access to important copying reading utilities
	Hardware controls (Chapter 14)
industrial espionage	Access control software
	Encryption as appropriate
	Full journalising
	Secured data media
	Secured print-outs
	Hardware controls (Chapter 14)
software for re-sale	Physical location of software media, Operating system limitation on copying utilities
	Full journalising
induced breakdown	Limited access to 'zap'-type utilities
	Full journalising
revenge	Limited access to 'zap'-type utilities
	Full journalising
industrial dispute	Limited access to 'zap'-type utilities
	Full journalising
ideological	Limited access to 'zap'-type utilities
	Full journalising
maintenance staff,	Same measures as for employees
fraud	
industrial espionage	
equipment for re-sale	
induced breakdown	
revenge	
industrial dispute	
ideological	
industrial espionage professionals	Access control software
	Encryption as appropriate
	Secured dial-in ports
	Full journalising
	Secured data media
	Secured print-outs
	Hardware controls (Chapter 14)
vandals,	Access control software
amusement	Encryption as appropriate
industrial dispute	Secured dial-in ports
ideological	Full journalising
	Hardware controls (Chapter 14)

CHAPTER SIXTEEN

Methods V: Controlling Fraud

In the report *The Incidence and Reporting of Commercial Fraud* prepared for the UK Home Office, The Police Foundation and Arthur Young in 1986, the author, Dr Michael Levi has this to say about how frauds are discovered:

> None of the frauds were detected by external auditors – an important point in the light of current policy discussions regarding the impact of obliging auditors to report – though many were discovered by routine internal audits. There was no consistent pattern in how the frauds came to light. The few frauds detected which involved directors or partners were detected because of (a) routine internal checks; (b) information from an ex-employee; and (c) when investors claimed interest and principal on money that was not there. The less senior management and accounting frauds were often discovered as a result of (a) routine checks of stock imbalances, or (b) chance queries from customers or from DHSS [Social Security] or Inland Revenue which prompted internal investigations. In some cases, discovery of the fraud was delayed by the failure of employees to report on variances in accordance with laid down procedures.

The UK Audit Commission in its rather limited surveys has come up with the following tables of method of discovery of fraud:

	1981	1984	1987
Internal control	28	40	48
Internal audit	4	9	13
External audit	1	–	–
Other means	34	23	52
Not disclosed	5	5	–
	67	77	118

Methods of seeking to restrict the amount of fraud an organisation can suffer from fall into a number of discrete headings:

- identifying the sorts of fraud to which the organisation could be susceptible
- selecting measures which will deter the perpetration of these frauds
- knowing how to detect fraud once it has taken place

Types of fraud

In Chapter 4 a description was given of common types of fraud and some attempt was made to develop a typology:

BY PERPETRATOR

Internal: Management
    Larcenous – no concealment
    Misrepresentation – falsified reality
    Manipulation of accounts
    Extortion

Internal: Staff
    Larcenous – no concealment
    Misrepresentation – falsified reality
    Manipulation of accounts
    Extortion

External: Business Contact
    Larcenous – no concealment
    Misrepresentation – falsified reality
    Manipulation of accounts
    Extortion

External: Opportunist Member of the Public or Criminal
    Larcenous – no concealment
    Misrepresentation – falsified reality
    Manipulationof accounts
    Extortion

Collusive
Employee and Outsider acting in concert
     Larcenous – no concealment
     Misrepresentation – falsified reality
     Manipulation of accounts
     Extortion

BY METHOD

Thefts – no concealment
A theft may not be concealed because:
- the victim's records will not disclose the loss
- although the loss is detected, there is insufficient evidence to point to any single perpetrator
- the victim condones the theft

Some thefts can't be concealed
Misrepresentation: falsified reality
The aim is to:
- hide or disguise an inventory discrepancy before, during or after a theft
- disguise, confuse or delay, identifying the thief
- enable the thief to obtain, or continue to obtain a dishonest advantage by deception

Manipulation of Accounts
This includes
- misrepresenting the value of physical inventory
- manipulating the company's books

Extortion and the use of force

For every business it is possible, if one is prepared to set out to do so, to identify particular points of weakness:

- cash transactions
- authorisations to make payments
- authorisations to move goods or release services
- payroll
- expenses claims

- commissions and discounts
- employment of casual staff
- mistake rectification/claims for damaged goods
- suspense accounts of any kind
- new, or extensively revised areas of business, or administrative procedures; often these are associated with computer-based facilities
- accounts staff
- computer operators
- management
- employees discontented of disaffected for any reason

Working from these traditional areas of weakness it is possible to home in on particular administrative procedures and see what can be done to strengthen and protect them.

Controlling before the event

The armoury of preventative measures includes the following:

Separation of duties. Job specifications should be designed to ensure that no single person can both authorise the making of payments and the receipt of goods, or the release of goods, or the acceptance of payment without receipts. Accounts staff should be concerned solely with the processing of payments; sales staff solely with the acquisition of orders; warehouse staff solely with the dispatch of goods; computer staff solely with the running of the electronic information systems; management staff solely with management.

Using twin-key authorisation for particularly sensitive procedures. Any transaction which involves an unusually large sum of money or a quantity of goods should require a counter-signature; if the transaction goes through a computer system, the counter-signature really ought to be confirmed via that system.

Using journalising. The function of journalising is to provide an adequate audit trail. To an extent it can be used as a substitute for other fraud control activities.

Checking the controls on input forms and direct methods of input into a computer. In very large numbers of 'computer frauds', the computer has worked faultlessly, or failed only in not spotting that misleading information was being fed into it. Whether someone is keying information direct into a computer or preparing a form which someone else uses in order to key information, great attention must be given to controlling what happens. Usually, the automatic numbering of each transaction together with journalising will provide adequate safeguards.

Controlling output forms and stationery. Official stationery can be used in forgery and other types of deception. Some output forms carry the authority to release goods or to make payment. All such forms should carry serial numbers. Test runs, training sessions and spoils should be properly logged.

Testing computer packages employed for the adequacy of the controls they provide. All computer programs used in a commercial environment, unless solely concerned with research work, should include extensive journalising. In the case of microcomputers, date-and-time stamping will come from the system clock. The facilities to re-set the clock should, if at all possible, be removed from the computer and only used when necessary, and after the event has been recorded in a written log. In an accounts package there should be several separate files from which an audit trail can be independently constructed. Word-processing packages should be administered so that automatic back-ups of all documents are kept for at least one year and for six years if there is any reference to contractual obligations.

If a new package is being used, particular care should be taken during initial installation when the company could be especially vulnerable as people may take advantage of the confusion; the usual advice to maintain the old system so far as possible for a while to run in parallel until problems have been identified and sorted out. Great care is required if the package has been custom-written, as there could be programming flaws.

Having good physical security on warehouses, etc. Most frauds require the acquisition of goods or cash as their final element. Deceiving or compromising a computer system is simply a step in this process. Good security on warehouses and other locations where goods are stored is an essential element in fraud prevention.

Having a system of internal audit. Very large numbers of frauds are detected as a result of routine stock checks and cash re-conciliations.

Having a good employee policy. All the surveys agree that at least 70 per cent of all fraud is committed by employees; the figure could be 90 per cent for computer-related fraud, depending on how you define the term. Well thought-out policies for recruitment, staff welfare, staff monitoring and security aware-ness are cited as among the most effective measures that can be taken. This theme is pursued in Chapter 20.

Detecting after the event

Almost all fraud investigators – policemen of all levels of senior-ity, accountants, private investigators – seem to agree on one thing: what counts is the investigator's 'nose'. In terms very similar to those used by the computer security surveyor men-tioned at the beginning of Chapter 13, there seems broad agree-ment that most investigations go through an initial process which is quite unmethodical. There are a number of common indicators that all is not well:

- people who appear to enjoy a more extravagant lifestyle than one might expect from their likely income must come under suspicion
- companies with poor internal accounting systems often not only do not know how much they owe and how much they own but may have a management that thrives on confusion as this gives opportunities for minor fiddles
- companies that are late in making statutory returns to the regulatory authorities
- situations where there appears to be a multiplicity of inter-locking companies with elements of common ownership but also trading extensively with each other
- employment situations where there is a considerable element of perks, covert rewards, large expense claims or cash-in-hand work

The important thing is not to forget the basic ingredients of information crime:

- opportunity to commit in terms of access and means of disposal
- technical skill to carry out the necessary concealment or deception methods
- a motivated individual or individuals

During an investigation, the following advice is particularly helpful during the early stage:

- Never overlook the obvious. The majority of frauds exploit glaring gaps in a system of control and leave obvious symptoms
- Look for deviations from the norms – never seek the most complex solution
- In a fraud, always concentrate on the weakest, most simple, point. Most frauds have three elements: theft act, conceal-ment and conversion. When suspected fraud appears unduly complex – the rule is 'follow the asset'
- If accounts have been manipulated or records destroyed, the person who is most likely to have carried out the act or had the opportunity is also likely to be responsible for the substantive act that the manipulation or destruction conceals
- See if there is any gossip among trade rivals or trade associ-ates which suggests that anything unusual might be going on: the availability of cheap supplies or spares on the market from a previously unknown source might be one indicator
- If, after an investigation of all available facts, guilt appears to point to one particular person, the chances are he is the guilty party

If these produce indeterminate results, there are methods with a little more rigour:

Order patterns, stock movement and stock loss patterns. The aim is to compare what a company was doing one or two years ago and to investigate if there had been any interruption to normal business; if there has, one wants a reason.

Examination of journals. Computer journals are examined for unusual activity. It is sometimes possible to carry out a compu-ter-aided search to look for, among other things, access at unusual times, an unusual number of transactions, the absence of expected transactions, breakdowns, spoils, mistake rectifications, unusual requests, an unusual number of failed accesses, or lost passwords.

Business ratios. These are ratios used by accountants and investment analysts to compare one company's activities with trade norms. For example, the current ratio, current assets divided by current liabilities, shows how far a company can meet its liabilities. An unusually long average collection period may indicate suppression of cash sales or opportunities for teaming and lading. An unusual turnover to inventory ratio may indicate a suppression of sales or an inflation of inventory.

Critical point auditing seeks to identify especially vulnerable areas in the perpetration of a fraud and to introduce additional checks on what could be happening. This could take the form of switching on additional computer journalising functions.

Created checks is one step further down the line; here the investigator takes a more active role and creates an opportunity for a fraud to take place, perhaps by marking money or goods. A less clandestine method is simply to introduce *spot checks* where unheralded audits of warehouse inventory or cash tills or paperwork are introduced, or where suspect staff are requested to submit to physical searches of their offices, desks, lockers and person.

Observation, if necessary by using closed-circuit television.

Some of these tests should be used with caution; often they will be insufficient to amount to the sort of evidence that can be produced in a court of law. At the most, they may form the basis of a suitable informal action against the perpetrator. However, legal advice should be sought before embarking on any course that might affect an employee's rights or which could give rise to an action for defamation of character. Some of these tests may also infringe employees' ideas of privacy and should only be used once definite results have been obtained from less sensitive testing methods.

There are particular problems with using evidence that has been obtained from a computer and it may be difficult to accumulate enough material to take full legal action. These matters will reappear in the next few chapters.

The consequences of a datacrime for a company may easily extend beyond the immediate harm of one individual incident as, rightly or not, many people think that to suffer such a crime indicates a weak and incompetent management. The next chapter addresses this specific issue.

CHAPTER SEVENTEEN

Limiting Damage

Sometime at the end of October 1984 a PR man employed by BT's Prestel service became aware that a popular national newspaper, the *Daily Mail*, had a lead for its front page: 'Codebusters spy on hidden royal messages.' The substance of the story was that 'three break-in experts – known as hackers' had managed to take almost complete control of the Prestel service. To demonstrate their success, they had been able to log on to the service under the password of the Duke of Edinburgh and had originated an electronic message under his name:

> I do so enjoy puzzles and games. Ta Ta. Pip! Pip!
> H R H Hacker

According to the newspaper story, they also managed to edit pages masquerading as one of Prestel's most prestigious publishers, *Financial Times International Financial Alert*

> FT NEWSFLASH!!!! £1 = $50

The story came at a bad time. Prestel had missed its highly-publicised targets for the number of users it had hoped to have connected by that date. Many of the original publisher-partners it had contracted with to provide services had left; new ones were coming along, but they were cautious. Prestel wanted to develop extensive electronic messaging services and to build up home banking, home shopping and to distribute large amounts of live information from the City's financial markets. It was extraordinarily vulnerable to crises of confidence. With all the benefit of hindsight, we can see how British Telecom consistently made all the wrong moves. Many computer crises which organisations will face will not come from hackers but, because Prestel's mishandling was so complete and because nearly all of the details came out in open court when two of the hackers involved were charged with forgery, it is worth spending some time in listing out their mistakes. There can be no doubt that the damage Prestel eventually suffered was considerably exacerbated by its own clumsiness and failure to think clearly what its priorities should be.[1]

There was nothing particularly wrong with the security facilities the Prestel system had, as it was delivered to those who had to operate it: users have to input a passnumber of fourteen digits before being admitted. They are given three tries; after the third they are disconnected and have to redial. Each *page* on Prestel (it is a page-orientated rather than file-orientated service) can be placed in any of a number of Closed User Groups which can be defined as to membership by Prestel staff or, for their own pages, by information publishers contracted to Prestel. However, like any other security system, it is only as good as those who administer it.

In December 1983, Prestel had received an assessment of BT's computer security prepared by the Manchester-based National Computing Centre; there is some dispute as to how far this report referred specifically to Prestel itself but in general it warned BT management that security awareness was low. In February 1984, one of the hackers found he was able to enter Prestel under the passnumber 2222222222 1234. No passnumber of this level of simplicity should have been allowed. He discovered he was logged on as a Prestel official and as such was a member of a number of exclusive Closed User Groups; among other things, he had access to hidden system information, including phone numbers to development computers. (In fact, though he didn't know it, some of this information was available, quite independently, on bulletin boards at the same time.) Between February and October the phone numbers to these computers remained unchanged. He and the friends he told could reach the log-on pages but, lacking passwords, could get no further. In early October, he discovered that the log-on page to the Gateway Test machine had written across it the system manager's password. This gave him access, not only to the Gateway Test machine at the most fundamental level, but also to the live public service. He and his colleagues spent two weeks exploring the extent of the breach they had discovered; among other things, they found they had access to *all* passwords for all users on the main public service, including those with the right to edit on the system. They informed BT (via an intermediary) on October 23rd. The following day BT appears to have told the intermediary that the matter was 'under control'.

Up to this point, the mistakes Prestel staff had made were all to do with extreme carelessness in handling security:

- they neglected to heed the warnings of the NCC about the poor level of computer security in December 1983
- they permitted a sensitive internal account to carry an 'obvious' pass-number
- they failed to realise that a phone number of their Gateway Test machine was published on bulletin boards – and was there for several months
- they tolerated a situation where the system-manager's pass-number to their development machine appeared on the log-on page so that all any caller had to do was copy it in order to gain admission
- the development machine held unnecessarily sensitive data which could be used on 'live' machines
- they failed to respond effectively when told privately of the security breach

In fact, the matter was not under control because the hackers – there were now four of them – could still enter the Prestel computers as they wanted. One of their number decided to tell the *Daily Mail* and, before running the story, the paper thought it ought to elicit a comment from Prestel. It is at this point that Prestel had to make some quick decisions about what their priorities should be and how, in consequence, they should act. One possibility for them would have been to issue a statement along the lines:

British Telecom is aware that a number of irresponsible individuals may have been able to access part of the Prestel facilities that are not normally available to ordinary users. British Telecom condemns such activities. It is not convinced that

> the *Daily Mail* story is entirely correct but is completing an
> urgent enquiry into what happened. If necessary, security
> procedures will be tightened up and, in so far as lapses by
> BT staff may have aided the situation, they will be disciplined.
>
> BT is not willing to discuss in public any specific security
> measures.

An unfortunate statement to have to make, but one that was
substantially true and which would effectively have killed off
press interest after a day or two. BT could have followed up
by testing the sincerity of the previously made offers of help
from the hackers and could have given their publisher-associates
a rather more detailed explanation in private.

Instead of this, Prestel appears to have fallen into a state of
high moral panic. On the day the story appeared, BT moved
into action and warned all users to change their passwords.
Thereafter the priority appears to have been to 'get' the hackers.
On the same day a call-logger was installed on the phone of
Robert Schifreen, the original discoverer of the 2222222222 1234
passnumber. This identified numbers dialled and the duration
of each call, but not the content. Four days afterwards a data-
logger was also attached; this machine captures the contents of
any data messages, but omits any conventional voice traffic.*
A call logger was attached to the phone of one of the others a
few days later still with a data-logger following shortly afterwards. Little attempt seems to have been made to ensure that
the substantive security loophole had been closed. The two
hackers continued to explore the system untroubled by the
security measures introduced by Prestel staff; Schifreen himself
appeared in silhouette on television a month later to demonstrate
Vampire, the device that monitors the port status of all the
Prestel computers and which should under no circumstances be
available to non-Prestel staff. By the third week of March 1985,
BT had accumulated enough evidence as a result of the taps
provided by the call-loggers and data-loggers to assemble

---

*Doubts have been expressed whether the use of what was in effect a tele-
phone tap without a properly issued warrant was quite legal; however the
events took place before the coming into force of the Interception of Communications Act 1985.

charges of forgery against the two; they, but not the others involved, were arrested and eventually charged.

A number of court appearances followed whilst evidence continued to be accumulated and assessed. Eventually there was a committal at a magistrates' court. On each of these occasions, there was considerable press interest and, no doubt, BT told themselves that the message that was coming over was 'Hackers Beware'. Equally strongly another message was being broadcast: 'Prestel has terrible security'.

Schifreen and his co-defendant Steve Gold were initially found guilty of forgery but, after hearings in the Court of Appeal and the House of Lords, the convictions were overturned. The view was expressed that, following the Lords' decision, English law was revealed as providing a 'Charter for Hackers' – an opinion shared by some hackers. In fact, the Lords' rejection of the forgery charge was extremely technical – forgery requires that an 'instrument' – piece of paper, a magnetic disc or somesuch, be manufactured. This does not happen when you type in a password which is immediately accepted by a computer. However, as we will see in the next chapter, there are plenty of remedies against most forms of computer crime under existing English law.

No one came well out of the sequence of events: the damage in terms of Prestel facilities abused during the hacks amounted to less than a few hundred pounds; the substantive damage was to Prestel's reputation and that they made worse by their actions; had they moved in time, no news story need ever have appeared. There may be additional reasons, but Prestel has not prospered and BT's 1987 strategy is to reposition the original concept by renaming it first BT Information Services and then parcelling it together with an electronic mail service under the joint name Dialcom, limiting the scope of its ambitions and changing the style of management. It was not only BT that suffered; one hacker lost his job and the other decided it was better to resign his; both had, by 1988, become computer journalists.

The two biggest mistakes BT made, once the breach was public and out of their control, were not to know what its priorities ought to be and not to have a disaster recovery plan.

Planning for disaster

A datacrime disaster can take many forms: it may be a phone call from a news organisation, it may be the discovery one morning that vast sums of money have disappeared, that a computer centre has been blown up, it could be an extorsive demand. The disaster may have happened in full public view; it may for the moment be private, but with the ever growing possibility that the matter becomes public. How should such a disaster be handled?

Any plan should revolve around five preoccupations:

- you must preserve the business as much as you can; any processes that have been stopped by the disaster must be re-started as soon as possible, if necessary by using stand-by equipment; all your actions must be directed to considering what the main goals of the business are
- some risks can be laid off by the taking out of appropriate insurance policies
- you should be able to identify a team of people with clear responsibilities to tide you over the crisis; some will see that the organisation's functions carry on as normal, some will be concerned with the recovery of damaged equipment, some with investigating what really happened, some with PR
- there could be extensive legal implications: a crime may have been committed, but contracts may have been broken, there could be civil liabilities to a variety of people and there may be insurance claims to be made. In all of these instances it is important that evidence of what has happened is accumulated
- if there is the slightest chance that matters become public, a carefully considered PR policy is essential to re-assure customers, trade associates, shareholders and the public

Above all, the aim must be to compartmentalise and contain the disaster so that as many of the organisation's regular staff can go about their normal business.

All companies that use computers ought to have computer disaster plans – for all those regular perils of fire, flood, electricity failure and equipment theft. Many of the plans that you put into operation for recovery from a datacrime disaster will be very similar to those for more natural calamities.

Disaster recovery plan

The aim of such a plan is to identify, in advance, priorities and to locate the resources needed after a disaster:

who needs to be involved?
internal staff
   disaster recovery team (see below)
   technicians and other line staff
external consultants
   lawyers
   auditors
   investigators
third-party suppliers
   hardware
   software
   comms links
   peripherals suppliers

what are the organisation's most important aims?
   which processes and products must be kept on the move?
   which customers and suppliers must be kept happy?
   is the mechanism for collecting, receiving and paying out money intact?
   does the organisation depend on having the confidence of customers, suppliers and the public?
   are shareholders nervous?

back-up files
   are there the usual arrangements for keeping back-ups?
   have these been damaged by recent events?
   how out-of-date is the last back-up?

stand-by equipment
   are there the usual arrangements for stand-by equipment?
   are they adequate?
   how soon can they be brought into being?
   what is the loss involved, in time, disruption to business, and money?

insurance cover

But extra considerations apply in the event of a datacrime: a number of the aims an organisation might set itself may conflict. Nowhere is this more likely than the twin requirements of keeping the business going and collecting evidence of what has happened.

DataCrime Recovery: immediate steps

Determine what has actually occurred
    accidental?
    deliberate?

Record all events as you discover what has happened and as you decide to take action

Pause before closing system down
    will system still function?
    is it possible evidence in temporary memory will be destroyed?

Decide whether act is in fact illegal before calling police
– do you need to call police immediately?

Attempt to determine level of sophistication

Attempt to produce preliminary list of suspects (or class of suspects) – do not make any accusations until you have full legal advice

Identify motives

Contact appropriate security staff, external consultants, if on retainer, perhaps lawyers

Identify any witnesses

Do not handle any evidence

Take advice from security consultant and EDP manager about possibility of re-starting normal operations

Take legal and other specialist advice before making any accusations

Locate insurance policy

Publicity

Time and again, a great deal of the damage organisations have suffered as a result of datacrimes has come, not so much from the immediate incident, as from the result of perceptions the rest of the world has had about the victim's level of competence and security. That some of these perceptions have been mistaken and the result of the general public's fear and lack of knowledge about 'computer crime' doesn't alter the quality and extent of the damage which can include:

- lack of confidence by customers and potential customers leading to lowering of turnover
- lack of confidence by trading partners leading to shorter and less good credit lines; perhaps earlier payment of debts and loans
- lack of confidence among investors leading to fall in share price; in extreme cases this can result in requests for swift management changes irrespective of what caused the 'computer crime' and to unwelcome take-over approaches
- anxiety among staff, both that suspicion may fall on them and that jobs may be lost. The anxiety may be quite prolonged if there are extensive internal investigations.

For these reasons, a carefully thought-out public relations policy is not an option but may be the difference between survival and death. No insurance policy covers an organisation for adverse publicity.

Public relations is not a question simply of 'putting the best face' on matters or employing some smooth press-massager; it requires an agenda of objectives. Even if you think it is possible that a particular incident may never become public, it is best to assume that somehow or other, a version of the truth will emerge. You must know how to handle it. Sometimes you may not even have this luxury, as when the organisation's management first hears of a calamity from the press.

There are a number of guidelines which can usefully be followed:

- decide who is in charge of PR; for preference it should

not be an organisation's chief executive, although he or she may be brought in to make a brief statement. The PR man should have the job of communicating to the press, both discovering how much they know and their level of interest as well as acting as the organisation's official voice. Everybody else should be forbidden to speak to the press but should be told to direct enquiries to the official PR man. All this is essential to prevent rumours and misunderstandings multiplying

- try and get the initiative as soon as possible. If news of the calamity emerges within the organisation, consider making a pre-emptive statement with angles that favour the organisation. If it is decided to wait and see if news leaks out, be ready with an explanation of the incident. If news comes from the press, ask for time to ascertain the facts in as rounded a fashion as possible, and use the time to work out a coherent strategy

- have a clear agenda of priorities in giving out news. The press's requirement is for as sensational a story as the facts appear to allow; an organisation's priorities are in maintaining the confidence of customers, trading partners, banks, investors and workforce. Each of these separate groups will need to hear different sorts of reassurance; it may be possible to use the press for this purpose, but more direct methods – phone calls, letters, and so on – may be more effective

- make sure that the PR man is given adequate technical information about the incidents and that he is competent to explain them to others. If getting to the bottom of the incident is taking time and the press are demanding explanations, tell them why the investigation appears to be moving slowly. Dismiss questions that are clearly speculative

- do not tell lies and do not make serious omissions from your explanations; if you do and you are caught out this will deepen the crisis, as no one will ever again believe what you say. What you can, and indeed should, do is present the events in context: if a computer has worked well but has been misled by the actions of an employee, say so. If a computer has had a breakdown but everything is fully backed up and duplicated, say so. If the potential loss is small in relation to the overall business, say so. If hackers, internal or external, have made a nuisance of themselves, explain that whilst the incident is regrettable, very little damage or breach of confidentiality actually occurred.

Wherever possible, seek to place the incident in as unimportant a light as possible; refer to other similar incidents and suggest that what has happened is an unfortunate but by no means abnormal hazard of doing business

- withholding a certain amount of information on the grounds of security is usually considered acceptable, provided that no information essential to assessing the level of damage to the company is later shown to have been withheld

It will, of course, be necessary to refrain from public comments that could impact on legal proceedings, either criminal or civil, or which could give rise to a claim for defamation.

It may be the case that the organisation acquires enough evidence to be able to lay information before the police or to bring a civil action of damages or breach of contract. In the case of suspected crimes, the 'upright citizen' advice is to report to the authorities and to support a prosecution. On reflection, this may not always be the best course:

- any court hearing will broadcast news of the incident; there is no guarantee that the story that emerges will show the organisation in a good light; indeed, because evidence is given under oath, all sorts of information about the company which it might prefer to keep to itself may come out
- because of the general absence of laws covering computer-related crime and in particular because of difficulties in handling computer-based evidence, any police investigation might be protracted, will involve many members of staff who could be employed in earning money for the company, may mean that vital computer resources are

kept unavailable while evidence is collected and may result in no prosecution following

- even if competent police investigators find what they regard as adequate evidence, the prosecuting authorities may decline to initiate a case; even if a case goes to court, there could be many hearings, at which senior company officials will be required, and the case could still fail at that point.

It is too easy for writers to suggest that victims should always prosecute; whilst the substantive law and the machinery of justice for computer-related crimes remains so inadequate, going to law can actually compound the victim's loss without offering much guarantee that perpetrators are punished or potential perpetrators deterred.

In England and Wales the police and Serious Fraud Office (see next chapter) have begun to recognise the necessity to encourage victims to report. They are doing so by offering discretion and promising that the mere *reporting* of suspicion to them will not inevitably lead to publicity. What remains to be seen is whether they actually deliver on these promises: the police and Serious Fraud Office have a dilemma when it comes to publicity. They also see it as a weapon in the fight against crime – every time there is a news headline to the effect that the police or SFO have swooped, they think, potential fraudsters are deterred.

Insurance

One of the most effective ways to limit exposure the financial consequences of any sort is to insure against those risks which cannot easily be eliminated by risk-control measures. There are a number of computer insurances on the market which address the various elements of exposure relating to computer systems, including property damage, business interruption and crime. A number of these forms of insurance were developed in the days when computers were in their infancy and these policies may not reflect the way in which businesses actually use computer-based information systems today. An organisation will probably need to arrange a number of separate policies to cover the variety of risks to which they are exposed. There are a number of risks for which no cover is available.

The following are traditional areas of available insurance coverage:

Physical damage, loss, through fire, flooding and other hazards. This type of cover is little different from that available to offices, factories, shops and the equipment therein contained. It is solely concerned with the physical incarnation of the computer and its peripherals. It includes:

- damage to hardware
- damage to data; it is assumed that back-ups are properly maintained, so that compensation would be for the media upon which the data is maintained, and for the costs of data restoration, including recent data for which there is no back-up. In some policies the cover for restoration of data appears in the 'business interruption' section.
- damage to blank media
- theft, of the physical incarnation of the computer, peripherals and disc media. Again, it is assumed that back-ups of data are available

Additional costs. Damage having occurred, there may be many short-term additional costs incurred to keep the business going and to avoid more serious loss of revenue or turnover. Typically insurance cover can handle these costs for periods up to six months. They would include the cost of hiring an alternate computer, temporary assistance from third-party suppliers, additional salaries and overtime for existing employees.

Interruption to business. The largest area of consequential loss is that due to loss of revenue or turnover, because the business is not able to function normally for a period following the damage. This type of insurance covers normal business operations and is usually calculated by estimating what the revenue or turnover would have been had the damage not occurred, comparing that with the revenue or turnover made in previous comparable business periods. There are very few computer-specific 'con. loss' policies available: insurances which make specific reference to losses that can only arise as a result of the failure of, or abuse of, a computer, such as software failure or logic bombs and viruses or the fall-out following a disruptive hack. One of the exceptions is the Lloyds Systems Perils Policy, but at the time of writing it is only available to financial institutions.

Fidelity. Fidelity insurance provides protection against the misbehaviour of employees and is the usual anti-embezzlement measure.

Employer's liability, occupier's liability. These are areas of standard business cover: employer's liability is for claims by employees for injury, disease, sickness or loss as a result of accidents at work or the working environment; occupier's liability covers claims by non-employees who suffer accident on the organisation's premises, provided that their presence there was lawful.

No insurances provide cover against industrial espionage, particularly if data has merely been copied and no data media has been stolen; in either eventuality, of course, insurance cover would be difficult to arrange since such losses are almost impossible to measure.

There are a number of specialist policies available for particular industries: financial services can use the Bankers' Blanket Bond and the Lloyds Electronic and Computer Crime Policy, and indeed this area is the one currently with the most highly developed sense of how computers and communications networks are used. Nevertheless these specialist covers only address the crime risks and there is still the need separately to insure the damage and interruption risks.

Many insurance companies and brokers are very interested in developing computer-related policies that are more comprehensive and reflect more accurately the increasing integration of computers within business. However, they are hampered by a lack of knowledge of how to assess risk in each case – and so set realistic premiums – and by the state of the law, which as

338

we will see in Chapter 18, has some difficulty in coping with evidence from computers.

CHAPTER EIGHTEEN

The Legal Response: The Law and the Police

In this penultimate chapter I want to move the subject-matter beyond the boundaries of the immediate concerns of managers seeking to limit the exposure of their organisations to data-crimes. It is time to consider what sort of laws, what sort of mechanism of justice and what sort of police force are necessary to cope with these new forms of crimes. It is time also to grasp the definitional difficulties any effective 'computer crime' law must tackle – beginning with defining what a 'computer' is.

In the Mercy College survey of 1985, 56 per cent of the participating companies said that they had experienced losses directly attributable to computer crime in the previous twelve months. In the Ernst & Whinney 1985 report *Attitudes of Companies in Britain to Fraud*, 56 per cent (by coincidence) said that they believed they had experienced fraud in the past or might do so in the future while 16 per cent thought they might be victims at the time they were being asked. Official US Federal publications have been prepared to lend credence to claims that computer crime is growing at the rate of 35 per cent per annum and that detected computer crime is as low as 1 per cent. The detailed examination of the surveys and claims that was undertaken in Chapter 3 should provide ample ammunition for doubting any of them, but at the very least there is evidence of the existence of considerable areas of wrong-doing and law-breaking that appear to bypass the machinery of justice. As we have seen, there are solid reasons why in the present circumstances it is often not worth the while of victims to report their troubles to the authorities; indeed taking the role of the upright citizen may actually compound the damage already suffered. It seems reasonable, therefore, to ask what should be 'done' about the situation.

The question, and the answers, are rather much more complicated than may at first be thought, for they go to the heart of issues about what you think the purpose of the law is, how the balance should be tilted between accused and alleged victim and what the public can reasonably expect of the police. Public attitudes to fraud in particular are highly ambiguous: condemnatory of its manifestation in general but capricious in deciding which of the many forms of fraud are the most serious. Can one blame the law – and the machinery for enforcing it – if it accurately reflects public equivocation?

One of the reasons why the earlier part of this book sought to place datacrime in a social and historic context is that, up to a point, datafraud, dataspying and datatheft are symptoms of profound changes that are taking place in the worlds of work and commerce. In the fifteen years between 1970 and 1985, the percentage of white collar workers rose from just over half of the working population to 65 per cent in both the USA and the UK, roughly a 1 per cent change each year. These figures conceal that in both blue-collar and white-collar occupations there have been considerable changes in the pattern of work. With them, as this book has tried to show, have come new opportunities for crime. On the face of it, in periods of such rapid social mutation, one would expect the law and the machinery of justice would need to respond rather rapidly.

Whilst the other chapters in this book have attempted to be as international in their appeal as possible, this chapter concentrates on the situation in England. One reason is that my own academic training, more than twenty years ago, was in English law, but there is a less self-centred justification. Although this book is not intended for lawyers,* I want to show the sort of policy arguments that must go on in most Western countries that try to tackle the problems; it seems to me they are more interesting if one can refer to specific legislation and institutions.

The arguments revolve around two areas: the extent to which existing law is adequate to cope with the changed circumstances of commercial life, and in particular the adequacy of the laws of evidence in relation to computer-based and computer-originated materials; and what sort of police force (using that term to

*The explanations of the law given here are for general guidance only; readers with specific problems must rely on professional advice.

embrace rather more than just those people who are actually policemen and women but to include inland revenue and other tax collectors as well as auditors) is required.

Three elements – the substantive law, the rules of evidence and the quality of the system of justice – have to support each other. There is little point in a fine-sounding set of 'computer crime' laws which are either so vague that no one is ever likely to be caught running foul of them or which require such difficult standards of proof that few prosecutions and court actions are likely to succeed. There is also little point in legislation which the police and the courts, through insufficiency of manpower, poor training and inadequate support, have difficulty in coping with. Or where victims think that results are so uncertain that they decide not to report what has happened to them.

There are really three attitudes which you can take towards producing laws which cope with the reality of datacrime:*

- you can introduce a set of new laws specifically labelled 'computer crime' legislation which assume that the situation with which we are presently faced is so radically different that few of the existing laws are adequate to deal with them. On the whole, this is the approach that has been widely favoured within the United States, both at a state and federal level. There is something of a tradition in the US for producing new laws for what are perceived to be new circumstances; two such examples are the concept of 'wire fraud', using a telecommunications device in pursuit of a fraud; and racketeering, which deals specifically with organised crime. It was an approach taken in an unsuccessful Private Member's Bill in England in 1989[1]

---

*In this next section I have drawn extensively from the Scottish Law Commission's *Consultative Memorandum* of 1986 and follow-up *Report* of 1987, the English Law Commission's Green and final Papers on *Computer Misuse* published in September 1988 and October 1989, the *Fraud Trials Committee Report*, 1986, chaired by Lord Roskill, *Some Legal Aspects of Computer Abuse*, by Andrew Tettenborn in The Company Lawyer Vol 2 No 4, the paper, *Legal Aspects of Computer Security*, produced by Colin Tapper, Reader in Law at Oxford University and a survey of legislation compiled by NCCCD, Los Angeles.

- you can suggest that existing laws are quite adequate. This is the line that appears to have been taken in the Netherlands and Belgium
- you can say that the present law needs extending and strengthening but that this means looking at a wide range of existing legislation and introducing a series of detailed reforms. There may or may not be a case for substantive new provisions. It is this view that has prevailed in Australia, Canada, Finland, France, West Germany, Sweden and to an extent in England

A broad distinction is made in most legal systems between the criminal law and civil remedies. In the first, activities are considered so appalling as to be an affront against society in general and it is the community at large that metes out punishment. Civil remedies are those available to one citizen who believes he has been wronged by another and where the courts adjudicate and adjust between them.

An examination of the present state of English law shows some of the problems would-be law reformers in most countries have to face.

How English criminal law copes

Many of the crimes described earlier in this book are straightforward examples of corporate fraud; the role of computer systems was to act as an aid in the deception. Often the computers themselves behaved faultlessly. The problem was to discover and then prove what happened. Where computers and peripherals suffer physical attack, the regular laws covering damage to property apply with no difficulty. All this leaves a number of outstanding areas where the application of the law is rather less clear:

Erasure or falsification of data or programs so as to obtain a pecuniary or other advantage. This, if you like, is one of the standard categories of computer crime. False data is fed into a computer which then passes it through so as to give a benefit to the perpetrator, or data is altered while in a computer, or programs are modified so that valid data is massaged to give the desired effect. English law has a number of existing weapons to bring to these situations. Many of them are only partially effective.

The first is Deception – under s 15 (4) of the Theft Act 1968: 'any deception (whether deliberate or reckless) by words or conduct as to a fact or as to law, including a deception as to the present intentions of the person using the deception or any other person'. The weakness of this provision is that it probably requires that a human mind be deceived. If the perpetrator gives an innocent person an instruction to enter something on to a computer which leads to a fraud, the section applies; if the perpetrator uses the computer direct, then no human may be deceived, and the section may not apply.

The next is False Accounting – under S 17 of the same Act, it is an offence to 'alter, conceal, destroy or falsify' any 'account or record or document made or required for any accounting purpose' with a view to gain for oneself or another, or loss to another. This could easily cover many of the typical frauds described in Chapter 7; unfortunately, the section only covers those records that are specifically for accounting; it would not include records kept for stock control, which is the prime target for warehouse and inventory-based frauds.

Forgery and uttering under the Forgery & Counterfeiting Act, 1981, can apply to material which is recorded or stored on a disc, tape or sound-track, but this recording must be more than a momentary process during the operation of a computer – something of permanence must come into existence.[2] It is probably the case that someone who uses a computer to make a 'false instrument', with the intention that he or another shall use it to induce another to accept it as genuine, and by reason of so accepting it to do or not to do some act to his own or another person's prejudice is guilty of forgery just as if the document were produced by other means. This would cover instances where the output of a computer has been manipulated, perhaps to print-out an authority to pay or to release goods. It could also cover word-processed letters which persuaded the reader that they ought to be completing the making of some commercial transaction. However, altering data within a computer which then processes it and subsequently issues a document which in turn causes a deception may not amount to forgery.

Then there is the offence of embezzlement, the felonious appropriation of property which is in the possession of the offender as trustee, agent, factor or other administrator. It is one of the main weapons against fraud by employees. Here the crime looks to the effect of the actions, rather than the actions themselves, and the principal problem, if a computer has been used, is to prove what has happened.

Obtaining unauthorised access to a computer. This can be either by an employee or by an outsider like an industrial espionage agent or hacker. Up to 1989, there has been no existing English legislation which aims directly at this problem. It had been thought that someone who uses a password to which they are not entitled is committing a forgery under the Forgery and Counterfeiting Act, but the result of the appeal in the Prince Phillip Prestel case seems to show that since no forged 'instrument' or 'document' ever exists, no forgery takes place.[2] However, it is possible that if a computer system required a magnetic or other identity card, and that was forged, securing a conviction might be easier. Even in this situation, however, it may be argued that since a computer is not a person, deception has not taken place.

Eavesdropping can take a number of forms: peeking over the shoulder of an authorised user of a computer and obtaining information, or a password, is not in itself an offence. Neither is listening at keyholes. Telephone tapping, in the sense of placing a direct tap onto a phone line is an offence under the Interception of Communications Act, 1985, whether it is a voice or a computer that is being intercepted. For a conviction, there has to be a strong evidential link between the tapping equipment and its installer. The offence concentrates on the fact of the interception, not on the information thereby obtained. Bugging, which implies the use of a radio transmitter to get the signal from the interception point to the eavesdropper, involves breach of the Wireless Telegraphy Acts, 1949 and 1967. However the level of proof required to secure a conviction is very high –

offenders nearly always have to be caught in the act and mere possession of the appropriate equipment is not an offence, which is why bugging is used with impunity in the UK.

Eavesdropping of radiation from vdus, other computer peripherals and even cpus probably involves no offence of any kind, as the Wireless Telegraphy Acts are concerned largely with radio transmissions that are intended, not accidental. (In fact, it is more likely that the *owner* of a vdu that radiates a signal is convicted for causing interference to others.)

Taking information without physical removal. If you remove a disc full of data or bundle of paper with information printed on it, the charge of which you can be convicted is theft of the disc or the paper. If you copy data from a computer onto your own disc or print-out, there is no theft. In English law 'theft' requires that property that is capable of being stolen is 'taken and carried away with the intention permanently of depriving the owner thereof'. The modern state of the law in regard to information theft was defined in 1978 when a student borrowed a proof of an exam paper, read it and then returned it. He was found not guilty.[3]

Unauthorised borrowing of computer discs or tapes. The distinction here is that the discs or tapes are actually taken away and then copied, prior to their return. Since the owner suffers no permanent deprivation, there is no offence. Although there is a provision to cover the 'borrowing' of property, it appears that it only applies if, in the course of the borrowing the original property has been damaged in some way. This is what the Court of Appeal concluded in a 1985 case involving the borrowing of material for two hours from which video tape material was generated. If the original is returned intact, there is no theft, notwithstanding the existence of large numbers of copies.[4]

However, protection of a limited kind for the victim may exist under S 21 of the Copyright Act, 1956, which imposes penalties (rather low ones) on any person who, knowing copyright subsists in a work, makes a copy for sale or hire, sells, or by way of trade exhibits in public. For a charge to succeed here, you have to show that there are copyrights in existence; easy enough for software, rather more difficult for data. The Act also contains a provision for copied material to be destroyed by order of the court; but this is an anti-piracy law, not one designed to protect against information theft.*

Making unauthorised use of computer time or facilities. This is another of the obvious 'big' crimes involving computers and again English law offers only partial solutions. The first of these is the offence of obtaining services by deception under s 1 of the Theft Act, 1978. The general view, however, is that the victim must be shown to have expected to be paid. The person who logs on to an electronic publisher's database under someone else's password would undoubtedly be found guilty, but if there is no tariff for the use of a machine, then proving that 'services' have been obtained could be rather more difficult.

The Telecommunications Act, 1984, which is primarily designed to cover the law as it affects telephone companies, has a section 42: a person who dishonestly obtains a service provided by means of a licensed telecommunications system with intent to avoid payment of any charge applicable to the provision of that service shall be guilty of an offence. This is essentially an anti phone-phreak provision, but it applies to telecommunications services, not to computers. Many of the crimes we have been describing have involved direct contact between the perpetrator and the computer; the provision would not apply if someone used the phone network – paying the appropriate rate – but then entered a computer in an unauthorised fashion.

You can steal electricity, and not only from the big Boards that supply it. S 13 of the Theft Act, 1968, was used by British Telecom against phone phreaks in the days before the Telecommunications Act, but it is a very indirect method of achieving the desired end.

In English law there is no equivalent of 'wire fraud' and also there is no general criminal offence in using someone else's

*The 1956 Act is being replaced.

property unlawfully,* though there are a number of individual, highly specific cases, such as joy-riding in a motor vehicle.

Malicious or reckless corruption of data or programs as a concept covers logic bombs and computer viruses as well as more direct and obvious types of destruction. English law recognises the crime of malicious damage under the Criminal Damage Act, 1971, but it is probably limited to damage to the media on which data is held rather than the data itself. Deliberately pour coffee on a floppy disc and your guilt is fairly clear; operate a program which wipes the data but leaves the floppy otherwise re-usable, and the courts may decide there is no offence. It may be slightly easier to gain acceptance for the idea of damage to software than damage to data. In an interesting 1986 case, someone erased a computer program from a plastic circuit card which was part of a computer-operated saw. The effect was to make the saw unusable.[5] This was held to be malicious damage. Again, if the damage to data has the consequence of causing damage to something physical, it is likely that the Criminal Damage Act, 1971, can then be successfully applied.

Denial of access to authorised users. A hacker, internal or external, or an extortionist, can seize control of a computer and then remove the passwords of authorised users, preventing them from logging on. This does not appear, of itself, to be a crime. However, depending on how the charge is framed, it could be criminal damage or, if extortion is involved – demanding money with menaces.

Conspiracy to defraud. English law has a rather unusual attitude towards conspiracy: if two or more people plan to do something 'unlawful' it is not necessary to show that any specific

---

*In English Law an act can be 'unlawful' without being 'illegal'. It is 'unlawful', for example, to enter on someone's land without their permission, but as such you commit no crime. The 'unlawful' element means the landowner can sue in the civil courts for trespass, but only if damage has occurred; it also means that if some accident befalls the unlawful visitor, the landowner is not liable. In contrast, the invited visitor can usually sue for damages. As will be seen later, some types of unauthorised access to computers is merely unlawful and not illegal.

crime has been committed. To take the example of the 'Prince Phillip' hackers: although no prosecution along these lines was ever launched, it would have been possible for British Telecom and the police to suggest that, although no offence or forgery was involved in their entry into the Prestel computer, the fact that they pooled information among themselves and that entry into the computer under passwords other than their own was not lawful, there was sufficient to make them guilty of conspiracy. In a case involving the borrowing of material in order to pirate videos, in the House of Lords the idea of conspiracy was upheld. However, academic comment on that case has suggested that an essential ingredient of conspiracy to defraud must be that the object was to cause loss to the victim, and if this is true, then the Prince Phillip hackers may not have been found guilty on such a charge.

Specific legislation. English law has a number of specific offences which cover the disclosure of certain types of information, whether in computer form or otherwise. Of these the most prominent are those in the Official Secrets Acts: policemen who are alleged to have sold information from the Police National Computer are usually charged under this provision.[6] Other legislation covers, among other things, the Atomic Energy Authority and some of the work of the European Economic Community.

Evidence in the criminal law. Until the arrival of the Police and Criminal Evidence Act, 1984, the presentation of computer-based evidence in court was not at all easy, although exceptions had been made for special situations like banking. In English law in general, any documentary evidence presented in court must be supported wherever possible, first-hand, by a witness. This is the requirement laid down by S 68 and it follows a long tradition of favouring evidence coming first-hand from human witnesses. S 69, however, provides an exception: if documentary records held on a computer cannot be presented in this fashion, it must be shown that 'there are no reasonable grounds for believing that the statement is inaccurate because of improper use of the computer' and that 'at all material times the computer was operating properly.' If the computer had some failure it must be shown 'that any respect in which it was not operating properly or was out of operation was not such as to affect the production of documents or the accuracy of its contents'. An expert witness is required to furnish a certificate to that effect and that witness faces a penalty for making statement known or thought to be untrue.

In practical terms, the Act provides defence lawyers with quite a bit of manoeuvre for shedding doubt on computer-based evidence: if the alleged crime was committed by manipulating the computer, how can one be certain that *any* evidence collected from the computer can be relied on? It is not clear at the moment whether the provisions of the Act reflect a proper balance between the interests of the accused and of the State and that what is needed is more experience in handling expert evidence or whether there needs to be some tilting in favour of one side or the other. The problem of expert evidence and the capacity of the courts – and jurors – to understand it is not unique to computing. One of the ideas explored by the *Fraud Trials Committee* under Lord Roskill was that trials of 'complex fraud' should no longer be held in front of regular juries but should use assessors advising a judge.

How English civil law copes

Civil protection of various sorts is available both against employees of the victim and third parties. Again, the coverage is less than complete.

Claims against employees. As we have seen, overwhelmingly the typical datacriminal is an employee, or contractor of the victim. In this situation, the principal civil protection the victim has is through the contract of employment which, in addition to its specific provisions can usually be extended to include some implied clauses. Such contracts would undoubtedly cover the right to dismiss staff for most of the offences described in this book, including misuse of computer resources for private benefit, revealing information confidential to the company, behaviour that showed so little care that it would be regarded as negligent, and malicious damage. The employee can be successfully sued even in the absence of specific contractual clauses, but you would probably need to show that the employee had a general obligation to behave in good faith and, if you can show breach of this, you could claim for any damage suffered, provided also you could demonstrate the damage was directly attributable to the breach of faith, provided that you persuade the courts of the precise monetary extent of the damage and, if it is a computer-based case, provided that acceptable evidence was forthcoming from the computer.

In particular, this general obligation to behave in good faith can cover information gathered by an employee in the course of employment and is a means of limiting employee-aided industrial espionage. The law of confidence extends to third parties: if someone acquired information knowing it to have been obtained via a breach of confidence, then they themselves are liable in damages. Further, the courts seem very willing to order injunctions preventing people from publishing information alleged to have been acquired by breach of confidence; so that a sufferer can sometimes get a gag ahead of a full hearing. The English law of confidence dates from a case in which Victoria and Albert successfully prevented the publication of private etchings which had been acquired by an employee; they were able to get the courts to act against the publisher.

In the alternative, you could sue the recalcitrant employee in the same way as any third party: using the torts of trespass or, if a duty of care can be shown, in negligence. Of course in all of these cases, what you can hope to extract from the perpetrator is limited by the extent of his personal wealth. In cases of large loss you would simply bankrupt him.

Claims against non-employees. The tort of Trespass is the usual route followed by plaintiffs who wish to claim for damage to property. Generally speaking, some element of physical interference or contact must be shown, so that whereas unauthorised access to a piece of land is trespass, unauthorised access to a computer is not.

The tort of Negligence requires that the offender has failed in a 'duty of care' which is owed to the victim. Both of these civil wrongs are well established in English law, and the basic standard of proof is only 'on the balance of probabilities'. However, as we will see, there are difficulties in introducing computer-based materials into court, particularly if there are grounds for believing that the computer has been interfered with.

Copyright law. Copyright law gives some protection against the loss of data and of software. Although there are criminal penalties for extreme infractions, the Copyright Act, 1956, and the Copyright (Computer Software) Act, 1985, are primarily concerned with giving remedies in the civil courts. The basic idea is that the plaintiff must show that there is in existence a 'work' in which copyright exists. Unlike what happens in the United States, there is no requirement to register a copyright: it is deemed to exist in, among other things, literary, dramatic, musical and artistic works and in sound recordings, cinematograph films, television and sound broadcasts and published editions. Since 1985 it also explicitly includes computer software. However there is considerable doubt that ordinary commercial documents can be considered 'works' of any kind, especially if there is no regular means of attaching a level of value to them. An internal memorandum would not be a work, neither would a mailing list, unless the company was in the habit of selling mailing lists on to third parties. To qualify as a 'work', it may be necessary to show that data is capable of being printed out so that it becomes a literary or artistic work. In any case, the extent of damage must be proved, because that is what the court will actually award.

Patent law. English patent law, in the 1977 Act, only covers 'inventions'. Software, let alone data, is explicitly excluded.

Trade secrets. English law does not recognise trade secrets as such, however you can bring an action for a breach of confidence to restrain the divulging by employees of any information obtained in the course of employment. The obligation, as we have seen, is said to 'travel' with the information, so that it can bind third parties.

Personal data held on computer. Here the person with the right to enforce is the individual whose data is maintained on computer and they can enforce that right against the computer owner for not taking care to keep the information secure.

Evidence in civil proceedings. Although the standard of proof in civil cases: 'on the balance of probabilities' is less onerous than that in criminal proceedings: 'beyond reasonable doubt', the test for the admissibility of computer-based evidence is tougher in civil cases. The requirements are laid down by the Civil Evidence Act, 1968 S 5 which says that in any civil proceedings a statement contained in a document produced by a computer shall, subject to the rules of court, be admissible as evidence of any fact stated therein of which direct oral evidence would be admissible, provided certain conditions are met. These conditions include: that the computer should have been regularly used for processing the type of information to be offered in evidence, that it should have been working properly during that period and that the evidence constituting the basis of the document should be of the sort normally supplied. Additional conditions apply if there are several computers working together. A certificate of compliance is required from a competent expert. It is not clear how far an activity journal* would be admitted in evidence, particularly as this may not be regarded as a 'normal' document. Activity journals can be one of the most effective methods of determining what has gone on within a computer.

Outstanding problems

What gaps does this survey of English criminal and civil law reveal, and how can they be plugged? During 1989 an extended public debate took place on the criminal aspects of computer misuse. Much of it was done in terms of 'hacking', a term that was used by different people to mean different things, so that the debate was less coherent than it might have been.

At the end, the Law Commission, the body responsible for suggesting legal reform measures, came up with proposals for three new offences:

*See Chapter 15, page 299.

- a 'basic' offence of unauthorised entry into a computer, to apply to anyone who, knowing he does not have authority to do so, seeks to enter a computer; the offence, punishable with a maximum of three months' imprisonment, applies whether the purpose was merely for fun or in order to interfere with a computer's working
- a more serious offence, punishable by up to five years' imprisonment, of unauthorised entry into a computer system with intent to commit, or assist the commission of, a serious crime. The idea of this offence is that it would be possible to convict someone even if they were unsuccessful in completing the intended serious crime, such as theft, blackmail or manslaughter
- a further serious offence of intentionally, and without authority, altering computer-held data or programs. This would also attract a maximum of five years in prison. This offence was designed to overcome weaknesses in the law of criminal damage as it applies to computers, and also to attempt to nail the writers of viruses who might have placed a destructive program in general circulation without necessarily aiming at a specific computer.

At the time this book went to press, the proposals had been broadly welcomed but there was neither a draft bill nor a legislative program.

The proposals fill in many of the gaps that had been perceived in English law and do so in an elegant way, dovetailing neatly with existing law. There are, however, still a number of gaps.

Making unauthorised use of computer time or facilities. In the criminal law, an offence can usually only succeed if 'services' have been stolen and it is necessary to show that these services have some agreed value. There is an offence of stealing electricity, but the punishment for that would presumably have to relate to the amount of *electricity* stolen and not to the value of the computer's processing time or data. The new 'basic' offence does not cover the situation of the person – typically an employee – who has authorised access but uses computer facilities in an unauthorised manner, for example running private programs or using a word-processor for personal correspondence.

Taking information without physical removal. The central problem here is that English law does not recognise the concept of theft of information. This is why industrial espionage, whether based on computer data, on paper-borne material, or held in someone's memory, is not an offence. The closest we get is in the law of confidence where the original breach must be committed by an employee with a general obligation to behave in good faith and where people who subsequently handle the information are aware that it must have been acquired by breach of confidence. However not only does the law of confidence exclude industrially secret information obtained by non-employees, the law itself is articulated not in clear Acts of Parliament but by a series of judge-made common law cases which have been frequently subjected to re-interpretation.

If we believe that information must now be regarded as an asset of businesses – there are enough people earning their living by producing and selling it – then it is time that English law looked seriously at giving it proper recognition. Other jurisdictions have not found the problems insuperable. Within the EEC, the Netherlands has a well-established concept of information crime and in West Germany industrial espionage is part of the Law of Economic Crime which has been developing since 1976. In fact, by 1986 it had been decided that it was no longer necessary to show that the secrets were actually used or sold by the industrial espionage agent, merely that they had been acquired; in addition, it had become an offence for third parties to make use of secrets originally obtained without authorisation. Finally, the law was strengthened so that it was no longer necessary for a victim to make a complaint: prosecution can take place simply in the public interest.

The problem is really to decide how the law ought to define an 'industrial secret' so as to give the company or individual protection without making the coverage so wide that, as sometimes happens under the Official Secrets Act, the owner can use the law to avoid revealing that which ought to be out in the public domain, or which might place an undue limit on the freedom of his employees.

Unauthorised borrowing of computer discs or tapes. Here again, there is no offence of theft, since there is no permanent deprivation. An offence of stealing information could be extended to cover unauthorised borrowing, but another approach would be to look to the damage that the victim suffers as a result of the event, so that the focus of the crime is not simply the fact of theft, but the theft plus demonstrable loss.

Eavesdropping. English law does not tackle the issue of eavesdropping directly either and some writers have suggested that specific legislation, covering old fashioned listening at keyholes as well as more modern techniques such as capturing vdu radiation, should be introduced. Again, the problem is what sort of test the law would require in order to demonstrate that eavesdropping has taken place. As we have seen, bugging by private detectives (or anyone else) is already illegal under the Wireless Telegraphy Acts; prosecutions are rare because of the standards of proof. One way of changing the present position would be to allow a prosecutor to suggest that, if someone has information which they could only have obtained via eavesdropping and can be shown to have had access to equipment appropriate to the circumstances, then the court is entitled to assume that eavesdropping has in fact taken place.

A quite different route would be to ban the manufacture, import, sale and possession of eavesdropping equipment. However, if US experience is anything to go by, many of the more popular and useful devices would simply be renamed as baby alarms, home security devices, telephone circuit testers and wireless microphones.

Civil Remedies. The Law Commission's 1989 Report was limited to the criminal law. One recommendation which they were not able to consider was the creation of a new tort (civil wrong) of computer trespass. Trespass – unauthorised access – to land requires physical entry whereas computer trespass would need to be defined differently. But the aim would be the same:

to provide victims with a civil remedy which relates directly to the amount of damage actually done.

Tilting the rules of evidence. Few of these amendments of the existing law and proposals for new laws will have much meaning if prosecutors and plaintiffs discover that their cases can be lost on questions of the admissibility of evidence. At the moment the criminal law, and to an even greater extent the civil law, requires that any evidence accepted from a computer must be accompanied by a certificate that at all times the computer (or that part of it which is relevant to the facts) has behaved normally. It is an entirely legitimate tactic for defence lawyers to seek to suggest that, since the computer has obviously been interfered with, *no* evidence from it can be admitted. At the moment, very few people accused of computer-related crimes do anything other than plead guilty. In the case of trials in front of a jury, there is the additional problem of presenting quite complex technical arguments to a lay public. The German Economic Crime courts are specialised and use the assistance of assessors. Yet the English legal system has recently rejected suggestions that complex fraud should be handled by special courts and there is a very powerful commitment towards the lay jury. Tilting the balance of the rules of evidence in favour of the victim is fraught with difficulty; no one wants a situation in which a prosecution witness is able to stand up in court and say, in effect, 'This person is guilty because, based on my experience, I have a sincere gut feeling that he is.'

Duty to disclose incidents of computer crime. It is widely believed that large numbers of computer crimes are deliberately concealed by victims and that there should be a duty to disclose all incidents. Indeed the US state of Georgia has just such a requirement. The argument in favour is that there really should not be an option whether a crime, which is by definition an offence against the whole community, is reported. One advantage of compulsory reporting is that it would make the statistics much more reliable.

However, there are two arguments against: first, in circumstances where victims really prefer to conceal the damage for fear of undermining confidence, the existence of a law of disclosure can provide an additional means of blackmail by the perpetrator. Secondly, large numbers of crimes of all kinds are, not so much concealed, as not reported, largely because the victims can't see that benefit will flow or consider that the police would not be able to do anything.

The theme of the role and effectiveness of the police is our next concern.

Policing datacrime

For a number of years now, senior policemen have gone to some trouble to explain that the public expect too much of police forces. There is a straight conflict between the demand that *all* incidents of crime be solved by the police and the desire to keep police strength down to numbers which are economically affordable and to maintain routine police presence at levels which, at the very least, are not intrusive to ordinary members of the public as they go about their normal affairs. What the police in fact do is attend to the very worst criminal excesses – no murder, serious assault, major theft will occur without being exhaustively investigated. In 1986, 92 per cent of homicides were cleared up, 71 per cent of offences against the person and 62 per cent of reported rapes. The police will investigate matters of major public concern, such as persons missing in mysterious circumstances. They will assist and indeed direct in major emergencies. They will see that road traffic flows freely. They have an important role in public order and it is felt vital that nothing approaching a riot should go uncontrolled. But after these main headings of what is essential, how far any of the many other crimes that are committed are tackled is a matter not of essence but of policy. And the police determine their priorities, by and large, as a result of what they think the public would like them to do.

One of the main problems the police have to face are the competing suggestions as to what is urgent: should it be theft from domestic dwellings, or muggings, or shop-lifters, or protection rackets, or robbery with violence, or drugs (and if so, which drugs), or vice, or drunk driving, or speeding, or untidy parking? Having decided a category is urgent, how do you tackle it? Are you after convictions for all those that commit offences? Do you want a high clear-up rate? Or do you want enough convictions to act as a deterrent? Or do you concentrate your activities on preventative measures, encouraging potential victims to protect themselves? The police do not have an entirely free hand in deciding the best use of the resources at their disposal: the public and politicians can *demand* a high clear up rate in particular categories of crime, even though the only realistic way in which this could be achieved is by pulling officers away from other activities. Even if the police had more self-determination there is no indication that senior officers would find it particularly easy to move their men and women away from the exciting action-orientated work of 'catching villains' to what may be more cost-effective areas of public education in crime prevention. The local Crime Prevention Officer does not always enjoy particularly high status and joining the Fraud Squad is not necessarily regarded as a particularly good career move.

There are further limitations in terms of what it is feasible to expect of the police. Like any other institution, they are a product of their history: they were formed to combat street crime and maintain public order. The way most of them are recruited, the emphases in training, and indeed their internal culture all continue to point to a strong emphasis on street crime. Perhaps it is unreasonable to expect that these self-same people can be transformed into effective operators in the office-bound world in which corporate and middle-class crime take place.

This explanation is necessary before one launches into a criticism of police effort in tackling datacrime; in faulting the police one must also include a massive reproach to the public. In England and Wales in 1988 there were approximately 144,000 police officers spread over 43 separate police forces. Of these, less than 600 belonged to specific fraud squads, perhaps 5 per cent of the total number of CID (criminal investigation) officers. Of the 600, less than 150 belonged to the Metropolitan Police Force (total strength 27,000) and just over 60 came from the City of London Police. The Met and the City run a joint fraud operation called the Metropolitan and City Company Fraud Branch, colloquially named 'The Fraud Squad'. It has been in existence since 1946. In 1984 they knew about frauds worth £867m; if insurance industry figures that only 30 per cent of employee fraud is reported to the police are correct, the total amount of London-based fraud could be in excess of £2,000m. However, the total 'recorded' figure was three times the total cost of all other property crimes in London. In fact, looking at England and Wales as a whole, the combined cost of theft, burglary and robbery was only £1,015m. The Fraud Squad has specialised groups that include cheque frauds, investment-related frauds, non-investment-related frauds, public sector corruption and intelligence. In June 1988 anonymous Fraud Squad officers from Scotland Yard were complaining to journalists that large numbers of officers were being tied up in a handful of big cases, including the then running Guinness affair.

Those officers who are drawn from the Met side of the operation usually serve a total of three years. This is part of a policy introduced by a former Metropolitan Commissioner, Sir Robert Mark. Mark had had to deal with a force in which there was a great deal of corruption in a number of the specialist squads, particularly those dealing with vice and serious crime. The basis of his reform was the idea of the 'all-round copper', that nearly all officers should have experience of all aspects of police work and in particular that there should be regular movement between the uniformed branch and those in plain clothes. The reforms, very necessary at the time, have been at the expense of building up specialised expertise.[7]

The Fraud Squad has a Computer Crime Unit run, in 1989, by a Detective Superintendent and three officers. At any one time, one or more of these may be seconded to other duties. One of their recent achievements has been to set up a specialist training course at the Bramshill Police College in Hampshire. It lasts four weeks and concentrates on how to extract information from a computer. By the beginning of 1987, apparently, a total of 18 officers, nationwide, had attended. By mid 1989 less than 100 officers had been through it. Most regional fraud squads did not have a single officer trained even to a basic level in tackling computer-related crime. At this very low level of manpower it is entirely idle to indulge in discussion whether police effort should be concentrated on how far officers should go out and attempt to detect crime in progress, carry out a program of preventative education, or simply react when someone decides to report an alleged crime to them.

There are a few elements which ameliorate this dire story. The police are anxious for the public to know that, as an organisation, they make considerable use of computers both for operations and administration. All officers are familiar with a variety of computers as users. Again, the police say that they can call on the aid of civilian staff or outsiders for help in particular investigations. The size and exact competence of this civilian support is not publicly known, nor how much they have in fact been used in recent years. The political problem senior police officers have in reconciling conflicting public demands for how they use their men is shown in the following statistic: whilst computer crime in London claimed, at most 5 officers for the year 1986, just one major industrial clash, the picketing outside News International's Wapping print plant, used up the equivalent of 350 man-years.

The police are not the only people who investigate fraud. 'Serious' fraud is, under a scheme which started in 1988, investigated by the Serious Fraud Office, a compromise product of one of the recommendations of the Roskill Report. The definition of 'serious' is – frauds where over £1m is at risk and frauds of a lesser amount that are of particular complexity or sensitivity. Run by a former Deputy Director of Public Prosecutions in July 1989 it had 20 posts of lawyers, 17 accountants and a support staff of 25. Twenty police officers from the City of London force are likely to be on *ad hoc* secondment for crimes which started in their area. When officers work for the SFO they are to that extent unavailable to their regular Fraud Squad commanding officer for deployment. After a period in which the police viewed the SFO staff with suspicion, relationships between the two now appear to be quite good. The First Annual Report of the SFO said that, in its first year, it was handling 66 cases out of an intended 60. Many of these, because of their very nature, are long-term projects which must be carried forward from initial investigation through to final trial.

Again in July 1989 the SFO had one senior staff member – a barrister – who was expert in computer crime, but this was only one of his duties: he was also responsible for seeing that the SFO could use computer-generated presentation techniques in court so as to explain complex frauds to lay juries as well as any other fraud that the SFO Director decided he could handle.

Less serious frauds are looked after by FIGs – Fraud Investigation Groups – which are part of the Crown Prosecution Service. The CPS is the entity which since 1986 has taken over the responsibility for initiating the vast majority of criminal prosecutions, a job formerly carried out by the police themselves. The CPS has never since its inception had a full complement of staff, largely, it is alleged, because of poor pay and conditions. It is not known if there is any specialist computer knowledge among its senior staff.

The Department of Trade and Industry has powers in relation to companies in general and also for the financial services industry, but these powers are to investigate, not to prevent. Investigations are carried out by inspectors, usually senior accountants and lawyers recruited for each instance from the leading accountancy practices and barristers well-known in the commercial bar. Also within the financial services sector, both the Securities and Investment Board (the UK's rough equivalent of the Securities and Exchange Commission) and individual self regulatory organisations (which includes the Stock Exchange) have staff to monitor compliance with their rules and to investigate complaints. The Bank of England has a regulatory role in relation to banks. Customs and Excise staff investigate frauds involving duty and VAT. The Inland Revenue maintains staff to check for tax evasion: approximately 550 are employed on PAYE audit, 100 in the Investigation Office and 100 in a Special Investigation Office, the latter being concerned with certain types of avoidance schemes.

There is one further specialist area of fraud investigation: that involving frauds on the social security system. This variety of fraud has often been identified as particularly unpleasant since the funds defrauded come from the tax-paying public. However, in order to have an opportunity to commit most social security frauds, you need to be a potential legitimate recipient, and that implies membership of the least well-off sector of the community. In 1987 there were 785 Department of Employment fraud investigators operating, a doubling in four years. As a result of their activities, savings in the year 1987/88 were claimed to be £55m. In the Department of Social Security which dispenses, among other things, Supplementary Benefit, in 1984/5 there were just over 1,500 specialist fraud officers and 564 special investigators. Sir Norman Price, a former Chairman of the Inland Revenue, who was also chairman of a NACRO working party on *Enforcement of the Law Relating to Social Security* estimates that there were 30 to 40 times more prosecutions for social security offences than for defrauding the Inland Revenue (where the public purse is also the victim) and the Customs and Excise.

Let it be said that both DoE and DSS fraud investigations are claimed to be cost-effective: the sums of money recovered exceed the costs of maintaining the investigators. However the imbalance of commitment of manpower as between these forms of fraud and all others is unforgivable.

A scheme of law and order is only really perceived as just if it applies to all members of society equally. It cannot be healthy for large areas of wrong-doing – actions which are almost identical to those of traditional theft and fraud, except that they involve computers – to go unpunished because the law lacks proper criminal offences, does not provide a full range of civil remedies, has unhelpful standards for the admissibility of evidence and a police force which, taken as a whole, has almost no chance of even understanding how many of the crimes were committed.

Yet laying blame, because that is the natural reaction, is not easy either. Each of the institutions involved believe that what they are doing is appropriate. There is a mechanism of law reform and it has produced results – only not enough and with a speed insufficient to respond to the rate of change in society which prompts the requirement for reform. Each of the police and quasi-police bodies that monitor fraud have developed along lines which have been suggested by circumstances as they see it. Indeed, one can identify a vicious cycle which ensures that change can only take place very slowly. The victim of a data-crime decides not to report what has happened because the results of going to law look so unpromising. The police's reaction to any area of crime is determined by the number of incidents reported to them. The impetus of legal reform depends heavily on the number of cases that have come to court and failed because the law is inadequate. It is only when the large picture is drawn that the unacceptable disparities of commitment and effort as between various forms of fraud and classes of fraudsters become apparent.

The next important step in computer law reform is to attend to the international dimension. The growth of global computer networks has made EFT fraud the preferred method of all serious international fraudsters. The problem is this: in the crime where an individual sits at a terminal in London, addresses a computer system based in Luxembourg and transfers money from Italy to Pakistan, where does the crime take place? Is it necessary to show that a loss has been sustained within a court's jurisdiction before the court can act? The situation is not limited to computer crime, of course. The legislatures of the UK, EEC countries and the Federal authorities in the USA are all working to redefine their local laws so that any 'fraudulent' event that touches their domestic territories can be caught within a criminal trap. The intentions are there, but the practical difficulties for implementation are considerable, both for framing substantive new laws and in deciding what evidence will be required in order to obtain a conviction.

But the course of law reform is not helped by shrill and ill informed campaigns. Individuals and organisations seize hold of one or other of the fashionable scare stories and demand instant action, apparently heedless for the need for sober research into the substance behind the scare, with little understanding of what the law might already deliver, and with scant regard for how the policing requirement is going to be resourced.

This book began with a concern that one of the largest problems in computer security was that attitudes to the subject seemed to be informed by a series of scare stories rather than a belief that computer risks can be made subject to rational management decisions. It is only right, therefore, to pick this issue up in the concluding chapter.

CHAPTER NINETEEN

Conclusion: Managing the Integrated Computer Resource

More computers mean more computer crime . . . yes, but what sort of computer crime? These are the thoughts that have pre-occupied this book.

How much 'computer crime' is really being committed? As we have seen, there are no truly believable statistics, but by taking a poll of those surveys where some evidence of intellectual discipline exists, by identifying those professionals whose opinions may be worth something we can come to some conclusions. First, while there is some evidence of a few wholly new crimes of considerable sophistication, there is no plague of them: nearly all 'computer crime' is regular white collar crime – with a computer dimension. There have been cases of computer-related extortion, perhaps there have even been cases of computer-related manslaughter. But in all of these cases the computer has been at the most a link in what was otherwise a conventional crime. Not that this is any reason for dismissing them.

The very first popular book on computer crime, Gerald Mc-Knight's 1973 effort, suggested: '. . . the underworld will soon make extensive use of the electronic vitals with which our world is allowing itself to become equipped, unless we can come sharply to our senses in the matter.' McKnight's prediction, though not unreasonable for the time in which it was written, has been repeated rather too often. Despite the existence of cases where the influence of some form of organised crime has been clear, the general absence of traditional criminal activity in 'computer crime' becomes something to be remarked on.

There is, however, a very great likelihood of the existence of large numbers of petty and not-so-petty offences which have taken advantage of the many opportunities offered by the ways in which information technology is now being used. In many instances, these crimes are much more akin to routine burglaries and muggings than carefully executed attacks on banks and armoured vans. That is to say, they are often opportunistic and, while their effects may be devastating to the victims, the rest of us have come to treat such events as mundane. The first difference is, whilst all of us who live in cities expect to be at the receiving end of burglary attempts and strengthen our homes and adjust our way of life accordingly, it appears that very few offices and factories take even the most rudimentary precautions to limit their exposure to datatheft. Whilst the law acknowledges burglary and street crime and the police make some attempt to limit them, no comparable awareness and effort attends the generality of datacrimes. Again, these crimes usually happen privately, within offices and businesses, rather than out on the street. The other difference is that, in datacrime, there is little correlation between the skill needed to perpetrate and the reward the criminal can expect. The largest amounts of money have gone to those with the best opportunities rather than those with the greatest technical skills.

How, in the absence of reliable statistics, can I be so confident that these datacrimes exist? I return to the classic ingredients of any crime: motive; opportunity to commit; probability of not being caught; skill to execute. By quite early in the 1970s, most of the classic forms of computer crime – theft of resources, theft of data, theft of software, theft of equipment, data manipulation, physical attack, logic bombs, software compromise, unauthorised access – had been discovered and had entered the casebooks; McKnight, to his credit, has examples of many of them. Indeed, apart from those methods that have involved the manipulation of the internal processes of computers, nearly all of these crimes are merely updates of crimes almost as old as criminality. The computer's role has been to expand and expedite the crimes. More computers means more computer crime . . .

How much unreported crime is there? Again we can only guess. I am fairly certain, however, that there are not a large number of concealed big-figure crimes, as is often suggested. You have to look at who the potential victims of multi-million-dollar crimes are and the range of external controls to which they must submit themselves. Overwhelmingly, the victims have to be financial institutions. These days such organisations are subject to rigorous scrutiny by internal and external auditors, internal compliance officers and external regulators. Too many people need to agree to any large-scale concealment. Financial institutions take out insurance, and whilst insurers do not insist that crimes are reported to the authorities, they do require to be told when the insurance is renewed: failure to make a truthful declaration can lead to voiding of the policy. An insurer may pay out a loss without informing the authorities, but the insurer will also simultaneously take the right to recover whatever can be of that loss – and details of the original crime may emerge during that process. So the probability is that concealed crimes tend to be under $2m in value. Depending on a company's size, however, in the case of crimes involving less than, say $500,000, it is almost certainly worth the while of the victim to conceal what has happened.

Traditionally, a fair proportion of the content of this book has in the past been written about under the heading 'computer security'. I have wanted to redefine the subject-area because it seemed to me that the words 'computer security' suggest that the fundamental problems are purely technical in nature, a question of getting the hardware and the software right, or working through a catalogue of 'computer security products' and selecting the right ones. It is an attitude which many members of the computer security industry have sought to encourage because the easiest way to sell products is to say: 'Here is a problem – I have the solution.'

It is still the case that most people who run businesses which depend on computers consider them a purely 'technical' matter: you acquire good computer systems by employing the right sort of specialists who will deliver, and be accountable for, the services you require. If there are problems with computers – and datacrime is perceived as one such – why then it ought to be solvable in the same technical way in which the purchase of computer hardware and software is carried out.

But, as I have sought to show, in 'computer security' the substantial issue is not computer hardware and software but information; information collected, compiled, processed, manipulated and finally used as a route to the better running of an organisation; and information as the representation of assets and money. It is what the computer handles and produces that needs to be protected, and what it contributes by way of added value to its owner's business, rather than its physical manifestation.

So worrying about 'computer security' is really worrying about a business as a whole – and planning for it requires the same level of careful system analysis that is needed in the first place to provide substantive computer systems. Indeed, the only truly safe course is to design security into a system as it is being specified – indicating not only functions you want the system to have, but also listing out eventualities which must not be allowed to arise. Just as a good system specification is designed around the culture of the company it is to serve, so should the security requirement – balancing the need to protect the company's assets against the virtues of giving the company's staff the flexibility to perform their tasks effectively.

But computer security isn't usually handled that way: it is treated as an add-on, an afterthought. Not only is it much more difficult to implement technically at this stage – because the essential functions of the computer system are already in place and no one wants to alter them too much – but by this time the systems analysis process is finished also and those who are charged with implementing 'computer security' are left to flounder without having the benefit of making the computer's owners and users think carefully about what risks they wish to guard against – and what price they will pay in order to secure their objectives.

If this sounds rather like country bumpkin's directions: 'Well if you want to get to X, I wouldn't be starting from here in the first place', it is not meant to: it is possible to set and implement objectives and controls for computer security after the event; it is just that the effort required, in terms of management commitment, will be found to turn out to be much greater.

As computer systems and the services demanded of them get more complex, the task of post-hoc security implementation gets steadily more difficult. Let us recall what has been happening in the last fifteen or so years:

There have been four outstanding changes: The move from

computer *installation* to computer *integration* has made very many organisations wholly dependent on the continuing sound functioning of their information systems, whereas before computers were simply a way of replacing older clerical processes with something more reliable and less costly. Computer systems and services have spread and multiplied throughout the organisations that use them: additional facilities can be purchased out of departmental petty cash; often there is no longer any central point from which anyone can exercise control and supervision. The arrival of end-user, or desk-top computing, has democratised the computer knowledge. Even those who were predicting such changes in the early 1970s over-estimated the length of time that would elapse before they were realised. What was also not realised was the rate at which such systems become obsolete and need updating – three years is not an unusually short period between installation and major modification; the obsolescence is not always in terms of computer technology; often it results from the organisation's demands to retain competitive edge. Alas, each time a computer system is altered, whatever security controls existed before have to be completely rethought. The phenomenal fall in the prices of both hardware and software – and no one predicted that – have created vast new classes of users who are able to purchase reliable products with which to run 'standard' businesses.

And perhaps the biggest 'computer security' problem of all is that those who run computer-dependent companies still do not make the effort to understand the implications if their company's computers fail or are compromised.

I believe that there are three reasons why there is such a ready audience for the sort of computer scare stories with which this book began. The first undoubtedly is that the stories are intrinsically interesting in themselves: they pass that first essential test of 'news' – they are unusual. In this book, by describing what is known of all of these phenomena, by inviting the reader to be sceptical about the way in which some stories and statistics are reported, and by setting them in the context of what is normal and mundane in datacrime, I hope I have helped readers achieve a balanced view of these exotic phenomena – as they are likely to impact the businesses and organisations in which they themselves are involved.

The second reason is that the scare stories are frequently repeated, not only by journalists, but also by many salesmen of computer security products. Authority for anecdotes is achieved by sheer repetition.

But it occurs to me that there is a third reason: these scare stories are a substitute for thinking coherently about computer crime and its causes. The readiness to accept the stories is a sad symptom of that belief of too many top managers that computers are purely a 'technical' matter.

It is quite evident that the fact of the computer-integrated company has made the range of management decisions that need to be exercised much more extensive. For many commercial enterprises, the detail and speed the computer can offer has made their existing operations vastly more efficient in their employment of capital and use of resources. But if an individual company has employed IT successfully, so will its most immediate rivals. Selecting the next correct step then becomes a matter of survival.

Each new development brings the prospect both of improved performance and of disaster, if the new facilities have been badly selected and installed. Each new development changes the existing relationships within the company; new power bases emerge, older ones decline. Managing technology also turns out to be about managing people. The particular problem is that the switch to the computer-integrated company has arrived unexpectedly rapidly, giving managers hardly any time to recognise what is happening, let alone adapt. The age-range of the people who run organisations is concentrated between 48 and 62, giving an 'average' of 55. Have they understood the extent to which their businesses have become dominated by information flows and dependent on computers? Most things in the fabric of our lives have not changed much in the last decade – we live in the same sort of houses, often the very same house; motor cars, tvs, air-travel, health care are scarcely different from what existed ten years ago. The one thing that has changed is the computer: its capabilities, its costs, its accessibility, its usefulness.

The process of this particular set of changes is not yet over. The rise of datacrime is a symptom of managers who have so far failed to make the full transition to the computer-dependent company.

To prevent this book concluding on too apocalyptic a note, let me summarise my own 'answers'. They revolve around the following issues:

- the management of information security
- the management of the employees in a company that is dependent on information technologies
- how information technology requirements in general are to be managed

These themes, which form the remainder of this chapter and this book, interact and intertwine.

The management of information security

Few companies as yet have a procedure of managing their information resources; they have very little clear idea of how much it costs to collect the information they use, nor what contribution it makes to their profitability. Perhaps one day the statutory annual audit will include a review and valuation of information assets.

But today very few companies even have a policy for classifying, let alone valuing, their internal information. Yet without these basic thoughts it is very difficult to develop a rational policy of information security. It means that there is no one person who directs or advises about what should be done. Such a role falls no more naturally to a DP manager than it does to the sort of individual normally recruited to handle the physical security of a set of premises.

Information security management involves more than the applying of a set of rules; it means the making of judgments, balancing the requirement to conserve the company's assets and secrets against the need to disseminate internal information widely in order that the company can prosper.

Basic Information Security Policy

System of the Classification of Information
Staff Pre-employment Vetting
Employee Exit Procedure
Continuous Information Security Awareness Program

The management of employees

Overwhelmingly, datacriminals are employees of their victims. Although there are many technical solutions which can limit the opportunities for employee fraud and datatheft, no collection of solutions, however carefully and expensively implemented, can offer full protection. The employee has on his or her side a detailed knowledge of how one aspect of the business operates, much more detailed than any systems analyst, programmer, accountant or consultant can ever hope to gain. The employee has time in which to discover opportunities and to decide when to exploit them. And the rate at which information systems keep on being changed ensures that there are always new opportunities for the motivated employee–datacriminal. There is an interesting paradox: a very common view is that the introduction of computers has resulted in the loss of many many jobs and the de-skilling of many others. Yet the impossibility of reaching the Holy Grail of the totally secure computer makes organisations *more* dependent on the staff they have.

Earlier in this book I suggested two routes to reducing an employer's risk from his employees: careful pre-employment vetting and in-employment monitoring. I said that both of these operations had to be carried out in a generally open way and to a level commensurate with the degree of risk that the employer felt he might be exposed to. I added that the employer should not indulge in practices which he would be unwilling to justify in public and in full. The issue of employee privacy is no trivial matter.

There is an additional policy which can be implemented: the introduction of an information security awareness programme. The object is to ensure that no employee is unaware of the value of the information they are handling. It can use a variety of methods – it can be part of the company welcoming procedure, it can form part of in-service training, it can be enshrined in booklets and, if appropriate, in warning notices. As we have seen, many datacrimes take place because datacriminals are able to persuade themselves that what is happening is not 'really' a crime. An effective information security awareness program removes this crutch; by linking the continued integrity of the information to the future of the company, and hence to the future of jobs, the help of the majority of employees can be enlisted to prevent a dishonest minority from taking an advantage. One of the standard features of much employee crime is that it is institutionalised: even those who don't participate directly become accomplices by tolerating what their workmates do.

Such a policy, if it is to work, must be more than a demand for 'stronger ethics in the workplace' and must be matched by an absence of corruption and greed among managerial staff. It has to call on the genuine enthusiasm and commitment of the work-force and as such, has to be part of the broader pattern of how managers and staff view each other. The need to protect a company's information assets can be a powerful reason for better industrial relations.

Managing information technology requirements

There are signs that some chief executives are recognising the enormous range of subtle changes that computers have wrought in the organisations they run. Writers on management science have sometimes sought to identify the dominant forces that impel various types of company forward. They might be manufacture-led, where what counts is innovation in products and methods of making. They can be marketing-led, where the Board's thoughts concentrate on finding out what people are willing to buy and then determining how to manufacture and sell it. Companies can be led by the concerns of the disciplines of financial planning: the emphasis is on return on investment. And there are beginning to be companies where the key element is mastery over information systems; where the fact of possessing large quantities of information and knowing how to exploit it, is what counts.

Whatever dominant discipline leads a company, the rational handling of computer crime has to be part of those skills.

The Obligations of Data Protection

Throughout this book we have been talking about datacrimes that might be committed against an organisation. There are, however, circumstances in which organisations may find that they themselves are committing datacrimes.

Objects and principles

Although this appendix concentrates on the UK Data Protection Act, 1984, which came into full effect at the end of 1987, the general principles apply in all countries with similar legislation.

The requirements of the act are as follows:

- All personal data and the uses thereof must be registered
- Personal data must not be used, disclosed or sent abroad except in accordance with the registered particulars
- Every computer bureau handling personal data must be registered
- The data subject (the person about whom data is held) is entitled to be told what the data is
- The data user (the owner of a computer which hold personal data) must abide by eight listed principles

These principles are:

1 The information to be contained in personal data shall be obtained, and personal data shall be processed, fairly and lawfully,

2 Personal data shall be held only for one or more specified and lawful purposes

3 Personal data held for any purpose or purposes shall not be used or disclosed in any manner incompatible with that purpose or purposes

4 Personal data held for any purpose or purposes shall be adequate, relevant and not excessive in relation to that purpose or those purposes

5 Personal data shall be accurate and, where necessary, kept up to date

6 Personal data held for any purpose or purposes shall not be kept longer than is necessary for that purpose or purposes

7 An individual shall be entitled,

(a) at reasonable intervals and without undue delay or expense

(i) to be informed by any data user whether he holds personal data of which that individual is the subject; and

(ii) to access to any such data held by a data user; and

(b) where appropriate, to have such data corrected or erased

8 Appropriate security measures shall be taken against unauthorised access to, or alteration, disclosure or destruction of, personal data and against accidental loss or destruction of personal data.

In interpreting this last principle, the Act has this to say:

Regard shall be had

(a) to the nature of the personal data and the harm that would result from such access, alteration, disclosure, loss or destruction as are mentioned in this principle; and

(b) to the place where the personal data are stored, to security measures programmed into the relevant equipment and to measures taken for ensuring the reliability of staff having access to the data

The effect of the eighth principle is that companies holding personal data are compelled to have adequate security measures, even if they have decided not to implement them for any other reason.

The act is only concerned with data about persons so that a company's research, marketing and manufacturing data is quite unaffected. There are a number of exemptions to the operation of the Act:

Exemptions for the ordinary business

- the Act does not apply to payroll, pensions and accounts data, nor to names and addresses held for distribution purposes
- Subjects do not have a right to access data if the sole aim of collecting it is for statistical or research purposes, or if it is held under the Consumer Credit Act (which does give the subject a right to see – the legislators wanted to avoid a duplicated right), or where it is simply for back-up
- Data can be disclosed to the data subject's agent (eg lawyer or acountant or other person), to persons working for the data user, and in response to urgent need to prevent injury or damage to health

Exemptions for special categories

These include data held:

- in connection with national security
- for individual use, including family and household affairs
- for club use, provided this is an unincorporated members' club and not a business of any sort
- for the prevention of crime – this may include data held by private detectives as well as that held by the police
- for the collection of tax and duty
- for health purposes
- for social work purposes
- for the regulation of financial services
- for judicial appointments
- for data available to the public by law (this includes the Electoral Register)
- for data held under professional legal privilege

There are two main criticisms of the Act: it only applies to material held on a computer; the same data written on card indexes is not subject to registration and there is no right of subject access. From a civil liberties point-of-view some of the most alarming aspects of incorrectly compiled data affect material held by the Security Services and police. There is no mechanism where a respected and independent third party can make a compulsory inspection as to necessity and accuracy.

Testing for Datatheft

These are some methods of testing for the possibility of datatheft: they should be used with caution – they may not produce sufficient evidence to satisfy a court of law and, in some cases, may infringe employee rights and privacy. The aim of the tests should be to satisfy an already-existing suspicion and the degree to which they are used should be commensurate with the depth of suspicion and the amount of harm the datatheft is actually likely to be causing[1]

Fraud

Critical point auditing
   stock losses
   inflation of assets
   inflation of expenses
   suppression of liabilities
   suppression of sales
   deviations from normal procedures
   missing documents
   broken control/measuring machinery
   distortion of historical or proportional trends

Key accounting ratios – comparison with similar organisations
vulnerability charts
increased use of activity logs
invigilation and created checks
observation
business intelligence
spot checking
undercover investigations
Computer fraud methods
   false inputting
   output manipulation
   forgery
   impersonation
   file manipulation

applications program manipulation
operating systems manipulation
piggy-backing

Information Theft

real-time data

    activity logs
    password checks
    access control check
    business intelligence

historic data

    activity logs
    password checks
    access control check
    business intelligence

on disc

    marked disc
    marked information (hidden code)
    business intelligence
    physical search

print-out

    business intelligence
    marked information
    watch on photocopiers
    physical search

unauthorised access/log-on

    activity logs
    password checks
    access control checks
    business intelligence
    enquiries among hackers

Resource Theft

software

    system – physical controls
    applications – physical controls

cpu processing time – activity monitors
network transport – activity monitors
hardware – physical controls
peripherals – physical controls
  modems
  printers
  monitors etc
stationery & media & supplies – physical controls

Preventative Methods

Coordinated Security Policy

Linked with general security policy

    written security policy
    management and staff training
    identification and allocation of responsibilities
    random checks

Identification of risks
Review machinery

Disaster Recovery Plan(s)

Contingency plans
Back-up facilities
Procedures
Teams
External expertise

Insurance

Loss of hardware & software
Interruption to business
Fidelity
Specialist

Physical Security

Buildings
Installations
Terminals & other peripherals

Data Security

End-users

   terminals
   printers
   discs
   print-outs

Operations
Systems
Applications
Access control

Communications Security

Access control systems
Encryption
Hardened comms lines

Personnel Practices

Recruitment
Screening procedures
Contracts of employment
Industrial relations
Staff morale
Assessments
Career development
Training
Turnover of staff
Termination procedures

Auditing facilities (computer)

Activity monitoring
Event reconstruction
Liaison with accounts audit
Procedures for development of new software
Procedures for acceptance and induction of new software

Notes

Chapter 1: Setting the Scene

1 *Financial Times*, 14 May 1986; *Sunday Times*, 17 May 1986; *Guardian*, 8 May 1987; *Datalink*, 27 Januay 1986; *Financial Times*, 4 November 1987; *Guardian*, 15 March 1988; *Computer Weekly*, 3 September 1987; *Independent*, 12 August 1987.
2 *Network*, January and February 1987; *Guardian*, 19 May 1986; *Datalink*, 1 December 1986; *Financial Times*, 4 February 1986; *Financial Times*, 23 September 1986; *Financial Times*, 6 June 1988; *Financial Times*, 26 May 1988; *Datalink*, 9 May 1988.

Chapter 3: The Extent of the Problem

1 *BIS Computer Related Fraud Casebook*, 1983
2 Versions of this crime can be found in *The Electronic Criminals*, Robert Farr, McGraw Hill 1975; *Time*, 25 December 1972; *Crime by Computer*, Donn Parker, Scribner's 1976; *Fighting Computer Crime*, Donn Parker, Scribner's 1983; *Computer Insecurity*, A R D Norman, Chapman & Hall 1983.
3 BBC2 *Horizon* film, 1976.
4 *Computer Capers*, Thomas Whiteside, Crowell 1978; *Computer Crime*, Gerald McKnight, Michael Joseph 1973; A R D Norman op cit; Donn Parker, 1976 op cit.
5 Whiteside, op cit; A R D Norman, op cit.
6 Whiteside, op cit; A R D Norman, op cit.
7 A R D Norman, op cit.
8 A R D Norman, op cit.
9 *BIS Computer Crime Casebook*, 1983; A R D Norman, op cit.
10 Whiteside, op cit; *BIS Computer Related Fraud Casebook*, 1983.
11 Whiteside, op cit.

12   *Observer*, 11 May 1989.
13   *Star*, 18 July 1985; BBC TV and ITN, 18 July 1985; and
     many others.
14   *2600 Magazine*, December 1985.

Chapter 4: DataFraud

1   *Audit Commission Computer Crime Survey*, 1985.
2   *Financial Times*, 14 April 1986.
3   *BIS Computer Related Fraud Casebook*, 1983.
4   *The Times*, 23 August 1986; *Datalink*, 1 September 1986.
5   *Guardian*, 26 June 1987.
6   *The Times*, 28 August 1986; *Home Office Research Bulletin*
     No 21, 1986.
7   *4—What It's Worth*, October/November 1986.
8   *Datalink*, 10 August 1987, 12 October 1987, 7 January
     1988, 31 October 1988.
9   *Sunday Times*, 1 November 1987.
10   *Observer*, 9 August 1987.
11   *Daily Telegraph*, 13 February 1981.
12   *Data Systems*, October 1975.
13   *UPI*, 11 March 1988.
14   *Daily Mail*, 7 February 1986; *Richmond & Twickenham
     Times*, 7 February 1986.
15   *Financial Times*, 31 March 1988; *Guardian*, 12 May 1988.
16   *Fighting Computer Crime*, Donn Parker, Scribner's 1983.
17   *Financial Times*, 2 September 1986, 3 September 1987;
     Guardian, 3 September 1987; *Daily Telegraph*,
     3 September 1987; *Datalink*, 1 September 1986, 8
     September 1986, 17 November 1986. 7 September, 1987
18   *Financial Times*, 14 March 1987.
19   *BIS Computer Related Fraud Casebook*, 1983.
20   *Audit Commission Computer Fraud Report* 1985.
21   *Fighting Computer Crime*, Donn Parker, Scribner's 1983.
22   *Datalink*, 6 April 1986.
23   *The Times*, 18 June 1987; *Independent*, 18 June 1987;
     Guardian, 18 June 1987.
24   *Financial Times*, 20 December 1986; *The Times*, 20
     December 1986.

Chapter 5: DataSpying: Industrial Espionage

1   *Computer Capers*, Thomas Whiteside, Crowell 1978;
    Computer Insecurity, A R D Norman, Chapman & Hall
    1983.
2   *See inter alia*, Peter Hamilton, *Espionage, Terrorism and
    Subversion in an Industrial Society*; Ronald Payne, *Private
    Spies*.
3   Figures from The World Almanac, *The New State of the
    World Atlas*.
4   *Fortune*, 7 March 1983.
5   *Independent*, 22 November 1987; *Guardian*, 2, 3, 4,
    February 1988; *Financial Times*, 4, 12 February 1988; *The
    Times*, 13 February 1988; *Daily Telegraph*, 23 January 1988;
    Observer, 15 February 1987.

Chapter 6: DataTheft: Stealing Resources

1   *The Times*, 26 April 1968; *BIS Computer Crime Casebook*,
    1983; *Computer Insecurity*, A R D Norman, Chapman &
    Hall 1983.
2   A R D Norman, op cit; *Crime by Computer*, Donn Parker,
    Scribner's 1976.
3   A R D Norman, op cit.
4   *Computer Capers*, Thomas Whiteside, Crowell 1978.
5   *BIS Computer Related Fraud Casebook*, 1983.
6   A R D Norman, op cit; a similar case appears in the *Audit
    Commission Report*, 1987.
7   *BIS Computer Crime Casebook*, 1983; A R D Norman, op
    cit.
8   *Computing*, 14 May 1987.
9   *Computing*, 25 June 1987.

Chapter 7: The Datathief

1   *Computer Weekly*, 21 December 1978.
2   *Daily Telegraph*, 9 July 1977.
3   *BIS Computer Related Fraud Casebook*, 1983.
4   *Ibid*.
5   The *Audit Commission Reports* of 1981, 1984 and 1987
    contain large numbers of similar instances.
6   *UPI*, 2, 7 November 1983, 16 October 1985 and many
    other places.

7   *Introduction to Computer Crime*, ed BloomBecker, various
    articles; *Newsweek*, 5 September 1983; *UPI*, 13 August,
    26 September 1983, May 1 1984
8   *Computer Weekly*, 29 May 1986; *Guardian*, 24 May 1986;
    The Times, 25 May 1986; *Information Security Monitor*, June
    1986.
9   *Computing*, 6 July 1989.
10 *Crime by Computer*, Donn Parker, Scribner's 1976.
11 *Computer Insecurity*, A R D Norman, Chapman & Hall
    1983.
12 *Computing*, 28 January 1988.
13 *Guardian*, 3 March 1988.
14 *The Times*, 7 August 1986; *Evening Standard*, 10 November
    1987; *Computing*, 21 April 1988; *Independent*, 8 February
    1989.
15 *Fighting Computer Crime*, Donn Parker, Scribner's 1983;
    A R D Norman, op cit.
16 There are too many accounts to list here, but for example:
    Daily Telegraph, 3 March 1989; *Independent*, 4 March
    1989; *The Times*, 4 March 1989; *Guardian*, 3, 4, March
    1989; *Financial Times*, 3, 4, March 1989; *Computing*, 9
    March 1989.
17 *Datalink, passim* issues, March to June 1989, followed the
    story in great detail.
18 *Observer*, 14 May 1989.
19 This account relies on *Sword and Shield*, Jeffrey T
    Richelson, 1986; *The New Wizard War*, Robyn Shotwell
    Metclafe 1988; *Financial Times*, 17 May 1986.
20 *Datalink*, 17 October 1988.

Chapter 9: Hardware at Risk

1   *Computer Capers*, Thomas Whiteside, Crowell 1978.
2   *Computer Insecurity*, A R D Norman, Chapman & Hall
    1983.
3   *Guardian*, 9 August 1986; *Financial Times*, 9 August 1986.
4   *BIS Computer Crime Casebook*, 1983.
5   *Computer Crime*, Gerald McKnight, Michael Joseph 1973.
6   *Sunday Times*, 2 July 1989.
7   *The Australian*, 8 September 1988.
8   See the case of David Coughlan, *Observer*, 2 April 1989;
    YTV *First Tuesday*, 4 April 1989.

9   *Fighting Computer Crime*, Donn Parker, Scribner's 1983.
10 Compare, for example, BBC2 *Micro Live*, November
    1986; BBC2 *Money Programme*, 23 October 1988, ITN,
    13 March 1989.

Chapter 10: Software at Risk

1   *BIS Computer Fraud Casebook*, 1983.
2   Accounts appear in *Crime by Computer*, Donn Parker,
    Scribner's 1976; *Computer Capers*, Thomas Whiteside,
    Crowell 1978 and numerous other books. Not one of
    them, that I have seen, contain names of actual victims
    or perpetrators.
3   *Datalink*, 5 October and 7 December 1987; *Computing*, 29
    October 1987.
4   See for example, BBC2 *Reportage*, 16 November 1988;
    BBC2 *Antenna*, 1 February 1989; *Computing*, 20 October
    1988; *Guardian*, 28 October 1988.
5   *Guardian*, 12 March 1987, 13 August 1987; *Financial Times*,
    13, 16 March, 14 August, 14, 21 September 1987;
    Datalink, 23 March 1987; *Economist*, 23 April 1987.
6   *Datalink*, 1 December 1986; *Guardian*, 7 March 1988;
    Channel 4 News, 27 November 1986.
7   *Computing*, 21 April 1988.
8   *Washington Post*, 8 November 1988, 5 February 1989.
9   *Telelink*, May 1986; *The Times*, 25 April 1986.

Chapter 13: Methods II: Personnel

1   *Computer Insecurity*, A R D Norman, Chapman & Hall
    1983.

Chapter 17: Limiting Damage

1   This account is based on the extended trial reports
    gathered by Micronet and personal interviews with
    Robert Schifreen and Steve Gold and with one of the
    defence barristers, Alistair Kelman.

Chapter 18: The Legal Response: The Law and the Police

1   The Anti-Hacking Bill, sponsored by Emma Nicholson MP.

2   Regina v Gold and Schifreen, *House of Lords*, (1988) 2 WLR 980.

3   Oxford v Moss (1978) 68 Cr App R 183.

4   Lloyd (1985) QB 829.

5   Cox v Riley (1986) 83 Cr App R 54.

6   eg *Computing*, 30 January 1987 and 27 October 1988; *Guardian*, 28 January 1988, 25 February 1988.

7   *Datalink*, 1 September 1986 and 4 July 1988; *Euromoney*, 17 November 1986; *Computing*, 8, 29 October 1987; *Guardian*, 8 January 1987; *The Times*, 7 May 1986 and 26 May 1988; *Computer Weekly*, 26 May 1988; *Sunday Telegraph*, 18 October 1987; *Sunday Times*, 3 April and 12 June 1988; *Financial Times*, 21 September 1988; First Annual Report of the Serious Fraud Office, 1989.

Bibliography

The publisher given is the original one; most US books have a separate UK publisher, and vice versa. A number of these titles have also appeared in paperback editions.

Allison, Dean & Henderson, Bruce B., *Empire of Deceit*, Columbus Books, London 1985, 1986.

Andrew, Christopher, *Secret Service*, William Heinemann Ltd, London, 1985

Arcagelis, Mario de, *Electronic Warfare*, Ugo Mursia Editore, Milan, 1981, Blandford Press, Dorset, 1985

Ardis, Patrick, and Comer, Michael, *The Tangled Web*, McGraw-Hill, London, 1987

Audit Commission, *Computer Fraud Survey*, HMSO, London, 1985

Audit Commission, *Computer Fraud Survey*, HMSO, London, 1987

Bamford, James. *The Puzzle Palace*, Houghton Mifflin Co, Boston, 1982

Bequai, August, *How to Prevent Computer Crime*, John Wiley & Sons, New York, 1983

Bernstein, Jeremy, *Three Degrees Above Zero*, Charles Scribner's Sons, New York, 1984

BloomBecker, Jay, *Computer Crime, Computer Security, Computer Ethics*, National Center for Computer Crime Data, Los Angeles, 1986

BloomBecker, Jay, (editor), *Introduction to Computer Crime*, National Center for Computer Crime Data, Los Angeles, 1985

Bolter, J. David, *Turing's Man*, North Carolina University Press, North Carolina, 1984

Bosworth-Davies, Rowan, *Too Good to Be True*, Bodley Head, London, 1987

Breton, Thierry, & Beneich, Denis, *SoftWar*, Editions Robert

Laffont SA, Paris, 1984, Holt, Rinehart and Winston, New York, 1985

Brunvand, Jan Harold, *The Vanishing Hitchhiker*, Pan Books, London, 1983

Buck, Edward, R., *Introduction to Data Security and Controls*, QED Information Sciences, Inc, Wellesley, 1982

Campbell, Duncan & Connor, Steve, *On the Record*, Michael Joseph, London 1986

Clarke, Thurston and Tighe, John J., *Dirty Money*, Simon & Schuster, New York, 1975

Comer, Michael J., *Corporate Fraud*, McGraw-Hill, London, 1985

Computer Security Institute, *Computer Security Handbook*

Corson, William R, *The Armies of Ignorance*, Dial Press, New York, 1977

Cronin, Daniel J., *Microcomputer Data Security*, Prentice Hall, New York, 1986

Cornwall, Hugo, *The Hacker's Handbook*, Century-Hutchinson, London, 1985, 1986, 1987, 1989

Daniel, W. W., *Workplace Industrial Relations and Technical Change*, Policy Studies Institute/Frances Pinter, London, 1987

Deitel, Harvey V., *An Introduction to Operating Systems*, Addison Wesley, Reading, Mass., 1984

Drucker, Peter, *The Changing World of the Executive*, William Heinemann, London,

Drucker, Peter, *Technology, Management and Society*, William Heinemann, London,

Ernst & Whinney, *Attitudes of Companies in Britain to Fraud* (Consensus Research), London, 1985 & 1987

Ernst & Whinney, *Computer Fraud* (Report presented to National Commission on Fraudulent Financial Reporting), New York, 1987

Evans, Christopher, *The Mighty Micro*, Victor Gollancz, London, 1979

Farr, Robert, *The Electronic Criminals*, McGraw-Hill, New York, 1975

Fernandez, E. B. and others, *Database Security and Integrity*, Addison Wesley, Reading, Mass., 1981

Fine, Leonard H., *Computer Security: A Handbook for Managment*, William Heinemann, London, 1986

Forester, Tom (editor), *The Information Technology Revolution*, Basil Blackwell, Oxford, 1985

Forester, Tom, *Hi-Tech Society*, Basil Blackwell, Oxford, 1987

Fraud Trials Committee Report (Lord Roskill), HMSO, London, 1986

Freemantle, Brian, *The Steal: Counterfeiting and Industrial Espionage*, Michael Joseph, London, 1986

Gibbons, Don G., *Society, Crime and Criminal Careers*, Prentice-Hall, Englewood Cliffs, NJ, 1968

Hamilton, Peter, *Computer Security*, Cassell/Associated Business Programmes, London, 1972

Hamilton, Peter, *Espionage and Subversion in an Industrial Society*, Hutchinson, London, 1967; 2nd edition, Peter Heims, Ltd, 1979

Hanson, Dirk, *The New Alchemists*, Little, Brown & Co, Boston, 1982

Henry, Stuart, *The Hidden Economy*, Martin Robertson, London, 1978

Hood, Roger and Sparks, Richard, *Key Issues in Criminology*, World University Library, London, 1970

Hougan, Jim, *Spooks*, William Morrow & Co Inc, New York, 1978

Institute of Chartered Accountants in England & Wales, *Countering Computer Fraud*, Chartac Books, London, 1987

Kahn, David, *The Codebreakers*, The Macmillan Company, New York, 1967, 1973

Kelman, Alistair, *Computer Fraud in Small Businesses*, Economist Intelligence Unit, London, 1985

Kidron, Michael & Segal, Ronald, *The New State of the World Atlas*, Pan Books, London, 1984

Kochan, Stephen G. & Wood, Patrick L., *Exploring the Unix System*, Hayden, Hasbrouck Heights, NJ, 1984

Kuong, Javier F. and others, *Microcomputer Security, Auditability and Controls*, Management Advisory Publications, Wellesley Hills, Mass., 1985

Landreth, Bill, *Out of the Inner Circle*, Microsoft Press, Bellevue, WA, 1984

Lane, V. P., *Security of Computer Based Information Systems*, Macmillan, London, 1985

Law Commission (for England and Wales), *Computer Misuse*, Working Paper No 110, HMSO, London, 1988

Laurie, Peter, *The Micro Revolution*, Futura, London, 1980

Leigh, L. H., *The Control of Commercial Fraud*, Heinemann Educational Books, London, 1982

Levi, Michael, *The Incidence, Reporting and Prevention of Commercial Fraud*, privately published by the Home Office and Arthur Young, London, 1986

Levy, Steven, *Hackers*, Doubleday & Co, New York, 1984

Macrae, Norman, *The 2024 Report*, Sidgwick & Jackson, London, 1984

Mars, Gerald, *Cheats at Work*, Allen & Unwin, London, 1982

M , James, *Security, Accuracy and Privacy in Computer Systems*, Prentice Hall, Englewood Cliffs, NJ, 1973

McKnight, Gerald, *Computer Crime*, Michael Joseph, London, 1973

McNeil, John, *The Consultant*, Weidenfeld & Nicholson, London, 1978

Metcalfe, Robyn Shotwell, *The New Wizard War*, Tempus/Microsoft Press, Redmond, WA, 1988

Moulton, Rolf T., *Computer Security Handbook*, Prentice-Hall, Inc, Englewood Cliffs, NJ, 1986

NACRO, *Enforcement of the Law Relating to Social Security*, London, 1986

Naisbitt, John, *Megatrends*, Warner Books, Inc, New York, 1982

Naisbitt, John & Aburdene, Patricia, *Re-inventing the Corporation*, Warner Books, Inc, New York, 1985

National Bureau of Standards (US Department of Commerce) *Security for Dial-Up Lines*, Washington, 1986

Norman, Adrian R. D., *Computer Insecurity*, Chapman and Hall, London, 1983

O'Donoghue, Joseph, *Mercy College Report on Computer Crime*, unpublished, Dobbs Ferry, NY, 1986

Office of Technology Assessment (US Congress), *Electronic Surveillance and Civil Liberties*, Washington, 1985

Office of Technology Assessment (US Congress) *Management, Security and Congressional Oversight*, Washington, 1986

Parker, Donn B., *Crime by Computer*, Charles Scribner's Sons, New York, 1976

Parker, Donn B., *Managers Guide to Computer Security*, Reston Publishing Inc, Reston, VA, 1981

Parker, Donn B., *Fighting Computer Crime*, Charles Scribner's Sons, New York, 1983

394

President's Council on Integrity and Efficiency, *Computers: Crimes, Clues and Controls*, Washington, 1986

Richelson, Jeffrey T. and Ball, Desmond, *The Ties that Bind*, Allen & Unwin, London, 1985

Richelson, Jeffrey T., *Sword and Shield: Soviet Intelligence and Security Apparatus*, Ballinger, Cambridge, Mass., 1986

Sanders, Norman, *Computer-aided Management*, Woodhead-Faulkner, Cambridge, 1985

Schweitzer, James A., *Computer Crime and Business Information*, Elsevier, New York, 1986

Scottish Law Commission, *Consultative Memorandum on Computer Crime*, Edinburgh, 1986

Scottish Law Commission, *Report on Computer Crime*, HMSO, Edinburgh, 1987

Sanders, Bruce D., *Computer Confidence*, Springer-Verlag, New York, 1984

Sutherland, Edwin H. *White Collar Crime*, Dryden Press, New York, 1949

Thomas, A. J. & Douglas, I. J., *Audit of Computer Systems*, NCC, Manchester, 1981

Thorsen, June-Elizabeth, (editor), *Computer Security: Equipment, Personnel & Data*, Security World Publishing Co. Inc, Los Angeles, 1974

Toffler, Alvin, *Future Shock*, Random House Inc, New York, 1970

Tuck, Jay, *High-Tech Espionage*, Sidwick & Jackson, London, 1986

US Department of Justice, *Computer Security Techniques*, Washington, 1980

US Department of Justice, *Electronic Fund Transfer Systems Fraud*, Washington, 1985

Weinberg, Geoff, *Understand Unix*, Que, Indianapolis, 1983

West, Nigel, *GCHQ: The Secret Wireless War 1900–1986*, Weidenfeld & Nicolson, London, 1986

Whiteside, Thomas, *Computer Capers*, Crowell, New York, 1978

Wingfield, John, *Bugging*, Robert Hale, London, 1984

Wong, Ken, *Computer Related Fraud Casebook*, BIS Applied Systems, London, 1983 and 1987

Wong, Ken, *Computer Disaster Casebook*, BIS Applied Systems, London, 1987

van Eck, Willem, *Electronic radiation from video display units*, PTT dr Neher Laboratories, Netherlands, 1985

Index

402

Also available from Mandarin Paperbacks

JANE R. HIRSCHMANN
CAROL H. MUNTER

Overcoming Overeating

- LOSE WEIGHT NATURALLY
- ENJOY THE FOOD YOU MOST DESIRE
- FORGET YOUR PREOCCUPATION WITH EATING AND WEIGHT
- DISCOVER THE FREEDOM OF NO RESTRAINTS
- GIVE UP DIETING FOREVER

Overcoming Overeating makes this all possible, for the authors have returned eating to its natural place in life, so that food becomes something to be enjoyed rather than feared.

Concentrating on the normal physiological hunger that we all experience. Jane R. Hirschmann and Carol H. Munter help you to break out of the lonely cycle of diet, binge, recrimination and self-loathing. Both practical and reassuring, they offer radical, realistic guidance on how to conquer an obsession and restore the compulsive eater's self-esteem.

'This is the best book on dealing with compulsive eating that I've read.'

Penelope Russianoff,
author of *When Am I Going To Be Happy?*

'*Overcoming Overeating*' will stand out from the crowd of diet books for its caring response to the compulsive eater.
Susie Orbach, author of *Fat is a Feminist Issue*

EDITED BY JAMES BEVAN

Sex & Your Health

The recent spread of AIDS has brought the relationship between sex and health to the forefront of public debate. It has also given rise to a maze of misinformation about sex and sexual problems.

In this book – the first encyclopaedic survey of the subject – nine experts disentangle the medical facts from the myths and explain, simple and authoritatively, the physiology and psychology of sex-related health problems.

- THE ANATOMY AND PHYSIOLOGY OF SEX
- MAIN METHODS OF CONTRACEPTION
- CAUSES OF MALE AND FEMALE INFERTILITY
- PHYSICAL PROBLEMS THAT AFFECT SEXUALITY
- AGEING AND SEXUALITY
- SEXUALLY TRANSMISSIBLE DISEASES
- THE PSYCHOLOGY OF SEX
- DEVIATION FROM THE SEXUAL NORM
- SEXUALITY IN THE SOCIAL CONTEXT

A Selected List of Non-Fiction Available from Mandarin Books

While every effort is made to keep prices low, it is sometimes necessary to increase prices at short notice. Mandarin Paperbacks reserves the right to show new retail prices on covers which may differ from those previously advertised in the text or elsewhere.

The prices shown below were correct at the time of going to press.

All these books are available at your bookshop or newsagent, or can be ordered direct from the publisher. Just tick the titles you want and fill in the form below.

Mandarin Paperbacks, Cash Sales Department, PO Box 11, Falmouth, Cornwall TR10 9EN.

Please send cheque or postal order, no currency, for purchase price quoted and allow the following for postage and packing:

UK	55p for the first book, 22p for the second book and 14p for each additional book ordered to a maximum charge of £1.75.
BFPO and Eire	55p for the first book, 22p for the second book and 14p for each of the next seven books, thereafter 8p per book.
Overseas Customers	£1.00 for the first book plus 25p per copy for each additional book.

NAME (Block letters) ....

ADDRESS ....

....